"Banayan's heart is poured into every page of this book. *The Third Door* is not only a guide to how the world's most remarkable pioneers succeeded, but it's also a magnificent story of one boy's journey to achieve his dream. *The Third Door* drips with passion and emotion—and it's a must-read for anyone wanting to turn their vision into a reality."

—ADAM BRAUN, *New York Times* bestselling author of
The Promise of a Pencil

"A wild ride . . . inspiring, hilarious, and insightful. Whenever you start to believe there's no other way to solve your problem, let Alex Banayan inspire you to think bigger."

—DAVID EAGLEMAN, *New York Times* bestselling author of *Incognito*,
host of PBS' *The Brain*, and adjunct professor at Stanford University

"As a Jewish mother, I don't want my teenage kids to read this book and get any ideas about dropping out of school. However, as someone who has served as a senior diplomat, tech executive, and social innovation entrepreneur, I want to put it at the top of their reading list! *The Third Door* is required reading for anyone in today's dynamic society who wants to learn success from the best."

—SUZI LEVINE, United States Ambassador to Switzerland and
Liechtenstein (Ret.)

"In just a few hours of reading this book, Alex Banayan taught me how to meet billionaires, leapfrog my associates, and achieve my dreams in record time. I've never read anything quite like this! Whether you are an entrepreneur or trying to jumpstart your career, *The Third Door* will open up your world of possibilities."

—TIM SANDERS, *New York Times* bestselling author of
Love Is the Killer App

"My grandfather used to tell me: 'If a problem has a solution, why worry?' And it's precisely that attitude of optimism and possibility that has so inspired me about Banayan's *The Third Door*. He wasted little time worrying: 'What if?' He went for it. And that made all the difference."

—JASON SILVA, Emmy-nominated host of
National Geographic's *Origins* and *Brain Games*

"Banayan personifies creativity, hustle, and passion. He's the embodiment of the next generation of the entrepreneurial leader, and *The Third Door* beautifully brings this mindset to life."

—JOSH LINKNER, *New York Times* bestselling author of *Disciplined Dreaming* and *Hacking Innovation*

"Banayan's approach to solving problems is as hilarious as it is brilliant. Whether you're an accomplished entrepreneur, an aspiring one, or an executive trying to get your employees to think outside the box, *The Third Door* is the way forward."

—MEREDITH PERRY, founder of uBeam

"A surprising combination of bildungsroman, spiritual journey, and caper comedy, *The Third Door* creates an opportunity for all of us to inspect what success means, what inspires us, and how we think about our paths through the world."

—MICHAEL SLABY, chief innovation officer of the Obama 2012 Presidential Campaign and executive director of Chicago Ideas

"Alex Banayan's *The Third Door* was absolutely worth the wait! He perfectly captures amazing insights while being funny and approachable. Banayan's journey leaves you not only inspired but also excited to pursue your dreams and define success in your own way."

—KAMAURI YEH, director of West Coast Brand Experience at Nike

"Banayan's hustle is insane. He crouched in bathrooms, chased people through grocery stores—he did whatever it took to make his dream happen. The extents he went through will inspire you to keep grinding on your path. If you are hungry to succeed, trust me: read *The Third Door*."

—JERMAINE DUPRI, Grammy Award–winning rapper and music producer

"Engrossing ... brilliantly insightful. Applicable and useful. I found myself nodding in places and re-reading passages. ... Banayan demystifies the hardest and scariest thing many of us have to do to succeed."

—DR. M. SANJAYAN, CEO of Conservation International and host of PBS' *Earth: A New Wild*

"Whether you are just beginning your first act or setting off on your twentieth, this may be the best and most thoroughly enjoyable career advice book you will ever read: fast moving, funny, big-hearted, and constantly insightful."

—MATTHEW BISHOP, author of *Philanthrocapitalism* and former business editor of *The Economist*

"Banayan's incredible journey, told with wit, warmth, and wisdom, explores his own search for meaning through the personal stories of his heroes. An inspiring read for anyone looking to find their purpose."

—RUMA BOSE, author of *Mother Teresa CEO: Unexpected Principles for Practical Leadership*

"I wish I had *The Third Door* when I was starting my first business. Thankfully, Banayan has delivered the book we've all been waiting for."

—MICHAEL LAZEROW, former chief strategy officer of Salesforce and founder of Buddy Media

"In this magnificent book, we the reader have the honor of following and witnessing an ambitious, resourceful, and very clever young man turn into a wise, astute, and very successful young adult. The twists and turns, the joys and disappointments, the letdowns and, ultimately, the victories and final realizations read like a movie that grips you with both hands and won't let go. The best part of all is the author's growth, self-reflection, and self-discovery. What does it really take to be happy? You really will find the answer in these pages as Banayan and his cast of friends gladly show us the way. Buy copies of this book, both for yourself and your entire family. You'll be glad you did. And so will they!"

—BOB BURG, coauthor of *The Go-Giver* and *The Go-Giver Influencer*

"A brilliant writer . . . I couldn't stop reading once I started. *The Third Door* is a must-read for entrepreneurs."

—VIVEK WADHWA, columnist for the *Washington Post* and Distinguished Fellow at Carnegie Mellon University

THE
THIRD
DOOR

THE
THIRD
DOOR

**THE WILD QUEST TO UNCOVER HOW THE
WORLD'S MOST SUCCESSFUL PEOPLE
LAUNCHED THEIR CAREERS**

ALEX BANAYAN

CURRENCY

NEW YORK

All rights reserved.
Published in the United States by Currency,
an imprint of the Crown Publishing Group,
a division of Penguin Random House LLC, New York.
crownpublishing.com

CURRENCY and its colophon are trademarks of Penguin Random House LLC.

The Equality Hurdles comic on page 244 copyright © by Emanu. Published with
permission of the artist.

Currency books are available at special discounts for bulk purchases for sales
promotions or corporate use. Special editions, including personalized covers,
excerpts of existing books, or books with corporate logos, can be created in large
quantities for special needs. For more information, contact Premium Sales at
(212) 572-2232 or e-mail specialmarkets@penguinrandomhouse.com.

Library of Congress Cataloging-in-Publication Data
Names: Banayan, Alex, author.
Title: The third door : the wild quest to uncover how the world's most successful
people launched their careers / Alex Banayan.
Description: 1 Edition. | New York : Currency, 2018. | Includes bibliographical
references and index.
Identifiers: LCCN 2018008522 | ISBN 9780804136662 (hardback) |
ISBN 9780804136679 (eISBN)
Subjects: LCSH: Success in business. | Motivation (Psychology) | BISAC: SELF-
HELP / Motivational & Inspirational. | BIOGRAPHY & AUTOBIOGRAPHY /
Personal Memoirs.
Classification: LCC HF5386 .B2293 2018 | DDC 650.1—dc23
LC record available at https://lccn.loc.gov/2018008522

ISBN 978-0-8041-3666-2
Ebook ISBN 978-0-8041-3667-9

PRINTED IN THE UNITED STATES OF AMERICA

Book design by Andrea Lau
Jacket illustration by Banayan International LLC

10 9 8 7 6 5

First Edition

To my mom and dad,
Fariba and David Banayan,
who made this all possible

And to Cal Fussman,
who turned this dream into a reality

CONTENTS

STEP 4
TRUDGE THROUGH THE MUD

STEP 5
TAKE THE THIRD DOOR

THE
THIRD
DOOR

STEP 1

DITCH THE LINE

Life, business, success . . . it's just like a nightclub.

There are always three ways in.

There's the First Door: the main entrance, where the line curves around the block; where 99 percent of people wait around, hoping to get in.

There's the Second Door: the VIP entrance, where the billionaires, celebrities, and the people born into it slip through.

But what no one tells you is that there is always, always . . . the Third Door. It's the entrance where you have to jump out of line, run down the alley, bang on the door a hundred times, crack open the window, sneak through the kitchen—there's always a way.

Whether it's how Bill Gates sold his first piece of software or how Steven Spielberg became the youngest studio director in Hollywood history, they all took . . . the Third Door.

CHAPTER ONE

Staring at the Ceiling

R ight this way . . ."
I stepped across the marble floor and turned a corner, entering a room with glistening floor-to-ceiling windows. Sailboats drifted down below, gentle waves lapped onto the shore, and the afternoon sun bounced off a marina and filled the lobby with a bright, heavenly glow. I followed an assistant down a hallway. The office had couches with the most plush cushions I'd ever seen. The coffee spoons sparkled in a way I'd never seen spoons sparkle before. The conference room table looked like it had been carved by Michelangelo himself. We entered a long corridor lined with hundreds of books.

"He's read every one," she said.

Macroeconomics. Computer science. Artificial intelligence. Polio eradication. The assistant pulled out a book on feces recycling and placed it in my hands. I flipped through it with sweaty palms. Nearly every page was underlined and highlighted with scribbles in the margins. I couldn't help but smile—the scribbles had the penmanship of a fifth grader.

We continued down the hallway until the assistant asked me to stay where I was. I stood there, motionless, looking at a towering frosted glass door. I had to stop myself from touching it to feel how thick it was. As I waited, I thought of all the things that led me here—the red scarf, the toilet in San Francisco, the shoe in Omaha, the cockroach in the Motel 6, the—

And then, the door opened.

"Alex, Bill is ready for you."

He was standing right in front of me, hair uncombed, shirt loosely tucked in, sipping a can of Diet Coke. I waited for something to come out of my mouth, but nothing did.

"Hey, there," Bill Gates said, his smile lifting his eyebrows. "Come on in . . ."

THREE YEARS EARLIER, MY FRESHMAN DORM ROOM

I flipped over in bed. A stack of biology books sat on my desk, staring back at me. I knew I should study, but the more I looked at the books, the more I wanted to pull the covers over my head.

I tossed to my right. A University of Southern California football poster hung above me. When I'd first taped it on my wall, the colors were so vibrant. Now the poster seemed to blend in with the wall.

I turned onto my back and stared at the silent white ceiling.

What the hell is wrong with me?

Ever since I could remember, the plan was for me to be a doctor. That's what happens when you're the son of Persian Jewish immigrants. I practically came out of the womb with "MD" stamped on my behind. In third grade, I wore scrubs to school for Halloween. I was "that kid."

I was never the smartest kid in school, but I was consistent. Like, I consistently got B minuses and consistently read CliffsNotes. To make up for my lack of straight As, I always had a sense of direction. In high school I "checked the boxes"—volunteer at a hospital, take extra science classes, obsess over the SATs. But I was too busy trying to survive to stop and wonder whose boxes I was checking. When I'd started college, I couldn't have imagined that a month later I would be hitting the snooze button four or five times each morning, not because I was tired, but because I was bored. Yet I continued dragging myself to class anyway, checking the premed boxes, feeling like a sheep following the herd.

That's how I found myself here: lying on my bed, staring up at the ceiling. I'd come to college looking for answers, but all I got were more questions. *What am I actually interested in? What do I want to major in? What do I want to do with my life?*

I flipped over again. The biology books were like dementors, sucking the life out of me. The more I dreaded opening them, the more I thought about my parents—running through the Tehran airport, fleeing to America as refugees, sacrificing everything to give me an education.

When I received my admissions letter from USC, my mom told me I couldn't attend because we couldn't afford it. Although my family wasn't poor and I grew up in Beverly Hills, like many families, we lived a double life. While we lived in a nice neighborhood, my parents had to take out a second mortgage to cover the bills. We went on vacations, yet there were times when I'd see notices on our front door saying our gas was going to be cut off. The only reason my mom allowed me to attend USC was because the day before the enrollment deadline, my dad stayed up all night, talking to my mom with tears in his eyes, saying he'd do whatever it took to make ends meet.

And this is how I paid him back? By lying in bed, pulling the covers over my head?

I glanced at the other side of the room. My roommate, Ricky, was at a small wooden desk doing his homework, spitting out numbers like an accounting machine. The squeak of his pencil mocked me. He had a path. I wish I had that. All I had was a ceiling that wouldn't talk back to me.

Then I thought about the guy I'd met the prior weekend. He'd graduated from USC a year earlier with a math degree. He used to sit at a desk just like Ricky's, spitting out numbers just like him, and now he was scooping ice cream a few miles from campus. I was beginning to realize that a college degree no longer came with guarantees.

I turned over to the textbooks. *Studying is the last thing I want to do.*

I rolled onto my back. *But my parents sacrificed everything so that studying would be the only thing I have to do.*

The ceiling remained silent.

I flipped over and planted my face in my pillow.

———

I TRUDGED TO THE LIBRARY the following morning, my biology books under my arm. But as much as I tried to study, my internal battery remained depleted. I needed a jump start, something to inspire me. So I pushed my chair back from the study tables, wandered to the aisles of the biography section, and pulled out a book on Bill Gates. I figured reading about someone as successful as Gates might spark something within me. And it did—just not what I'd expected.

Here was a guy who started his company when he was my age, grew it into the most valuable corporation in the world, revolutionized an industry, became the richest man alive, and then stepped down as the CEO of Microsoft to become the most generous philanthropist on earth. Thinking about what Bill Gates accomplished felt like standing at the base of Mount Everest and staring up at the peak. All I could wonder was: *How did he take his first steps up the mountain?*

Before I knew it I was flipping through the biographies of one successful person after another. Steven Spielberg climbed the Mount Everest of directing, so how did he do it? How did a kid who'd been rejected from film school become the youngest major studio director in Hollywood history? How did Lady Gaga, when she was nineteen years old and waiting tables in New York City, get her first record deal?

I kept returning to the library, searching for a book that held the answers. But after a few weeks, I was left empty-handed. There wasn't a single book that focused on the stage of life I was in. When no one knew their names, when no one would take their meetings, how did these people find a way to launch their careers? That's when my naive eighteen-year-old thinking kicked in: *Well, if no one has written the book I'm dreaming of reading, why not just write it myself?*

It was a dumb idea. I couldn't even write a term paper without half the page coming back covered in red ink. I decided not to do it.

But as the days pressed on, the idea wouldn't let me go. What interested me wasn't writing a book so much as embarking on "a mission"—a journey to uncover these answers. I figured if I could just talk to Bill Gates myself, he had to have the Holy Grail of advice.

I ran the idea by my friends and found out I wasn't the only one staring at the ceiling. They were dying for answers too. *What if I go on this mission on behalf of all of us?* Why not just call up Bill Gates, interview him, track down some other icons, put what I discover in a book, and share it with my generation?

The hard part, I figured, would be paying for it. Traveling to interview all these people would cost money, money I didn't have. I was buried in tuition payments and all out of Bar Mitzvah cash. There had to be another way.

———

TWO NIGHTS BEFORE FALL SEMESTER final exams, I was back in the library when I took a break to scroll through Facebook. That's when I saw a friend's post about free tickets to *The Price Is Right*. The game show was filmed a few miles from campus. It's one of those shows I watched as a kid when I stayed home sick from school. Audience members would get called down to become contestants, they'd be shown a prize, and if they guessed closest to the actual price without going over, they'd win. I'd never seen a full episode before, but how hard could it be?

What if . . . what if I go on the show to win some money to fund the mission?

It was absurd. The show was taping the next morning. I had to study for finals. But the thought kept crawling back into my mind. To prove to myself it was a horrible idea, I opened my notebook and wrote a list of the best- and worst-case scenarios.

WORST-CASE SCENARIOS

1. Fail my finals
2. Ruin my chances of going to med school
3. Mom will hate me
4. No . . . Mom will kill me
5. Look fat on TV
6. Everyone will make fun of me
7. Not even make it onto the show

BEST-CASE SCENARIO

1. Win enough money to fund the mission

I searched online to calculate the odds of winning. Out of three hundred people in the audience, one wins. I used my cellphone to do the math: a 0.3 percent chance.

See, this is why I didn't like math.

I looked at the 0.3 percent on my phone, then at the stack of biology books on my desk. But all I could think was, *What if . . . ?* It felt as if someone had tied a rope around my gut and was slowly pulling.

I decided to do the logical thing and study.

But I didn't study for finals. I studied how to hack *The Price Is Right*.

CHAPTER TWO

The Price Is Right

Anyone who's watched *The Price Is Right* for even thirty seconds and has heard the announcer say "*COME ON DOWN!*" knows the contestants are colorfully dressed and have wild personalities that fill the television screen. The show makes it seem like the contestants are randomly selected from the audience—but at around 4:00 a.m., as I'd Googled "how to get on *The Price Is Right*," I discovered it was far from random. A producer interviews each audience member and picks the wildest ones. If the producer likes you, he puts your name on a list that's given to an undercover producer who observes you from afar. If the undercover producer puts a check mark by your name, you're called on stage. It wasn't luck: there was a system.

The next morning, I swung open my closet and threw on my brightest red shirt, a big puffy jacket, and neon-yellow sunglasses. I pretty much looked like a chubby toucan. *Perfect.* After driving to the CBS studio, I pulled into the parking lot and approached the check-in table. Because I couldn't tell who the undercover producer was, I assumed it could be anyone. I hugged security guards, danced with janitors, flirted with old ladies—I break-danced, and I don't know how to break-dance.

I got in line with the other audience members in a maze of railings outside the studio doors. The line moved forward, until finally, it was almost my turn to be interviewed. *There's my guy.* I'd spent hours researching him the night before. His name was Stan and he was the producer in charge of casting contestants. I knew where he was from, where he went to school—and that he relied on a clipboard, but it was never in his hands. His assistant, who sat in a chair behind him, held it. When Stan selected a contestant, he would turn to her, wink, and she'd write the name down.

An usher motioned for ten of us to step forward. Stan stood ten feet away, walking from one person to the next. "What's your name? Where are you from? What do you do?" There was a rhythm to his moves. Officially, Stan was a producer; but in my eyes, he was the bouncer. If I didn't get my name on his clipboard, I wouldn't get on the show. And now the bouncer was right in front of me.

"Hey, my name's Alex, I'm from LA and I'm a premed at USC!"

"Premed? You're probably always studying. How do you have time to watch *The Price Is Right*?"

"The . . . what? Oh! Is that where I am?"

He didn't even give a pity laugh.

I needed to redeem myself. In one of the business books I'd read, the author said that physical contact speeds up a relationship. I had an idea.

I had to touch Stan.

"Stan, Stan, come over here! I want to make a secret handshake with you!"

He rolled his eyes.

"Stan! Come on!"

He stepped forward and we slapped hands. "Dude, you're doing it all wrong," I said. "How old are you?"

Stan chuckled and I showed him how to pound it and blow it up. He laughed some more, wished me luck, and walked away. He didn't wink to his assistant. She didn't write anything on the clipboard. Just like that, it was over.

This was one of those moments when you see your dream in front of you, you can almost touch it, and then just like that, it's gone, slipping through your fingers like sand. And the worst part is you know you could've seized it if you just had another chance. I don't know what got into me, but I started shouting, at the top of my lungs.

"STAN! STAAAAN!"

The entire audience whipped their heads around.

"STAAAAAAAAAAN! Come back!"

Stan ran over and nodded slowly, giving me that "all right, kid, what now?" look.

"Uh . . . uh . . ."

I scanned him up and down: he was wearing a black turtleneck, jeans, and a plain red scarf. I didn't know what to say.

"Uh . . . . . . uh . . . . YOUR SCARF!"

He squinted. Now I *really* didn't know what to say.

I took a big breath, looked at him with every bit of intensity I could muster, and said, "STAN, I'M AN AVID SCARF COLLECTOR, I HAVE 362 OF THEM IN MY DORM ROOM, AND I'M MISSING THAT ONE! *WHERE DID YOU GET IT?*"

The tension shattered and Stan burst into laughter. It was as if he knew what I was really doing, and he was laughing less at what I said than why I said it.

"Oh, in that case, you can have my scarf!" he joked, taking it off and offering it to me.

"No, no, no," I said. "I just wanted to know where you got it!"

He flashed a smile and turned to his assistant. She scribbled something on the clipboard.

———

I STOOD OUTSIDE THE STUDIO DOORS and waited for them to open. A young woman walked by and I noticed she was looking around, staring at people's nametags. A laminated badge peeked out of her back pocket. She had to be the undercover producer.

Locking eyes with her, I made funny faces and blew her some kisses. She started to laugh. Then I did the 1980s sprinkler dance move and she laughed more. She looked at my nametag, slipped a sheet of paper out of her pocket, and made a note.

I should've felt on top of the world, but that's when I realized I'd spent my all-nighter figuring out how to get *on* the show—I still didn't know how to play. I took out my phone and Googled "how to play *The Price Is Right.*" Thirty seconds later, a security guard snatched my phone from my hand.

I looked around and saw security was taking everyone's phone away. After passing through metal detectors, I plopped down on a bench. Without my phone, I felt unarmed. An old, gray-haired woman sitting beside me asked what was wrong.

"I know this sounds crazy," I told her, "but I had this idea to come here and win some money to fund my dream, but I've never seen a full episode of the show before, and now they've taken my phone, so I don't have a way to figure out how the show works, and—"

"Oh, honey," she said, pinching my cheek. "I've been watching this show for forty years."

I asked for advice.

"Sweetie, you remind me of my grandson."

She leaned in and whispered, "Always underbid." She explained that if you overbid by even a dollar, you lose. If you underbid by

$10,000, you still have a chance. As she continued, I felt like I was downloading decades of experience into my head. That's when the light bulb went off.

I thanked her, turned to the guy on my left, and said, "Hey, my name is Alex, I'm eighteen, and I've never seen a full episode of the show before. Do you have any advice?" Then I turned to another person. Then to a group of people. I jumped throughout the crowd and spoke to almost half the audience, crowdsourcing their wisdom.

The doors to the set finally swung open. I stepped in and the place smelled like the 1970s. Turquoise and yellow drapes flowed down the walls. Gold and green flashing light bulbs danced between them. Psychedelic flowers were painted on the back wall. All that was missing was a disco ball.

Theme music began to play and I took my seat. I stuffed my jacket and yellow sunglasses under the chair. To hell with the toucan—it was game time.

If there was ever a time to pray, it was now. I dropped my head, closed my eyes, and put a hand over my face. Then I heard a deep, rumbling voice from above. Every syllable was elongated. The voice got louder and louder. But this wasn't God. It was TV God.

"HERRRRE IT COMES, FROM THE BOB BARKER STUDIO AT CBS IN HOLLYWOOD, IT'S THE PRICE IS RIGHT!... AND NOWWWWW, HERE'S YOUR HOST, DREW CAREY!"

TV God called down the first four contestants. I wasn't the first, second, or third, but for the fourth, I felt it coming. I inched forward in my chair, and . . . it wasn't me.

The four contestants stood at flashing podiums. A woman wearing mom jeans won the opening round. She advanced to a bonus round. Four minutes into the show, a fifth contestant was called to fill Mom Jeans' vacant podium.

"ALEX BANAYAN, COME ON DOWN!"

I leapt out of my seat and the crowd exploded along with me. As I flew down the stairs slapping high fives, it felt like the audience was my extended family and all my cousins were in on the joke—they knew I had no idea what I was doing and they were loving every second of it. I got to my podium without a second to breathe and Drew Carey said, "Next prize, please."

"A CONTEMPORARY LEATHER CHAIR AND OTTO-MAN!"

"Go ahead, Alex."

Underbid. Underbid.

"Six hundred!"

The audience laughed and the other contestants bid next. The actual retail price: $1,661. The winner was a young woman who jumped up and hollered. Nearly everyone who's been to a bar on a college campus has seen someone like her: the Woo Girl. She's the one slamming back tequila shots and shouting *"WOOOOOOO!"* after each one.

Woo Girl played her bonus game and then it was time for the next round.

"A BILLIARDS TABLE!"

My cousins have a pool table. How expensive could it be?

"Eight hundred dollars!" I said.

The other contestants bid higher and higher. Drew revealed the retail price: $1,100. The other contestants had all overbid.

"Alex!" Drew said. "Come on up here!"

I raced up to the stage. Drew glanced at the USC logo on my red shirt. "Nice to meet you," he said. "You go to USC? What do you study there?"

"Business administration," I said without thought. It was half true: I was also studying business administration. But why did I choose not to mention premed when put on the spot on national television? Perhaps I knew myself more deeply than I wanted to admit. But I didn't have time to notice, because TV God was already revealing the prize for my bonus round.

"A NEW SPA!"

It was a hot tub with LED lights, a waterfall, and lounge seating for six. For a college freshman, this was gold. How it would fit in my dorm room? I had no idea.

I was shown eight prices. If I picked correctly, the hot tub was mine. I guessed $4,912. The actual retail price . . . $9,878.

"Alex, at least you've got a pool table," Drew said. He looked into the camera. "Don't go away. We're going to spin the Wheel!"

The show cut to commercial break. Production assistants carted a fifteen-foot wheel onto the stage, which looked like a giant slot machine covered with glitter and flashing lights.

"Uh, excuse me," I said, turning to one of the assistants. "Sorry, quick question. Who spins the Wheel?"

"Who spins? *You* spin."

He explained that the three of us who'd won opening rounds would spin the Wheel. There were twenty numbers on it: every multiple of five, up to one hundred. Whoever landed the highest number would move on to the final round. If someone spun a perfect one hundred, he or she would win an extra cash prize.

The theme music started and I ran to my position between Mom Jeans and Woo Girl. Drew Carey stepped over and lifted his microphone.

"Welcome back!"

Mom Jeans went first. She stepped forward, grabbed the Wheel, and . . . *TICK, TICK, TICK* . . . eighty. The audience let out a cheer and even I knew that was an unbelievable spin.

I inched forward, gripped the handle of the Wheel, and pulled down . . . *TICK, TICK, TICK, TICK* . . . eighty-five! The crowd erupted and the commotion was so loud it might as well have shaken the ceiling.

Woo Girl stepped forward, spun, and . . . fifty-five. I was about to celebrate but I noticed the audience was quiet. Drew Carey was giving her another chance to spin. I learned that this was like blackjack. She could hit again, and if her numbers added up to a higher total than mine, without going over one hundred, she would win. She spun once more and . . . another fifty-five.

"Alex!" Drew exclaimed. "You're on your way to the Showcase! More *Price Is Right* is coming up."

———

I WAS USHERED TO THE SIDE of the stage as a new batch of contestants battled to determine who'd go against me in the final round. Twenty minutes later, I found out. Her name was Tanisha and she had demolished the competition as if she'd spent her whole life walking through Costco studying price tags. She'd won a thousand-dollar luggage set, a ten-thousand-dollar trip to Japan, and on the Wheel, she'd spun a perfect one hundred. Going up against Tanisha felt like David facing Goliath, except David forgot his slingshot.

During the commercial break before the final round, I realized I'd never watched this far into the show. And on top of that, no one in the audience had given me advice on this part because no one thought I'd get this far.

Tanisha walked by. I reached out my arm to shake her hand.

"Good luck," I said.

She looked me up and down. "Yeah, *you'll need it.*"

She was right. I needed help fast, so I stepped over to Drew Carey and threw my arms up. "Drew! I loved you on *Whose Line Is It Anyway!*" I gave him a hug and he pulled back, giving me an awkward one-armed pat.

"Drew, any way you could explain to me how the Show-Room Showdown works?"

"First of all," he said, "it's the *Showcase* Showdown."

He explained it in a way someone would talk to a kindergartner, and before I knew it, the theme music started again. I dashed to my podium. Six machine gun–sized cameras aimed at my face. Blinding white lights shot down from above. To my left, Tanisha was dancing. *Shit, I still have to go to the library and study tonight.* To my right, Drew Carey stepped forward and adjusted his tie. *Oh my God, Mom is going to kill me.* The music grew louder. I spotted the old lady who'd pinched my cheek. *Focus, Alex, focus.*

"Welcome back!" Drew said. "I'm here with Alex and Tanisha. Here we go! Good luck."

"YOU'RE IN FOR A ROLLER-COASTER RIDE OF ACTION AND ADVENTURE! FIRST UP, A TRIP TO MAGIC MOUNTAIN IN CALIFORNIA!"

With all the stimulation, I didn't hear the rest of the details. *How expensive could a theme park ticket be? Fifty bucks?* What I hadn't heard was that it was a VIP package, with a limousine, front-of-the-line passes, and all meals included—for two.

For my second prize, all I heard was "Blah, blah, blah, a trip to Florida!" I'd never purchased a plane ticket before. *What is it? Like a hundred bucks? No . . . a couple hundred?* Again, I'd missed that it also included a rental car and a five-night stay in a first-class hotel.

"PLUS, YOU'LL FLOAT WEIGHTLESSLY AT THE ZERO-G EXPERIENCE!"

It sounded like a carnival ride. *How much could that cost? Another hundred?* I later found out this is how NASA trains astronauts. Fifteen minutes in zero gravity costs five thousand dollars.

"AND FINALLY . . . THERE'S ADVENTURE ON THE HIGH SEAS, THANKS TO THIS STUNNING NEW SAILBOAT!"

The doors slid open, a supermodel waved her arms, and there it was: a glowing, pearl white sailboat. When I finally calmed down and looked closer, the boat seemed relatively small. *Four, no, five thousand dollars—tops?* Once again, what I hadn't heard was that it was an eighteen-foot Catalina Mark II boat with a trailer and a cabin inside.

"WIN THIS SHOWCASE AND THERE'LL NEVER BE A DULL MOMENT WITH THE TRIP TO MAGIC MOUNTAIN, THE VACATION IN FLORIDA, AND THE NEW SAILBOAT. AND THEY'LL ALL BE YOURS IF THE PRICE IS RIGHT!"

The audience's cheers echoed off the studio walls. The cameras swung back and forth. As I tallied the total, one number came to mind, and it just felt right. I leaned forward, grabbed the microphone, and with all the confidence I could summon, said, "Six thousand dollars, Drew!"

Dead silence.

I stood there, for what felt like minutes, not understanding why the audience had gone quiet. Then I realized Drew Carey hadn't locked in my answer. I turned to him and he had a baffled, almost dumbfounded look on his face. I finally got the hint. I hunched my shoulders, reached for the microphone, and sheepishly said, "Just . . . kidding?"

The audience erupted into applause. Drew sprang back to life and asked for my real answer. *Well, that was my real answer.* I looked at the sailboat, then back to the audience. "Guys, you've got to help me out!"

Their shouts blended into a roar.

"Alex, we need an answer," Drew pressed.

The audience slowly began to chant one number over and over, but I could barely make it out. I heard a *th* sound.

"Alex, we need an answer."

I grabbed the mic. "Drew, I'm going with the audience on this one. Thirty hundred dollars!"

Drew immediately said, "You know there's a difference between thirty *hundred* dollars and thirty *thousand* dollars, right?"

"Uh . . . of course I know that! I was just messing with you." I pretended to think out loud. "I'm feeling $20,000. Higher than $20,000?"

The audience shouted *YESSSSS!*

"Thirty thousand?"

YESSSSSSSSSSS!

"How about $29,000?"

NOOOOOOO!

"All right," I said, looking at Drew. "The audience is saying $30,000, so I'm saying $30,000."

Drew Carey locked in the price.

"Tanisha," he said. "Here's your Showcase. Good luck."

She was in the zone. Tanisha kept dancing; I kept sweating.

"A NEW ATV, AN OFF-ROADING VACATION IN ARIZONA, PLUS A BRAND-NEW TRUCK, AND IT'S ALL YOURS IF THE PRICE IS RIGHT!"

She bid, and then it was time to reveal the prices.

"Tanisha, we'll start with you," Drew said. "A trip to Phoenix, Arizona, and a 2011 Dodge Ram. You bid $28,999. Retail price . . . $30,332. A difference of $1,333!"

Tanisha leapt back and shot her hands to the ceiling.

Okay, I thought, *I still have twenty-four hours until my first final. If I drive from the studio straight to the library, that gives me six hours to study for bio, three hours for . . .*

Drew revealed my retail price and the audience cheered louder than they had all day. The producers motioned for me to smile. I leaned over to check the number on the front of my podium.

I'd guessed $30,000. Retail price . . . $31,188.

I had beaten Tanisha by $145.

My face went from day-before-finals dread to just-won-the-lottery hysterical. I leapt from my podium, high-fived Drew, hugged the supermodels, and ran to the sailboat.

Drew Carey spun around and looked back into the camera.

"Thanks for watching *The Price Is Right*. Bye-bye!"

CHAPTER THREE

The Storage Closet

I sold my sailboat to a boat dealer for sixteen thousand dollars, which for a college student feels like a million bucks. I felt so rich I kept buying Chipotle for all my friends—*free guacamole for everyone!* But after the holidays, when I returned to school for spring semester, the party was over. It was hard for my eyes not to gloss over in my premed classes as I imagined what it would be like to instead learn from Bill Gates. I counted down the days until summer, when I could finally focus all my time on the mission.

Just before school let out, I had a routine meeting with my premed adviser. She clicked away at her computer and scrolled through my transcript, studying my "unchecked boxes."

"Uh-oh, Mr. Alex, we have a little problem."

"What is it?"

"Looks like you're behind on credits. To stay premed, you'll have to take chemistry this summer."

"No!" I blurted, the word slipping out before I could catch it. "I mean, I've got other plans."

My adviser slowly swiveled in her chair, turning away from her computer and leveling her gaze at me.

"No, no, Mr. Alex. Premeds don't *have* other plans. You either sign up for chemistry by next Wednesday or you're no longer a premed. You're either on the track, or you're not."

I dragged myself to my dorm room. All the usual suspects were there: the white ceiling, the USC football poster, and the biology books. Except this time, something felt different. I sat at my desk to draft an email to my parents, telling them I was switching from premed to a business major. But as I tried to type, the words wouldn't come. For almost anybody else, switching majors isn't a big deal. But for me, after my parents had told me for years that being at my medical school graduation was their biggest dream, each time my fingers hit the keyboard, I felt I was shattering their hopes, one stroke at a time.

I willed myself to finish the email and pressed send. I waited for my mom's response, but it never came. When I called, she didn't answer.

That weekend, I drove home to visit my parents. As I walked through the front door, I found my mom sitting on the couch, sniffling, a crumpled tissue in her hand. My dad was beside her. My sisters, Talia and Briana, were in the living room too, but as soon as they saw me, they scattered.

"Mom, I'm sorry, but you just have to trust me."

"If you're not going to be a doctor," she said, "what are you going to do with your life?"

"I don't know."

"What are you planning to do with a business degree?"

"I don't *know*."

"So how are you going to support yourself?"

"I don't know!"

"You're right: you *don't* know! You don't know *anything*. You don't know what it's like in the real world. You don't know what it's like to have to start over in a new country with nothing. What I *do* know is that if you become a doctor, if you can save people, you can do that anywhere. Going on an adventure is not a career. You can't get this time back."

I looked at my dad, hoping he'd support me, but all he did was shake his head.

The emotional barrage went on all weekend. I knew what I had to do. I did what I'd always done.

I called my grandma.

My grandma is like a second mother to me. When I was a kid, my favorite place in the world was her home. I felt safe there. Her phone number was the first one I'd memorized. Anytime I argued with my mom, I'd tell my grandma my side of the story and she'd get my mom to cut me some slack. That's why when I called, I knew she'd understand.

"I think," she said, her voice landing softly on my ear, ". . . I think your mom is right. We didn't come to America and sacrifice everything, just so you could throw it all away."

"I'm not throwing it away. I don't understand what the big deal is."

"Your mom wants a life for you that we never had. In a revolution, they can take your money, they can take your business—but if you're a doctor, they can't take away what you know.

"And, if it's medicine you don't like," she added, "then fine. But an undergraduate degree is not enough in this country. You have to get your master's."

"If that's what it's about, I can get an MBA or go to law school."

"If you do that, then, okay. But I'm telling you: I don't want you to become one of these American kids who gets 'lost' and then tries to find himself by traveling the world."

"I'm just switching my major! And I'll still get my MBA or something like that."

"Well, if that's your plan, then I'll talk to your mom. But I need you to promise me, that no matter what, you'll finish undergrad and get your master's."

"Yeah, I promise."

"No," she said, her voice hardening. "Don't tell me: 'Yeah, I promise.' Tell me *jooneh man* that you'll get your master's."

Jooneh man is the strongest promise in the Persian language. My grandma was asking me to swear on her life.

"Fine. I swear."

"No," she said. "Say: *jooneh man.*"

"Okay. *Jooneh man.*"

⸻

THE DAYS GOT WARMER and summer finally arrived. I cleaned out my dorm room and moved home. But on my first day back, I felt restless. If I wanted to be serious about the mission, I needed a serious place to work.

Late that evening, I grabbed my mom's keys off her nightstand, drove to her office building, climbed the stairs to her storage room, and flicked on the lights. The space was tiny and covered in cobwebs. There were old filing cabinets, run-down storage boxes, and a beat-up chair crammed behind a rickety wooden desk.

I packed the storage boxes into my car and put them in our garage. The next morning, I moved in a few bookshelves, vacuumed the dusty carpet, and taped a USC banner above the door. Then I installed a printer and made cutout business cards with my name and number. As I took a seat behind my desk, I kicked my feet up and smiled—it felt like a corner office of a Manhattan high-rise. Although, in reality, it looked more like Harry Potter's cupboard.

That first week, dozens of brown Amazon packages arrived. I tore them open and pulled out books I'd bought using my *Price Is Right* money. I lined an entire row with books about Bill Gates.

Another row on politicians, then a row on entrepreneurs, writers, athletes, scientists, and musicians. I spent hours on the floor, arranging the books by height on the shelves, each one another piece of my foundation.

On the top row, I placed one book on its own, the cover facing out as if it were a shrine: *Delivering Happiness* by Tony Hsieh (pronounced *shay*), the CEO of Zappos. When I had first been hit by the "what do I want to do with my life?" crisis, I had volunteered at a business conference where copies of his book were given out. I didn't know who he was, or what his company did, but college students don't say no to anything free, so I took one. Later, when my parents became hysterical over my decision to switch majors and I was torn about whether I'd made the right decision, I saw Tony Hsieh's book on my desk. It had the word "happiness" in the title, so I reached for it as a distraction. But then I couldn't put it down. Reading about Tony Hsieh's journey—about the leaps of faith he took despite everything that could go wrong—helped me find the courage within myself I didn't know I had. Reading about his dream fueled me to pursue my own. That's why I put his book on the top shelf. Whenever I needed to remember what was possible, all I had to do was look up.

WHILE PUTTING THE FINISHING TOUCHES on the storage closet, it dawned on me that I'd never asked myself exactly who the "most successful" people are. How was I going to decide whom to interview for the mission?

I called up my best friends, explained my problem, and asked them to meet me at the storage closet. Later that night, they walked in, one by one like a starting lineup.

First came Corwin: his messy hair dangling past his shoulders, a video camera in his hand. We had met at USC, where he was studying filmmaking. I felt like I could always find him either meditating or crouching on the ground, peering through the viewfinder of a camera. Corwin was our fresh eyes.

Then came Ryan: staring down at his phone and studying NBA statistics, as usual. We'd met in seventh-grade math class and Ryan was the reason I'd passed. He was our numbers guy.

Next was Andre: also looking down at his phone, except knowing Andre, he was definitely texting a girl. We became friends when we were twelve, and for as long as I've known him, he was the ladies' man.

Brandon followed next: holding an orange book in front of his face, reading as he stepped in. Brandon could read an entire book in a day. He was our walking Wikipedia.

And lastly, there was Kevin: a giant smile on his face, his presence making the storage closet come alive. Kevin was the energy that held our crew together. He was our Olympic flame.

We sat on the floor and began brainstorming: If we could invent our dream university, who would be our professors?

"Like, Bill Gates would teach us business," I said. "Lady Gaga, music—"

"Mark Zuckerberg for tech," Kevin yelled out.

"Warren Buffett for finance," Ryan said.

We went on for half an hour. The only person who hadn't suggested a name was Brandon. When I asked what he thought, he just lifted his orange book and pointed to the cover.

"This is who you need to talk to," Brandon said, his finger on the author's name. "Tim Ferriss."

"Who?" I asked.

Brandon handed me the book.

"Read it," he said. "He's going to be your hero."

The brainstorm continued—Steven Spielberg for film, Larry King for broadcasting—and before long, we had the list. After my friends headed home, I wrote the names on an index card and put it in my wallet for motivation.

I jumped out of bed the next morning, more determined than ever. I took the index card out of my wallet and stared at the names. My certainty that I could interview each of them by the end of summer was the fuel that got me going. If I'd known then how my journey would unfold—how beaten and broken I'd soon find myself—I may never have started. But that's the upside of being naive.

STEP 2

RUN DOWN THE ALLEY

CHAPTER FOUR

The Spielberg Game

With my list in hand, I charged straight to the storage closet, sat behind my desk, and flipped open my laptop. But as I stared at the screen, a cold, empty feeling ran through me. My only thought was . . . *Now what?*

This was the first time I didn't have a teacher telling me when to show up for class. No one was telling me what to study or what the homework was. I'd hated checking boxes, but now that they were gone, I realized how much I'd relied on them.

Only later would I learn how pivotal these moments are for anyone who sets out to start something new. Many times the hardest part about achieving a dream isn't actually achieving it—it's stepping through your fear of the unknown when you don't have a plan. Having a teacher or boss tell you what to do makes life a lot easier. But nobody achieves a dream from the comfort of certainty.

Because I had no idea how to get my interviews, I spent the day emailing every adult I knew, asking for advice. I reached out to professors, parents of friends—anyone I'd met who seemed relatively put together. The first person who agreed to meet with me was an administrator who worked at USC. We met at a café on campus a few days later. When she asked whom I wanted to interview, I took the index card out of my wallet and handed it over. Her eyes scanned the names and a smile spread across her face.

"I shouldn't be telling you this," she said, lowering her voice, "but Steven Spielberg is going to be at the film school in two weeks for a fundraising event. Students aren't allowed to attend, but . . ."

It wasn't until much later that I learned the full extent of this rule. On the first day of school for film students, the dean makes it clear that they can never, ever attend fundraising events and pitch the donors. But I didn't know that then, so as I sat in that café my only question was "How can I get in?"

It's a small event, she said, and if I showed up dressed in a suit, she could bring me in as her "assistant."

"Look, I can't guarantee I'll get you next to Spielberg," she added, "but getting you through the door shouldn't be hard. Once you're in there, it's all on you. So if I were you, I would prepare. Go home and watch all of Spielberg's movies. Read everything you can about him."

I did just that. I pored over a six-hundred-page biography by day and watched his movies by night. Finally, the day arrived. I swung open my closet, threw on my only suit, and headed out.

———

THE FILM SCHOOL'S OUTDOOR PATIO had been transformed to look like anything but a school. A red carpet flowed along a walkway, tall cocktail tables lined the manicured gardens, and waiters in tuxedos glided around carrying trays of hors d'oeuvres. I stood among the crowd of donors, listening as the film school dean began her opening remarks. The dean wasn't much taller than the podium, but her presence gripped the crowd.

With trembling hands, I straightened my suit jacket and inched forward. Just ten feet in front of me, standing shoulder to shoulder, were Steven Spielberg, *Star Wars* director George Lucas, Dream-Works Animation CEO Jeffrey Katzenberg, and actor Jack Black. I'd walked in nervous, but now I was in a full panic. How could I approach Spielberg when he was in the middle of a conversation with the man who'd created Darth Vader and Luke Skywalker? What would I say? *"Excuse me, George, out of the way"*?

As the dean continued her speech, I inched nearer. Spielberg was so close I could see the stitching of his graphite-gray blazer. He wore an old-fashioned newsboy cap atop a head of wispy hair; soft, kind-looking wrinkles surrounded his eyes. There he was— the man behind *E.T.*, *Jurassic Park*, *Indiana Jones*, *Jaws*, *Schindler's List*, *Lincoln*, *Saving Private Ryan*—and all I had to do was wait for the dean to finish.

Applause took over the patio. I tried to take the remaining steps toward Spielberg, but my feet turned to stone. A large lump formed in my throat. I knew exactly what was happening. This was the same sensation I felt whenever I approached a girl I had a crush on in school. I called it The Flinch.

The first time I remember feeling The Flinch was when I was seven. During lunchtime, I sat at a long table in the school cafeteria and looked around: Ben had chips and granola bars, Harrison had a turkey sandwich with the crust cut off, and then there was me, taking out a heavy plastic container of Persian rice covered in green stew with red kidney beans on top. When I opened the lid, the smell spread everywhere. The kids around me pointed and laughed, asking if I had rotten eggs for lunch. From that day on, I kept my Tupperware in my backpack, waiting to eat my lunch until after school when I was alone.

The Flinch started out as my fear of being seen as different, but as I grew up, it mushroomed into so much more. I felt it every time the kids at school called me Fatty Banayan, every time my teachers yelled at me for speaking out of turn, and every time a girl bit her lip and shook her head when I told her I liked her. These little moments added up, one on top of another, until The Flinch was a living, breathing being.

I was terrified of rejection and mortified of making mistakes. Because of that, The Flinch would paralyze my body at the worst possible times, hijack control of my vocal cords, and turn my words into a stuttering, stammering slur. And The Flinch never had a stronger hold on me than when I was standing a few yards from Steven Spielberg. I stared at him, hoping to find an opening. But before I did, Spielberg was whisked away.

I watched him glide from one group to another, smiling and shaking hands. The party seemed to orbit around him. I looked at my watch: I still had an hour left. I headed to the men's room to splash cold water on my face.

The only comfort I had was knowing that Spielberg could probably relate to what I was experiencing. Because what I was trying to do was pull a Spielberg, on Spielberg.

———

STEVEN SPIELBERG GOT HIS START when he was right around my age. I'd read varying accounts, but according to Spielberg, this is what happened: he boarded a tour bus at Universal Studios Hollywood, rode around the lot, and then jumped off, sneaking into a bathroom and disappearing behind a building. He watched the tour bus drive away then spent the rest of the day on the Universal lot.

Wandering around, he bumped into a man named Chuck Silvers who worked for Universal TV. They spoke for a while. When Silvers found out Spielberg was an aspiring director, he wrote him a three-day pass. Spielberg came for the next three days, and on the fourth, he showed up again, this time dressed in a suit and carrying his dad's briefcase. Spielberg walked up to the gate, threw a hand in the air, and said *Hey Scotty!*—and the guard just waved back. For the next three months, Spielberg arrived at the gate, waved, and walked right through.

On the lot, he would approach Hollywood stars and studio executives and ask them to lunch. Spielberg snuck onto soundstages and sat in editing rooms, soaking up as much information as he could. Here was a kid who had been rejected from film school, so in my eyes, this was his way of taking his education into his own hands. Some days he'd smuggle an extra suit in his briefcase, sleep overnight in an office, and change into the fresh clothes the next morning and walk back onto the lot.

Chuck Silvers eventually became Spielberg's mentor. He advised him to stop schmoozing and come back when he had a high-quality short film to show. Spielberg, who'd been making short films since he was twelve, began writing a twenty-six-minute film called *Amblin'*. After months of directing and grueling editing, he finally showed it to Chuck Silvers. It was so good that when Silvers saw it, a tear ran down his cheek.

Silvers reached for the phone and called Sid Sheinberg, Universal TV's vice president of production.

"Sid, I've got something I want you to see."

"I've got a whole goddamn pile of film here . . . I'll be lucky to get out of here by midnight."

"I'm going to put this in the pile for the projection booth. You really should look at it tonight."

"You think it's that goddamn important?"

"*Yes*, I think it's that goddamn important. If you don't look at this, somebody else will."

After Sid Sheinberg watched *Amblin'*, he asked to meet Spielberg immediately.

Spielberg rushed over to the Universal lot and Sheinberg offered him a seven-year contract on the spot. And that's how Steven Spielberg became the youngest major studio director in Hollywood history.

When I'd read that story, I originally thought Spielberg had played the "people game"—networking around the lot and making connections. But the word "networking" made me think of exchanging business cards at a career fair. This wasn't simply a people game. It was more than that. This was the Spielberg Game.

1. Jump off the tour bus.
2. Find an Inside Man.
3. Ask for his or her help to bring you in.

The most important step, I realized, was finding that "Inside Man"—someone inside the organization willing to put his or her reputation on the line to bring you in. If Chuck Silvers hadn't offered Spielberg a three-day pass, or called the VP of production and demanded he watch the film, Spielberg never would have gotten the contract.

Of course, Spielberg had incredible talent, but so do other aspiring directors. There was a reason he got that contract when so many others didn't.

It wasn't magic. And it wasn't just luck. It was the Spielberg Game.

I LOOKED AT MYSELF IN the bathroom mirror. I knew if I couldn't approach Spielberg while he was standing in front of me, the mission would be over before it started.

I drifted around the party until I spotted him again. When Spielberg moved to one side of the patio, I moved to the other. When he stopped to talk to someone, I stopped to look at my phone. After heading to the bar to grab a Coke, I scanned the patio and my stomach dropped—Spielberg was heading for the exit.

Without thinking, I slammed my glass down and chased after him. I swerved through the crowd of donors, dodging waiters and cutting around tables. Spielberg was a few feet from the exit. I slowed down, trying to time my approach perfectly. But I had no time for perfect.

"Uh, excuse me, Mr. Spielberg. My name's Alex and I'm a student at USC. Can I . . . can I ask you a quick question as you head to your car?"

He stopped walking and swung his head over his shoulder, his eyebrows shooting over his metal-framed glasses. He lifted his arms in the air.

He gave me a hug.

"I've been on a college campus for hours and you're the first student I've seen all day! I'd love to hear your question."

His warmth melted The Flinch away, and as we walked to the valet, I told him about the mission. The words spilled out almost unconsciously. This wasn't an elevator pitch. This was what I believed.

"I know we just met, Mr. Spielberg, but"—the lump came back in my throat—"would you . . . would you be willing to do an interview?"

He stopped again, then slowly turned toward me. His lips pressed and his eyelids clenched like heavy iron gates.

"Normally, I'd say no," he said. "I usually don't do interviews unless they're for my foundation or to publicize a movie."

But then his eyes softened. "Even though I'd normally say no . . . for some reason, I'm going to give you a maybe."

He paused and looked at the sky, squinting although the sun wasn't bright. I'll never know what he was thinking, but eventually he lowered his head and locked his eyes onto mine.

"Go make this happen," he said. "Go out and get your other interviews. Then come back to me and we'll see what we can do."

We spoke for another minute and then he said goodbye. He stepped toward his car, but then suddenly turned around, facing me one last time.

"You know," he said, holding my gaze, "there's something about you that tells me you're actually going to make this happen. I believe in you. I believe you can do this."

He called over his assistant and told him to get my information. Spielberg climbed into his car and drove away. His assistant asked for my business card so I reached into my back pocket, taking out one of the printout cards I'd made in the storage closet. Then a single word sliced through the air.

"*NO!*"

It was the film school dean. Her arm shot between us. She snatched the card out of my hand.

"What is this regarding?" she asked.

I wished I could've calmly said, "Oh, Mr. Spielberg asked his assistant to get my information," but instead I just stood there, frozen. I glanced at Spielberg's assistant, hoping he'd help explain, but as soon as the dean saw me looking at him, she motioned for him to leave—without my card, my number, or even my name.

"*You should know better,*" she snapped, her stare shooting straight into my bones. "We don't do these types of things here."

She asked if I was a film student, the rage in her voice almost pushing me back. I stuttered, which even to me sounded like an admission of guilt.

"*I told you,*" she railed. "I told you on day one that we don't tolerate this type of behavior!"

I apologized profusely, not even knowing what I was apologizing for. I said whatever I could to escape her wrath. The dean continued to berate me until my eyes welled up. Although she wasn't much taller than five feet, it felt like she towered above me. A minute later, she stormed off.

But before I could move, the dean spun around and marched back.

She glared at me once more. *"There are rules here."* She lifted her arm and pointed for me to leave.

CHAPTER FIVE

Crouching in the Bathroom

I woke up the next morning, the dean's voice still ringing in my ears. By late afternoon I still couldn't shake my gloom, so I dragged myself to the storage closet and scanned the shelves, looking for inspiration.

An orange-colored book was sticking out: *The 4-Hour Workweek* by Tim Ferriss. It was the book Brandon had given me. I grabbed it and stretched out on the floor. As I turned to the first page, it felt like Tim Ferriss was talking just to me. His words sucked me in so deeply that I didn't lift my head for the next hour except to reach for a pen to mark my favorite parts.

The opening scene was of Tim Ferriss competing in the Tango World Championships.

The next page had Ferriss racing motorcycles in Europe, kick-boxing in Thailand, and scuba diving off a private island in Panama.

Two pages later I discovered a line that almost made me scream "yes!" out loud: *"If you picked up this book, chances are that you don't want to sit behind a desk until you are 62."*

Chapter two was called "The Rules That Change the Rules."

Chapter three was about conquering fear.

Chapter four had a passage so powerful it felt like Tim Ferriss whacked my "what do I want to do with my life?" crisis with a wooden bat:

> "What do you want?" is too imprecise to produce a meaningful and actionable answer. Forget about it.
>
> "What are your goals?" is similarly fated for confusion and guesswork. To rephrase the question, we need to take a step back and look at the bigger picture ...
>
> What is the opposite of happiness? Sadness? No. Just as love and hate are two sides of the same coin, so are happiness and sadness ... The opposite of love is indifference, and the opposite of happiness is—here's the clincher—boredom.
>
> *Excitement is the more practical synonym for happiness, and it is precisely what you should strive to chase. It is the cure-all.* When people suggest you follow your "passion" or your "bliss," I propose that they are, in fact, referring to the same singular concept: excitement.

Three pages after that was an entire section titled "How to Get George Bush Sr. or the CEO of Google on the Phone."

Thank you, God!

I went to Tim Ferriss' website and saw he'd written a second book. I bought it immediately. If *The 4-Hour Workweek* was about hacking your career then *The 4-Hour Body* was about hacking your health. I flipped to a chapter called "The Slow-Carb Diet: How to Lose 20 Pounds in 30 Days Without Exercise." It sounded as if it were written by a snake-oil salesman, but Ferriss had used his body like a human guinea pig to prove it worked, so what did I have to lose? The answer: a lot—*a lot* of weight. Following his instructions, I shed forty pounds over the course of the summer. Bye-bye, Fatty Banayan. My family was shocked and jumped headfirst on the Tim Ferriss bandwagon too. My dad lost twenty pounds; my mom, fifty pounds; my cousin, sixty.

We were just a few of the millions of people following Tim Ferriss online, reading his every blog post and liking his every tweet. The Internet had changed the world, and a new world needs new teachers. Tim Ferriss was that guy.

His name was now at the top of my list, and *The 4-Hour Workweek* gave me just the clue on how to reach him.

As I was going through the book a second time, I noticed something on the dedication page that I hadn't caught at first.

> 10% of all author royalties are donated to educational not-for-profits, including DonorsChoose.org

Wait a minute . . . DonorsChoose . . .

I had my Inside Man.

When I'd volunteered at that business conference during my freshman year, the one where I'd gotten Tony Hsieh's book, I saw an attendee wobbling on crutches, so I asked if he needed help. "No, no, don't worry about it," he said. He told me his name was César and that he was the COO of DonorsChoose. We kept running into each other over the next few days and we had stayed in contact ever since.

César had explained that DonorsChoose.org is a site where anyone can donate to classrooms in need. Potential donors could search through requests from across the country—picture books for kindergartners in Detroit or microscopes for high schoolers in St. Louis. You pick whichever project resonates with you and donate as little or as much money as you like.

After some Googling, I learned that Tim Ferriss and the CEO of DonorsChoose had been on the same high school wrestling team. Ferriss even sat on the nonprofit's advisory board.

I emailed César and asked him to lunch. Once we got together, I asked if there was any way he could help me reach out to Ferriss. César said he was sure his CEO would pass along my interview request.

"Consider it done," he said.

A week later, César emailed me saying his boss had sent along my request to Ferriss. And to top it off, César also mailed me a stack of DonorsChoose gift cards to give out as thank-yous to the people I interviewed. They were each valued at one hundred dollars—a large donor had put up the money—and Stephen Colbert even gave out the same cards to all the guests on his show.

As summer rolled by, the gift cards arrived, but a response from Tim Ferriss did not. I found the email address of Ferriss' assistant and sent her a note. But there was no reply. So I sent a follow-up. Still nothing.

I didn't want to bother César by asking for more help, and soon enough, I wouldn't have to. Late one night, while clearing my inbox, a newsletter caught my eye:

Evernote Conference: Register Now | The Evernote
Trunk Conference will feature bestselling authors
Tim Ferriss and Guy Kawasaki, and sessions for
developers and users.

The event was being held in San Francisco. *If I can meet Tim Ferriss and tell him about the mission in person, I'm sure he'll say yes to an interview.*

I used my *Price Is Right* money to book my plane ticket. I was so excited I even went to Niketown and bought a jet-black duffel bag for my travels. I packed it up the morning of the conference, and as I was running out the door, I grabbed a DonorsChoose gift card from the top of the stack, slipped it in my pocket, and took off.

———

THE CONFERENCE HALL IN SAN FRANCISCO was packed. As far as I could see, there were hundreds of young people in hoodies searching for seats. I looked closer and saw that many of them had *The 4-Hour Workweek* clutched under their arms. My insides twisted as reality set in: I wasn't the only one here trying to approach Tim Ferriss.

Perhaps 99 percent of the world hasn't heard his name. But to a certain niche, and probably everyone at this event, Tim Ferriss is bigger than Oprah Winfrey.

Not wanting to leave anything to chance, I paced the aisles, searching for a chair with the closest path to approach Ferriss after his speech. There was an open seat beside the stairs that led to the stage, on the far right. After I sat, the lights dimmed, the event began—and Tim Ferriss stepped on stage from the far *left*.

My eyes frantically scanned the room again. I moved to the back of the conference hall to get a better vantage point, and then I spotted it: a bathroom beside the left side of the stage.

I crept toward the men's room and slipped into a stall. Crouching next to the toilet, I pressed my ear against the tile wall, listening to Ferriss' speech so I could time my exit. I continued crouching, the smell of urine stinging my nostrils. Five minutes went by . . . ten . . . finally, thirty minutes later, I heard applause.

I raced out the bathroom door, and there he was, two feet in front of me, all alone. Once again, at the worst possible time, The Flinch wired my mouth shut. Desperate to break its hold, I reached into my pocket and shoved the gift card right at Ferriss' face.

"Oh," he said, stepping back. He glanced at the card. "Awesome! How do you know DonorsChoose? I'm on their advisory board."

Ah, you don't say.

The Flinch released its grip and I told Ferriss about the mission. I said I hoped to interview everyone from Bill Gates and Lady Gaga to Larry King and Tim Ferriss.

"Very funny," he said at the mention of his name.

"I'm serious." I reached into my other pocket and pulled out printouts of the emails I'd sent him. "I've been emailing your assistant about it for weeks."

Ferriss looked at the emails and laughed, and we ended up talking about the mission for the next few minutes. At the end, he squeezed my shoulder and told me it sounded great. He couldn't have been nicer. He said he'd get back to me in a few days.

But after I got home, days turned into weeks, and there was no word from Tim Ferriss.

What I wasn't aware of was that Ferriss *had* replied to my original interview request a month earlier, telling the DonorsChoose CEO, "Thanks, but no thanks." I guess the CEO didn't have the heart to break the news to me, so I wouldn't learn this until years later.

I continued emailing Ferriss' assistant, hoping to get an answer. Business books claimed persistence is the key to success, so I kept writing email after email, sending a total of thirty-one messages. When brief emails didn't get a response, I sent a nine-paragraph message. I wrote another telling Ferriss' assistant that doing an interview with me "would be one of the best investments of an hour Tim's ever made." I tried to remain upbeat and grateful, ending every email with "Thanks in advance!" But no matter how thoughtfully I tried to word my messages, they fell flat. Eventually I received an email from Ferriss' right-hand man saying his boss wouldn't be doing the interview anytime soon, if at all.

I couldn't understand where I'd gone wrong. Ferriss had squeezed my shoulder. I had my Inside Man.

If I can't get to Tim Ferriss, how the hell am I going to get to Bill Gates?

I continued emailing Ferriss' assistant, hoping something would change. Then one day, seemingly out of the blue, Ferriss said yes. And not only did he say yes, but he wanted to do the interview by phone the next day. I practically leapt into the air, yelling, *"Persistence! It works!"*

Much later, when it was far too late, I found out the real reason Ferriss said yes. He had called the CEO of DonorsChoose, asking what the hell was wrong with me. Thankfully, the executive's response was that, while I was rough around the edges, my heart was in the right place. And that led Ferriss to say okay. But I didn't know that, so I became completely convinced that, no matter my problem, persistence would be my answer.

———

LESS THAN TWENTY-FOUR HOURS LATER, I was on the phone with Tim Ferriss. My notepad was full of questions, and not surprisingly, the first one was about persistence. I'd read a brief mention in *The 4-Hour Workweek* that Ferriss got his first job out of college by emailing the CEO of a start-up over and over until he got a position. I wanted to know the full story.

"It wasn't just one-two-three and then you're hired," Ferriss told me.

Toward the end of his senior year in college, Ferriss did his final project on that start-up in an attempt to build a relationship with its CEO, who'd been a guest speaker in one of his classes. But when he mustered the courage to ask for a job, he was turned down. Ferriss sent the CEO more emails. After the CEO said no a dozen times, Ferriss decided it was time for a Hail Mary. He emailed the CEO saying that he'd "be in the neighborhood" next week—even though he was in New York and the CEO lived in San Francisco—and said it'd be great to stop by. "All right," the CEO wrote back. "I can meet you on Tuesday."

Ferriss got a standby ticket, flew to California, and arrived at the start-up's office early for his meeting. One of the other executives asked him, "So you're not going to stop bothering us until we give you a job, huh?"

"Sure," Ferriss told him, "if you want to put it that way."

He got the job—and, naturally, in sales.

"It's important to note," Ferriss told me, "that I was never rude. I also didn't push the density. It's not like I emailed him six times a week."

Ferriss' tone shifted, as if he was hinting at something, though embarrassingly, I couldn't figure it out. But I could sense something was off because his tone was making my head snap back as if I was getting punched.

"Where do you think that fine line is?" I asked.

"If you sense someone getting annoyed, you need to back off." *Jab.* "You need to be polite and deferential and recognize that, if you're emailing someone like that, you should have your hat in hand." *Jab.* "There's a fine line between being *persistent* and being a *hassle*." *Uppercut.*

If I had more experience interviewing, I would've dug deeper to uncover what Ferriss was trying to tell me. Instead I just fled to safer ground, looking down at my notepad in search of a different topic.

"How did you gain credibility before you were a well-known author?"

"Well, volunteering for the right organizations is an easy way to get some credible association," Ferriss said.

His tone lightened and I relaxed. Ferriss explained that when he was an entry-level employee, he volunteered at the Silicon Valley

Association of Startup Entrepreneurs where he produced large events, giving him a credible reason to email successful people. Rather than saying, "Hi, I'm Tim Ferriss, recent college graduate," he could say, "I'm Tim Ferriss, an event producer with the Silicon Valley Association of Startup Entrepreneurs." That legitimacy made a big difference.

"A second step would be writing for or being featured in known publications," he continued. "And that could be as easy as doing a Q and A with someone—interviewing them and publishing the answers online."

In other words, Ferriss didn't build credibility out of thin air, but *borrowed* it by associating himself with well-known organizations and publications. The phrase "Borrowed Credibility" stuck in my mind.

When Ferriss began writing *The 4-Hour Workweek*, he said, he had no prior experience in publishing, so he cold-emailed authors asking for advice. He said it worked well, so I asked for cold-email tactics.

"The general composition of my emails," Ferriss said, "when I'm emailing a busy person, is:

> Dear So-and-So,
>
> I know you're really busy and that you get a lot of emails, so this will only take sixty seconds to read.
> *[Here is where you say who you are: add one or two lines that establish your credibility.]*
> *[Here is where you ask your very specific question.]*
> I totally understand if you're too busy to respond, but even a one- or two-line reply would really make my day.
>
> All the best,
> Tim

Ferriss was giving me exactly the kind of advice I craved. He told me to never email someone and ask to "jump on the phone," "get coffee," or "pick your brain."

"Put your question right in the email," he said. "It might be as simple as, 'I'd like to discuss a relationship of some type that could take this-and-this form. Would you be willing to discuss it? I think a phone call might be faster, but if you prefer, I could throw a couple of questions your way via email.'

"And never write lines like, 'This is perfect for you,' or 'You'll love this because I know this-and-this about you.' Don't use super-lative or exaggerated words because"—he let out an almost mock-ing laugh—"they don't know you and they'll assume, quite fairly, it's hard for you to determine if something's perfect for them.

"I'd also not end with something like, 'Thanks in advance!' It's annoying and entitled. Do the opposite and say, 'I know you're super busy, so if you can't respond, I totally understand.'

"And certainly, watch your frequency of emailing. Don't email a lot. It really"—he let out a heavy breath—"does not make people happy."

I wasn't self-aware enough to see that Ferriss was trying to save me from myself. Over a year later, when I was rummaging through old emails, I came across the messages I'd sent Ferriss' assistant. Only then did I realize how much of an idiot I'd been.

"All right, man," Ferriss said as our conversation wrapped up. "I've got to go." He said goodbye and hung up.

A part of me wishes I could go back in time and shake my teen-age self and explain what just happened. If I'd learned my lesson then, things would have gone a lot differently when I found myself in Omaha with Warren Buffett.

CHAPTER SIX

Qi Time

Steve Jobs once said, "You can't connect the dots looking forward. You can only connect them looking backwards. So you have to trust that the dots will somehow connect in your future."

Those words couldn't have applied more to the business conference where I met César. One evening, I was feeling out of place as a student volunteer in a room full of executives when one of the speakers, Stefan Weitz, said hello to make me feel comfortable. He was a director at Microsoft and we talked for a while that night. I emailed him at the start of the summer about the mission, and when we had lunch, he insisted I add one more person to my list.

"Qi Lu."

The name was pronounced *Chee Loo* and I'd never heard of him. While I was grateful for Stefan's help, I figured I hadn't explained the mission well enough to him.

"The people I'm trying to talk to are, well, people my friends want to learn from, people everybody knows—"

"Trust me . . ." Stefan said, lifting his hand. "Qi Lu is someone you want to know."

He set up the interview, and that's how I found myself in Seattle, during the last week of summer, walking across the top floor of a Microsoft high-rise. It was a Saturday and the hallways were empty. Every desk was deserted. The lights were off in every office except one. At the end of the hall, a shadow behind the glass stood up and moved toward the door. Qi Lu opened it and bowed me in.

He was thin and in his mid-forties. Qi wore a T-shirt tucked into faded jeans, white socks with sandals. He shook my hand with both of his and told me to make myself comfortable. Instead of going back behind his desk, he pulled out a chair and sat beside me. The office was sparsely furnished. There was no art on the walls, no framed accolades. *Amazing.*

Qi Lu grew up in a rural village outside of Shanghai, China, with no running water or electricity. The village was so poor that people suffered deformities from malnutrition. There were hundreds of kids, but only one schoolteacher. At age twenty-seven, Qi Lu was making the most money he'd ever earned—seven dollars a month. Fast-forward twenty years: he's president of online services at Microsoft.

———

I ALMOST SHOOK MY HEAD in disbelief. Barely able to think of a coherent question, I just threw my hands up and asked, "How did you do it?"

Qi smiled humbly and said that when he was a kid he wanted to be a shipbuilder. He was too scrawny to pass the weight requirement, which forced him to focus on his studies. He got into Fudan University, a top college in Shanghai, where he majored in computer science—and it was there he had a realization that changed his life.

He began thinking about time. Particularly, the amount of time he felt he wasted in bed. He was sleeping eight hours a night, but then he realized that one thing in life doesn't change: whether you're a rice farmer or the president of the United States, you only get twenty-four hours in a day.

"In some ways," Qi said, "you can say God is fair to everybody. The question is: Will you use God's gift the best you possibly can?"

He read about notable people in history who'd reengineered their sleep patterns and set out to create his own system. First he cut out one hour of sleep, then another, and another. At one point, he was down to a single hour a night. He forced himself awake with ice-cold showers, but he wasn't able to sustain it. Eventually he found that the least sleep he could optimally function on was four hours a night. To this day, he hasn't slept in since.

The consistency is part of his secret.

"It's like driving a car," Qi told me. "If you always drive at sixty-five miles per hour, it doesn't wear and tear the car that much. But if you speed up and slam the brakes often, that wears the engine down."

Qi wakes up every morning at four o'clock, goes on a five-mile run, and is in the office by six. He eats small meals throughout the day of mostly fruits and vegetables, which he packs in containers. He works eighteen hours a day, six days a week. And Stefan Weitz had told me that the word around Microsoft was that Qi works *twice as fast* as everyone else. They call it "Qi Time."

Qi Time seemed like a fanatical, even unhealthy lifestyle. But when I thought about it through the lens of Qi's circumstances, I saw it less as a quirky experiment and more as a means of survival. Think about it. With so many brilliant college students in China, how else could Qi have found an edge to break through? If you cut 8 hours of sleep down to 4, then multiply the saved time by 365 days, that equals 1,460 extra hours—or *2 additional months* of productivity per year.

During his twenties, Qi spent the extra time he created writing research papers and reading more books, striving toward his biggest dream of studying in the United States.

"In China," he said, "if you wanted to go to the United States, you had to take two tests. The fees to take them were sixty dollars. My salary each month, I think, was equivalent to seven dollars."

That was eight months' salary just to take the entrance exams.

Qi didn't lose hope, though, and all his hard work paid off on a Sunday night. He usually spent Sundays riding his bike to his village to visit his family, but it was pouring rain and the trip took hours, so Qi stayed in his dorm room. That evening, a friend came by to ask for help. A visiting professor from Carnegie Mellon University was about to give a lecture on model checking, but because of the rain, attendance was embarrassingly low. Qi agreed to help fill the seats, and during the lecture, he asked some questions. Afterward, the professor complimented Qi on the points he'd raised and wondered if he'd done any research on the topic.

Qi hadn't just done some research—he'd published five papers. That's the power of Qi Time. It enabled him to be the most prepared person in the room.

The professor asked to see the papers. Qi sprinted to his dorm room to fetch them. After the professor looked them over, he asked Qi if he'd be interested in studying in the United States.

Qi explained his financial constraints and the professor said he would waive the sixty-dollar qualification tests. Qi applied, and months later, a letter arrived. Carnegie Mellon offered him a full scholarship.

Every time I'd read about Bill Gates, Warren Buffett, or other examples of meteoric success, I wondered how much their achievements were a result of seemingly miraculous coincidences. If it hadn't rained that Sunday night, Qi would have been home with his family, wouldn't have met the professor, and none of this would have happened. At the same time, there was nothing coincidental about Qi having published those five research papers. I asked Qi about luck, and he said he believes it isn't completely random.

"Luck is like a bus," he told me. "If you miss one, there's always the next one. But if you're not prepared, you won't be able to jump on."

———

TWO YEARS AFTER QI FINISHED at Carnegie Mellon, a friend invited him to lunch. There was a person at the table Qi didn't know. The new acquaintance asked what he was working on and Qi said he worked at IBM researching e-commerce platforms.

The friend-of-a-friend worked for Yahoo, which at the time was known for its prominent Web directory. He asked Qi to stop by his office on Monday and Qi agreed. When he arrived at Yahoo headquarters, there was a job offer on the table.

Yahoo had secret plans to build an e-commerce platform and sought someone to build it. Qi joined the company, took on the project, and spent nearly every second he had coding. For three months, he cut his sleep down even more to just one or two hours a night—working so hard he got carpal tunnel syndrome and had to wear a brace. Qi felt it was worth it, though, because he ultimately created what we now know as Yahoo Shopping.

Qi was promoted to head the company's next major initiative: Yahoo Search. That turned out to be another home run, but Qi didn't slow down. In addition to taking on more engineering projects, Qi spent his weekends holed up in a library, reading stacks of books about leadership and management.

I realized Qi Time wasn't just about sleeping less. It was about sacrifice—sacrificing short-term pleasure for long-term gain. In just eight years at Yahoo, Qi became an executive vice president, overseeing more than three thousand engineers.

After nearly a decade at the company, Qi decided the ten-year mark would be a good time to finally take a break. During Qi's last week at Yahoo, his staff handed out T-shirts at his going-away party that read: "I worked with Qi. Did you?"

Qi was considering heading back to China with his family when he got a call from Microsoft CEO Steve Ballmer. Microsoft was looking to build a search engine. Qi met with Ballmer and decided not to go back to China, accepting Ballmer's offer to become president of online services.

As Qi told me about working through the nights to create the Bing search engine, a weird feeling sank into my stomach. My thoughts began to wander, and then a distant memory flashed in my mind.

I was five years old. In the middle of the night I'd had a bad dream, so I climbed out of bed to go to my parents' room. As I made my way down the dark hallway, I saw a blue light seeping through the bottom of their door. I poked my head in and saw my mom sitting at her tiny desk, typing on the computer. Night after night, I'd crawl out of bed and spy on my mom working as the rest of the family slept. I would later learn that my dad had just filed for bankruptcy for his used-car lot, which meant my mom had to keep our family afloat. Perhaps, in her own way, my mom's sacrifice was like Qi Lu's sacrifice.

Only now, while listening to Qi Lu, did I understand why my mom had been crying when I'd said I was leaving premed. To her, I was turning my back on everything she'd worked for. The guilt of how ungrateful I'd been was so painful I began to squirm. Then, Qi took the conversation to one of the last places I expected.

"By the way," he said, "thank you for doing what you're doing. What's motivating you to go on your mission is, in some ways, similar to what motivates me. Every minute of every day, it's about empowering people to know more, do more, and be more. I think what you're doing, in many ways, is a great example of that."

He offered to help in any way he could. I pulled the index card out of my wallet with the names of the people I hoped to interview and handed it over. Qi nodded his head as his finger slowly went down the list.

"The only person I know personally," he said, "is Bill Gates."

"Do you . . . do you think he'd be interested?"

"Yes, you absolutely should have a chance to talk to him. I'll mention your book to him."

"Maybe I could write an email?"

Qi smiled. "I would be happy to forward it to him."

CHAPTER SEVEN

The Hidden Reservoir

*B*ILL FUCKING GATES!" Corwin hollered.

He raised his glass to toast the news. Brandon, Ryan, and I lifted our glasses too. We clinked them together and continued celebrating in the dining hall all night.

Sophomore year couldn't have started better. I was so happy I had to hold myself back from dancing as I walked to class. Even lectures were more enjoyable now. A few days later, as I was headed to the library, I saw an email from Qi Lu's assistant on my phone.

Hi Alex,

I have reached out to BillG's office and they unfortunately cannot accommodate this request . . .

I read the message again, but my mind refused to accept it. I called Stefan Weitz, my Inside Man at Microsoft. He explained that Bill Gates probably didn't turn me down himself; his Chief of Staff makes most of these decisions.

"Is there any way you can get me in front of the Chief of Staff?" I asked. "All I need is five minutes. Just let me talk to him myself."

Stefan told me to sit tight and he'd see what he could do.

But I couldn't sit tight. That night I decided to channel all my frustration into Qi Time. Qi wasn't born on Qi Time—he chose to do it. And now I was making that choice too. Every morning that followed, I jumped out of bed at six o'clock, went straight to my desk, and wrote cold emails, requesting interviews from everyone on my list. When I got rejected by all of them, I reached out to people beyond my initial list. I woke up even earlier and worked even harder, but that only led me to getting rejected twice as fast. *No, no, no, no, no, no, no.*

Some of the no's hurt more than others, like the one with Wolfgang Puck. I'd answered a trivia question on Twitter, won tickets to a food and wine red carpet event, and then I approached the acclaimed chef there. When I asked for an interview, he said, "I'd love to! Come by the restaurant and we can do it over lunch!" He hugged me like we were old friends. The following day, I emailed his representative as if she were my old friend too.

> Hey *****,
>
> My name is Alex and I'm an undergraduate student at USC. I spoke with Wolfgang last night at the LAFW red carpet event and he told me to contact you about setting up a meeting time for an interview. He said it would be best if I come over for lunch at "the restaurant" (in all honesty, I'm not sure which one he was referring to! haha) . . .

She didn't reply. So I followed up once, twice, and even a fourth time. Clearly, I hadn't learned my lesson from Tim Ferriss. Puck's representative responded a month later.

> hey alex—
>
> yes, we did receive your emails, and hey, I've been thinking of the proper response. so hey, I know you will take the advice as constructive when I tell you that when you contact the world's most successful people, I might suggest you do not say, hey larry king, or hey george lucas. typically, such queries would start as "dear mr. king" or "dear mr. lucas" out of respect.
>
> but hey, I digress . . .
>
> I spoke to wolfgang about this before he left for new york, and although it sounds like an interesting opportunity, unfortunately, he will not have time to do this because he has a full schedule now until the end of the year with his recent opening of CUT in london and his ongoing opening activities at the hotel bel air. wolfgang asked that I respond to you on his behalf to tell you that he is sorry, but he cannot participate . . .

As the days of fall dragged on, I felt more and more despondent, each rejection beating away at my self-worth. Getting up before sunrise morning after morning, just to get rejected, felt like I was lying on a road so a truck could run me over, reverse, then run me over some more. But there was one person who didn't turn me into roadkill, and I thank God for him, because he may have saved the mission.

Most people know Sugar Ray Leonard as the six-time world champion boxer with the bright smile in the 7 Up and Nintendo commercials. If you know the sport well, you know him as the slick, quick-punching artist who became a global sensation at the 1976 Olympics.

After attending his book signing and getting pushed aside by security, I used the Tim Ferriss cold-email template to reach out to someone who did public relations work for Sugar Ray. We met and she became my Inside Man. I wrote Sugar Ray a letter explaining that I was nineteen, and after reading his autobiography, I sensed his advice was exactly what my generation needed. As soon as my Inside Man passed along the note, Sugar Ray invited me to his house.

He met me at the door wearing a black tracksuit and showed me to his home gym. The second I stepped in, it felt like I'd entered the Cave of Wonders in *Aladdin*—except the gold covering the walls wasn't buried treasure, but gold medals and glimmering plaques engraved with the words WORLD CHAMPION. A punching bag hung from the ceiling. Dumbbells and treadmills surrounded the plush leather couch in the middle. All the sparkle coming off the gold fit into my image of Sugar Ray—but when we sat and started talking, I soon realized I had no idea what was underneath that sparkle.

Sugar Ray told me he grew up in a family of nine in Palmer Park, Maryland. Money was so tight that one Christmas the only gifts under the tree were the apples and oranges Ray's dad stole from the supermarket stockroom where he worked. His dad had boxed in the navy, so when Ray was seven he decided to give the sport a try. He climbed into the ring at the No. 2 Boys Club outside of Palmer Park, and within seconds, he was getting pounded in the face. Blood gushed from his nose. His legs burned as he moved around the mat. He walked away defeated, head pounding, and returned home to his comic books.

Six years later, his older brother urged him to give boxing another try. Ray returned to the gym and got beat up again. This time, though, he decided to stay with it. He was younger, shorter, skinnier, and less experienced than the other boys, so he realized he needed an edge.

He dressed for school one morning and walked with his brothers and sisters to the bus stop. As the yellow bus pulled to the curb, the other kids stepped on, but Ray held back. He threw his backpack on the bus, tightened his shoelaces, and as the bus drove away, he chased after it, running behind it all the way to school. That afternoon, he ran behind the bus again all the way home. He did it the next day as well. And the next. He ran in the heat, the rain, the snow—some days were so cold that ice froze on his face. He chased the school bus day after day after day.

"I didn't have the experience," Sugar Ray told me, "but I had the heart, the discipline, and the desire."

As soon as that last word left his mouth, he looked at me a bit differently and asked what was motivating me to chase my dream. We talked about the mission, and Sugar Ray made me feel so comfortable that I admitted to him how defeated I'd felt trying to arrange interviews. He asked to see my list. While looking it over, Sugar Ray subtly shook his head and smiled, as if he understood something that I didn't. He then began telling me the story of one of the biggest fights of his life, and the lesson was exactly what I needed to hear.

Five years after he'd turned pro, Sugar Ray stepped into the ring with Thomas "The Hitman" Hearns. Not only was The Hitman undefeated, but he'd also won nearly every fight by knockout. He famously had a far-reaching left jab that would snap his opponent's head back, which then set up the real terror that seemed to come out of nowhere: The Hitman's deadly right hand.

Tens of thousands filed into Caesars Palace and millions tuned in on pay-per-view. The bout was billed as "The Showdown." The winner would be named the undisputed welterweight champion of the world.

After the opening bell rang, The Hitman's far-reaching jab

zoned in on Sugar Ray's left eye. *Jab* after *jab* after *jab*, to the point where Ray's eyelids became black and purple and swollen shut. Sugar Ray rallied back in the middle rounds, but by the twelfth, he was still behind on the scorecards. He slumped forward on his stool in the corner of the ring, his left eye throbbing. He tried to force it fully open, but he couldn't, leaving him with only half his vision in that eye.

The only way he could win was by stepping through the strike zone of The Hitman's right hand. That was crazy to begin with, but without being able to fully see out of his left eye, it was practically suicide. Sugar Ray's trainer crouched in front of him and looked him square on.

"You're blowing it now, son. You're blowing it."

Those words triggered a powerful feeling within Ray that spread throughout his body. Thirty years later, as we sat on his couch, he made those words come alive.

"You may have the heart—you keep fighting, you keep fighting, you keep fighting—but your mind is saying, 'Man, forget this. I don't need this.' The head and the heart aren't going together; but they *have to* go together. It all has to connect. Everything has to connect to reach that level, that pinnacle.

"You may have a desire, a wish, a dream—but it's got to be more than that—you've got to want it to the point that it hurts. Most people never reach that point. They never tap into what I call the Hidden Reservoir, your hidden reserve of strength. We all have it. When they say a mother lifted up a car off a trapped child, *that's* that power."

The bell for the thirteenth round rang and Sugar Ray exploded out of his corner as if the blood in his veins had turned into pure, concentrated adrenaline. He shot off twenty-five consecutive punches and The Hitman flew into the ropes, dropped to the floor, and then stumbled up. Ray sprinted after him. The Hitman stumbled back again but the bell saved him. When the next round began, Ray ran out in overdrive again and pummeled Hearns with a blizzard of punches to the head. Then, with just a minute to go in the fourteenth round, The Hitman went limp into the ropes. The referee stopped the fight. Ray was the undisputed champion of the world.

The story hung in the air, and then Sugar Ray stood up from the couch, stepped toward the door, and motioned for me to follow.

"I want to show you something."

We headed down a dimly lit hallway. He told me to stay put and disappeared around a corner. A minute later, he returned holding his gold world-championship belt. Soft light shimmered off its ridges. Sugar Ray stepped over and put it around my waist.

He stepped back, giving me a moment to let the feeling sink in.

"How many times have people told you, 'You can't interview these types of people'? How many times have they said, 'No way'? Don't let *anyone* tell you your dream isn't possible. When you have a vision, you've got to hang in there. You've got to stay in the fight. It's going to get tough. You're going to hear no. But you've got to keep pushing. You've got to keep fighting. You've got to use your Hidden Reservoir. It's not going to be easy, but it's possible.

"When I saw in the letter that you're nineteen, I remembered how I felt when I was your age. I was eager. I was excited. I was hungry. I wanted that gold medal more than anything. And when I look at you"—he paused and stepped toward me, pointing his finger at my face—"don't let *anybody* take that away from you."

STEP 3

FIND YOUR INSIDE MAN

CHAPTER EIGHT

The Dream Mentor

I t was a good thing Sugar Ray gave me that talk, because rejections pounded me for the rest of fall. The holidays flew by faster than I liked and it was now January, the first week of spring semester, and the prospects of reaching the people I dreamed of were grim.

I was standing in a CVS parking lot one afternoon, a heavy sheet of gray clouds overhead, and a chocolate-brownie ice cream cone in my hand. When life beats you down, at least there's always ice cream.

My phone buzzed in my pocket. My eyes widened when I saw the Seattle area code. Instantly, it felt like the gray clouds were parting and white light was shining down on me.

"So, you want to interview Bill, huh?"

On the line was Bill Gates' Chief of Staff.

Stefan Weitz, my Inside Man at Microsoft, had managed to arrange the call. To preserve the Chief of Staff's privacy, I'll leave his name out.

I started telling him about the mission, but he said there was no need because Stefan and Qi Lu had already told him all about it.

"I love what you're doing," the Chief of Staff said. "I love your initiative. I love that you're doing this to help others and I'd love to support this"—just hearing that made me feel like I was 99 percent there—"but, the thing is, you're only about five percent there. I just can't take this to Bill. You don't have enough momentum."

Momentum?

"Look," he added. "I can't present an interview request to Bill for a book that doesn't even have a publisher. Even when Malcolm Gladwell came to us for *Outliers*, it wasn't a sure thing. Now—if you can get more interviews done, if you can get a publishing deal from Penguin or Random House—then we can sit down and discuss presenting this to Bill. But before any of that can happen, you need to engineer more momentum."

He said goodbye and hung up, leaving me in a haze, two words echoing in my head. *Five percent?* The next thing I knew I was in the storage closet, my head in my hands, those words still reverberating in my mind.

At this rate, my friends would be in rocking chairs by the time the mission was completed. If Qi Lu's introduction only got me 5 percent of the way there with Bill Gates, then I must be at negative 20 percent with people like Warren Buffett or Bill Clinton. And with all the tests and homework I have for school, I'll be—

Wait, Bill Clinton . . .

A vague memory came to me as though there was an itch on my mind.

Didn't someone tell me over the summer that Bill Clinton and Richard Branson spoke on a cruise ship or something? And some young guy organized it?

I reached for my laptop, Googled "Bill Clinton Richard Branson cruise ship," and found an article on FastCompany.com:

In 2008 Elliott Bisnow, an entrepreneur with several companies to his name, started Summit Series, an "un-conference conference" that would serve as a mutual aid society for young entrepreneurs. It started with 19 people on a ski trip, and has grown to more than 750 people who attended their latest event in May. Part networking, part TED, part extreme sports, these invitation-only events have become the epicenter of social entrepreneurship. And along the way, Summit Series had raised over $1.5 million for not-for-profits. Participants include Bill Clinton, Russell Simmons, Sean Parker, Mark Cuban, Ted Turner, and John Legend.

I kept reading and then did a double take: Elliott Bisnow, the CEO of Summit Series, the man who brought all these leaders together—was only twenty-five years old. How was that possible? That was my cousin's age.

I typed in "Elliott Bisnow" and ripped through the search results. Dozens of articles mentioned him, but not one was about him. He had a blog with hundreds of posts, but all they had were pictures—Elliott surfing in Nicaragua; hanging with supermodels in Tel Aviv; at the Running of the Bulls in Spain; at the Tour de France in Belgium; at the White House standing with the co-founder of Twitter and the CEO of Zappos. There were photos of him building classrooms in Haiti, giving vision tests in Jamaica, delivering shoes to kids in Mexico. There was even a video of him in a Diet Coke ad.

In one article, I learned that CNN founder Ted Turner was his hero and that Elliott hoped to meet him one day. Then I discovered a picture of Elliott and Ted Turner shaking hands a year later at the United Nations. There were images of Elliott Bisnow living on a beach in Costa Rica and on a houseboat in Amsterdam. In all the photos, he wore T-shirts and jeans and had a scruffy beard and thick brown hair. I found an article in the *Huffington Post* titled "Tech's Biggest Party Boys." Elliott ranked sixth. The closing line threw me back in my chair. "Bisnow's latest plan: Buy a $40 million mountain in Utah."

I continued clicking and missed two meals without noticing. I found a picture of him laughing with President Clinton in someone's living room, another of him presenting Clinton with an award, and a third with Clinton on stage at a Summit event. Yet there was nothing online that told me exactly who Elliott Bisnow was. It was like going through the blog of the guy from *Catch Me If You Can*.

I couldn't wrap my head around this guy. Though at the same time, I experienced a deep, almost overwhelming feeling of connection with him. Elliott's dream was to bring together the world's top entrepreneurs, and somehow, he'd pulled it off.

Bill Gates' Chief of Staff had said I needed to engineer momentum. Clearly, Elliott had figured out how. I felt I was looking at the one person who held the answer.

I lowered my head, closed my eyes, and thought, if there is one thing I want more than anything right now, it's Elliott's guidance. I pulled out my journal, turned to a fresh page, and scribbled "Dream Mentors" across the top. On the first line, I wrote: "Elliott Bisnow."

———

MY PILE OF HOMEWORK and tests grew even more, so I spent every night that week in the library, just trying to survive. But each day I caught my mind wandering, imagining what it would be like to talk to Elliott Bisnow. One afternoon, three days before my accounting final, I couldn't hold myself back anymore. *Screw it, I'll just send him an email.* It's not like I wanted to interview him. I just had one question to ask Elliott so I could get to Bill Gates: How do I engineer momentum?

I began writing a cold email. Two hours later, I was still at it, weaving in details about Elliott so he'd know I'd gone to the twenty-third page of a Google search to find them. I figured he must be the king of cold emails, so it had to be perfect.

> From: Alex Banayan
> To: Elliott Bisnow
> Subject: Mr. Bisnow—I could really use some advice from you
>
> Hi Mr. Bisnow,
>
> My name is Alex and I'm a sophomore at USC. I know this is pretty out-of-the-blue, but I'm a big fan of yours and I could really use your advice on a project I'm working on. I know you're really busy and that you get a lot of emails, so this will only take sixty seconds to read.
>
> My story is that I'm a nineteen-year-old who is writing a book with the hope of changing the dynamic of my generation. The book will feature some of the world's most successful people and will focus on what they were doing early on in their careers to get to where they are today. I'm truly humbled by the people who have already jumped on board for this mission—from Microsoft president Qi Lu to author Tim Ferriss. I'm determined to combine the greats from the older generation along with the new generation, and integrate their wisdom and practical advice into one book that changes people's lives. Like you say, "make no small plans" :)

Mr. Bisnow, being nineteen years old and pursuing my vision does have some obstacles, so it would be unbelievably helpful to get some guidance from you on the topic of: How did you effectively bring all these luminaries together behind a single vision? You did it masterfully with your first ski trip in 2008, and you've continued to do it better and better as the years have gone on.

I'm sure you're really busy, but if there is any chance we can connect so I can soak up some guidance, that would mean the world to me. If you'd like, I could field some specific questions your way via email, we can talk via telephone for a few minutes, or if your schedule permits, I'd love to meet you either at a coffee shop, or ... if the planets align ... at the world-famous Summit House :)

I totally understand if you're too busy to respond, but even a one- or two-line reply would really make my day.

Dreaming big,
Alex

I spent thirty minutes searching online for his email address, but I couldn't find it. Three hours later, I still had nothing. So I typed out my five best guesses of what it could be and put them all in the "To:" field. I prayed to God, and to the holy spirit of the Tim-Ferriss-cold-email, that it would work.

Twenty-four hours later, Elliott replied:

great email
    r u in LA tomorrow or thurs?

I checked my calendar. Thursday was my accounting final. "I'm completely free both days."

I hoped he wouldn't want to meet Thursday. At USC, anyone who misses a final exam fails the course.

Elliott replied right back:

> can u meet me at 8am in long beach on thurs in the lobby of the renaissance hotel? sorry to make u come so far, i am at a conference here
>
> and u should read "when I stop talking you'll know I'm dead" and get to the part about the star of ardaban before we meet, maybe it's a chapter or two in . . . u will love the book

Go on *The Price Is Right*—not study for finals. Meet Elliott—risk missing a final. It was as if someone was playing a video game of my life and sitting back, laughing, and flinging banana peels at my feet. Each impossible decision was a checkpoint, testing to see where my heart truly was.

For the first time though, I didn't hesitate.

CHAPTER NINE

The Rules

Two days later, I sat on a couch in the middle of the hotel lobby, glancing between my watch and the main entrance. If our meeting lasted twenty minutes, and it took half an hour to get back to school, that gave me two hours to cram before my final. And if our meeting lasted an hour, I would still have—

My mental calculations stopped as Elliott strode in, right on time.

He cut across the lobby. Even at a distance, Elliott's eyes were sharp and piercing. They scanned the room slowly, almost too slowly, like a panther's eyes scouring the jungle floor. As he walked closer, he seemed to never blink. He spotted me and threw me a nod, then sat beside me.

"Give me a second," he said without making eye contact.

He took out his phone and typed away.

One minute passed . . . then two . . . then . . .

He glanced up and caught me staring at him. My eyes darted

away. I checked my watch. We were five minutes into our meeting and we'd barely spoken.

As I snuck another look at Elliott, I couldn't help but smile when I saw his shoes. My prediction was right.

I'd noticed at USC during fraternity rush that students gravitated toward people they looked similar to, which made me think that the more you look like the other person, the easier it is to strike up a friendship. So I spent some time that morning wondering what Elliott would wear. I put on blue jeans, a green V-neck shirt, and brown TOMS shoes, because I'd read that the founder of TOMS went to Summit events. Elliott was wearing gray jeans, a blue V-neck, and gray TOMS. But with his head down and eyes glued to the screen, I felt that what I wore would be the last thing he'd notice.

"You still in school?" he asked, not lifting his head.

"Yeah. I'm a sophomore."

"You going to drop out?"

"What?"

"You heard what I said."

My grandma's face flashed in my mind. *Jooneh man.*

"No," I blurted. "No. I'm not."

Elliott let out a soft laugh. "Okay. We'll see."

I changed the subject. "So, I can tell you're really good at bringing people together and building momentum for your Summit events, and I'm really curious how you do it. So my one question for you is—"

"You don't have to ask just one question."

"Okay, so, I guess my first question is: What was the tipping point in your career that allowed you to build so much momentum?"

"There is no tipping point," he said, still typing away. "It's all just little steps."

To someone else, that might've been a good answer. But I'd spent weeks dreaming of Elliott offering an entire monologue on the subject, so the fact he didn't give more than a five-word explanation made me feel like he was blowing me off.

"Well, okay, so I guess my next question is—"

"Did you read the 'Star of Ardaban' chapter? Did you even open the book yet? Or can you not even handle reading two chapters on a day's notice?"

"I read it," I said, "and I finished the whole book."

Elliott finally looked up. He put his phone away.

"Man, I was just like you when I was your age," he said. "I hustled just like you're hustling. And that cold email you sent me, you probably researched for a whole week to write that, huh?"

"Two weeks. And then it took another three hours just trying to find your email address."

"Yeah, man. I did that kind of stuff all the time."

I finally relaxed, which was a mistake, because Elliott immediately turned on me, firing a machine gun of questions about the mission. He asked them so intensely, so rapidly, I felt I was being interrogated. I answered the best I could, unsure how our conversation was going. Elliott laughed when I told him about the time I crouched in the bathroom.

He checked the time on his phone.

"Listen," he said. "I only expected this to last thirty minutes. But maybe— Wait, don't you have class today?"

"I'm all good. What do you have in mind?"

"Well, if you want, you can stick around for a bit and sit in on my next meeting."

"That sounds amazing."

"Okay, cool," he said. "But first, we need ground rules. These five things aren't just for today. They're for the rest of your life." He locked his eyes onto mine. "Write these down."

I took out my phone to type them into the notepad.

"Rule number one: *Never* use your phone in a meeting. I don't care if you're just taking notes. Using your phone makes you look like a chump. Always carry a pen in your pocket. The more digital the world gets, the more impressive it is to use a pen. And anyway, if you're in a meeting, it's just rude to be on your phone.

"Rule number two: Act like you belong. Walk into a room like you've been there before. Don't gawk over celebrities. Be cool. Be calm. And never, *ever* ask someone for a picture. If you want to be treated like a peer, you need to act like one. Fans ask for pictures. Peers shake hands.

"Speaking of pictures, rule number three: Mystery makes history. When you're doing cool shit, don't post pictures of it on Facebook. No one actually changing the world posts everything they do online. Keep people guessing what you're up to. Plus, the people you're going to impress by posting things online aren't the people you should care about impressing.

"Now, rule number four," he said, slowly stressing each word, "this rule is the most important. If you break it"—he moved his hand across his neck in a slicing motion—"you're done.

"If you break my trust, you're finished. Never, ever go back on your word. If I tell you something in confidence, you need to be a vault. What goes in does not come out. This goes for your relationships with everyone from this day forward. If you act like a vault, people will treat you like a vault. It will take years to build your reputation, but seconds to ruin it. Understood?"

"Understood."

"Good." He stood up and looked down at me. "Get up."

"But I thought you said there were five rules?"

"Uh, oh yeah. Here's a last one: Adventures only happen to the adventurous."

Before I could ask what that meant, Elliott walked away. I followed. He turned his head back to me. "Ready to play with the big boys?"

I nodded.

"By the way," he added, looking me up and down, "nice TOMS."

———

ELLIOTT'S MEETING BEGAN and I found myself sitting with my forearms on my knees, listening more intently than I ever had to a professor in class. Elliott started it casually, making jokes and asking his guest how her morning was going. Then almost unnoticeably, he shifted the full force of his focus on her: What was she passionate about? What was she working on? When she was polite and asked Elliott about himself, he laughed and said, "Oh, I'm not that interesting," and posed another question. For essentially the entire interaction, Elliott barely spoke about himself. Finally, at what seemed like the last 10 percent of the meeting, Elliott shared his story: "The city of my dreams didn't exist, so I'm setting out to build it." He was buying the largest private ski mountain in North America in a city called Eden, Utah, and creating a small, residential community on the backside of the mountain for entrepreneurs, artists, and activists. Then just as she was hooked, Elliott ended the conversation.

He gave her a hug and she headed off. Then another guest arrived. The second meeting flowed as smoothly as the first. I was mesmerized by how Elliott controlled their interaction. I didn't want to take my eyes off him, yet I kept sneaking looks at my watch. I had to be on the road within the hour.

After the second meeting ended, Elliott stood up and motioned for me to do the same.

"Having fun?" he asked.

I let out a giant grin.

"Great," he said. "You're going to love this next one."

I trailed close behind as he headed for the exit. All I could see in my mind was an enormous hourglass, the sand trickling down until my final exam.

We crossed the street to the Westin hotel, which wasn't just any hotel. This week it was the main lodging of the TED conference, one of the most exclusive gatherings in the world. We made our way to the lobby restaurant. It was intimate, no more than fifteen tables. Classical music played in the background, accented by the chimes of tiny spoons against porcelain cups.

Elliott walked directly to the host. "Table for four, please."

As we were escorted through the dining area, I figured I should tell Elliott that I might have to leave this meeting early, but right then Elliott greeted a man at a nearby table. I recognized him instantly: Tony Hsieh, the CEO of Zappos. His book *Delivering Happiness* was still on the top row of my bookshelf.

Elliott continued walking. "You see that guy over there," he whispered to me. "That's Larry Page, the CEO of Google. That guy to your left is Reid Hoffman. He's the founder of LinkedIn. Now look over there. The table in the far back—the guy with the glasses, he created Gmail. On your right, in the blue running shorts, that's Chad. He's the cofounder of YouTube."

We got to our table and Elliott's guests arrived. First came Franck, the cofounder of Startup Weekend, one of the world's largest entrepreneurial organizations; then Brad, the cofounder of Groupon, which at the time was valued at thirteen billion dollars. The three of them chatted. Throughout the meal, Elliott's gaze kept darting my way as if he was judging me. I couldn't tell if he wanted me to speak up more or if the one time I did was one too many.

Halfway through breakfast, the cofounder of Groupon went to the restroom, then the cofounder of Startup Weekend stepped to the side to take a call. Elliott turned to me and continued the interrogation.

"So where are you getting your money from? How are you paying for all your travels?"

I told him I was using the money I won on a game show.

"You what?" he said.

"Have you heard of *The Price Is Right*?"

"Everyone's heard of *The Price Is Right*."

"Well, last year, two nights before finals, I pulled an all-nighter and figured out how to hack the show. I went the next day, won a sailboat, sold it, and that's how I'm funding my mission."

Elliott put his fork down. "Hold on. You're telling me that we've been together for over two hours now and you never told me that you *funded your entire adventure by hacking a game show*?"

I shrugged.

"You idiot!" he said.

He leaned in and lowered his voice, enunciating each word. "Never again will you sit in a meeting with someone and not tell them that. Your mission is nice, but this story tells me more about who you are than anything else you could possibly say. This story commands attention.

"Everybody has experiences in their lives," he added. "Some choose to make them into stories."

I was so transfixed by Elliott's words I barely noticed that his guests had sat back down.

"Alex, tell them what you just told me," Elliott said. "Tell them how you funded your mission."

I stumbled through the story. Despite my stutters, by the end the dynamic of the table had changed. The cofounder of Groupon cut me off. "That's . . . *incredible*." He spoke to me for the rest of breakfast, sharing his stories and advice, then giving me his email address and telling me to stay in touch.

I snuck another look at my watch. If I didn't leave in a few minutes, I was dead.

Excusing myself from the table, I stepped to the side and looked up the number for the USC business school office. As the dial tone rang in my ear, I looked over my shoulder at all the CEOs and billionaires I'd dreamed of learning from.

A secretary picked up, and with an overwhelming sense of urgency I blurted, "Patch me through to the dean." For some reason, she did. The business school's associate dean—not the film school dean who had stopped me with Spielberg—answered the phone.

"It's Alex Banayan. I need to explain to you where I'm standing right now. Within ten feet of me is . . ." and I went on to list everyone in my vicinity. "I don't need to explain to you how rare of an opportunity this is. Now, I have an accounting final in an hour, and I would have to leave right this second to get to campus on time. I can't make this decision—*you* have to make this decision. And I need an answer within thirty seconds."

She didn't respond.

After thirty seconds, I asked if she was still there.

"You didn't hear this from me," she said, "but email your professor tomorrow morning saying your flight from San Francisco to LA was delayed, you had no control over the matter, and that's why you missed the final."

Click. She hung up.

To this day, it's hard to fully express how grateful I am for what the associate dean did for me that morning.

When I returned to the table, breakfast continued and the energy kept building. The cofounder of Groupon invited me to visit him in Chicago. Then Reid Hoffman stopped by our table. Eventually, Elliott's two guests left and I sat there, looking around the restaurant, taking it all in.

"Hey, big shot," Elliott whispered. "You want to interview a tech mogul, don't you? There's the CEO of Google, twenty feet away from you. This is your chance. Go talk to him. Let's see what you got."

A wave of panic washed over me.

"If you want it," Elliott said, "there it is."

"I usually prepare for weeks before I ask someone for an interview. I don't know anything about him. I don't think this is such a good idea."

"Do it."

It was almost as if Elliott could smell The Flinch.

"Come on, tough guy," he went on. "Let's see what you got."

I didn't move.

"Come on. Do it," he said, sounding like a drug dealer. With each sentence, his shoulders rose higher and chest grew broader, as if he was fueling off my discomfort. He bore into me with his panther-like eyes.

"When it's in front of you," Elliott said, "make your move."

Larry Page, the CEO of Google, pushed his seat back. I could barely feel my legs. Page began walking away. I stood up.

I shadowed him out of the restaurant and down some stairs. He entered a restroom. I cringed . . . *Not again.* I stepped in and saw six urinals. Larry Page was at one end. The other five were empty. Without thinking, I chose the one farthest from him. As I stood there, I tried to come up with something clever to say. But all I could hear in my head was Elliott's voice: *When it's in front of you, make your move.*

Page stepped over to wash his hands. I followed, again choosing the farthest sink. The more I thought about failing, the more I failed.

Page was drying his hands. I had to say something.

"Uh, you're Larry Page, right?"

"Yes."

My face went blank. Page looked at me, confused, and then walked out. And that was that.

I dragged my feet back to the breakfast table where Elliott was waiting. I slumped in my seat.

"What happened?" he asked.

"Uh . . . well . . ."

"You've got a lot to learn."

CHAPTER TEN

Adventures Only Happen
to the Adventurous

Bill Gates' Chief of Staff had said I needed a publishing deal, so I set out to get one. I began Googling and it didn't take long to learn the basics. First you write a book proposal, which you use to attract a literary agent, who then secures a publisher. Every blog post I read stressed that you can't land a deal with a major publisher without a literary agent, so the way I saw it was: no agent, no Bill Gates.

I bought more than a dozen books about the process—*How to Write a Book Proposal*, *Bestselling Book Proposals*, *Bulletproof Book Proposals*—and stacked them in a gigantic tower on my desk. As I plowed through them and started my proposal, I used the Tim Ferriss cold-email template to reach out to dozens of bestselling authors for advice, and miraculously, the guidance flooded in. They answered my questions over email, spoke with me on the phone, and some even met me in person. Their kindness blew me away and they helped me understand the obstacles I was up against. I was a young, unknown writer, with no prior experience, entering the publishing industry at a time when it was shrinking and difficult for even successful writers to get deals.

Because of that, the authors I spoke to stressed how important it was to focus on marketing ideas, both in my proposal and when I spoke to agents. They told me to use every fact and statistic I could to prove the book would sell, because without proof, why would an agent waste his or her time? But first, I needed to figure out exactly which agents to approach.

One author told me how.

He said to buy twenty books similar to the one I wanted to write, study the acknowledgments, and make notes of whom the authors thanked as their agents. I spent weeks compiling my list, researching what other books the agents represented and determining which agents might be best.

Then one night in the storage closet, I grabbed a sheet of white printer paper, uncapped a thick black marker, and wrote across the top: NO AGENT, NO BILL GATES.

One by one, I scrawled the names of twenty agents, starting with my favorite and working my way down. I taped the list on the wall. After I finished my proposal, I began reaching out to them, a few at a time. As sophomore year ended and summer began, their responses trickled in.

"Books like this don't sell," one told me. I drew a line through her name.

"I don't think we're a right fit," another said. I crossed him off too.

"I'm not taking on any additional clients."

Each rejection stung more than the last. One day, as I racked my mind wondering what I was doing wrong, my phone buzzed on my desk. It was a text from Elliott. Just seeing his name made me immediately grab my phone.

I'm in LA . . . come hang for a bit

Desperate for a break, I headed straight to Elliott's Santa Monica apartment. When I got there, I found him and his twenty-four-year-old brother, Austin, on a couch, each with a laptop in hand.

"Yo!" I said.

Elliott shot down my enthusiasm with a dismissive stare. He turned his attention back to his laptop.

"We're going to Europe tonight," he said.

"Oh, cool. What time are you going?"

"We don't know yet. We just decided to go a minute ago. We're looking for tickets."

How did he live like this? When my parents traveled, they planned six months in advance. My dad would give thick packets with photocopies of his passport, emergency contact numbers, and itinerary to three different people.

"You should come with us," Elliott said.

I assumed he was joking.

"You have any big plans this weekend?" he asked.

"Not really."

"Good. Come with us."

"Are you serious?"

"Yes. Book your ticket right now."

"There's no way my parents will let me go."

"You're nineteen. Why do you need to ask your parents?"

Clearly, Elliott had never met my mom.

"Are you in?" he pressed.

"I can't. I have a . . . a family thing tonight."

"Okay, fly out tomorrow morning. Meet us there."

I didn't respond.

"Are you in?" he repeated.

"My *Price Is Right* money is low. I don't have enough cash for flights and hotels and all that."

"Get your plane tickets and I'll cover the rest."

I ran out of excuses.

"Great," he said. "You're coming with us."

I hadn't made up my mind, but I didn't want to close off the possibility, so I nodded.

"Perfect. Get on a flight tomorrow morning and meet us in London."

"How am I going to find you?"

"Just text me when you land. I'll send you the address. It's easy. Just get on the Tube from the airport and I'll tell you which stop to get off."

"What's the Tube?"

Elliott sneered.

He turned to Austin. "Oh my God, how funny would it be if we tell him to meet us in London, but instead of being there we leave him a note with a riddle that tells him we're now in Amsterdam, then he goes there and finds another riddle that tells him we're in Berlin, and then another, and another!"

My face went flush.

"We're kidding, we're kidding," Elliott said.

He looked at Austin and they laughed hysterically.

———

I HEADED TO SHABBAT DINNER at my grandma's house, which is far from a calm family gathering. It's thirty cousins, uncles, and aunts all around a table, shouting on top of each other, which is why I knew better than to tell my mom about Europe during dinner.

After our meal, I asked my mom if we could talk in a side room. We closed the door and I told her about Elliott, why I so desperately wanted to learn from him, and how our first meeting went.

"Wow," she said, "that's so nice."

Then I told her I was meeting him in London the next day.

"What do you mean you're going to London? You're pulling my leg. You don't even know this guy."

"I do know him. And he's not just some guy. He's well known in the business world."

She Googled Elliott on her phone, which I quickly remembered was a bad idea.

"What are all these pictures?"

"Well . . ."

"Where's his home? Why doesn't his website say what he does?"

"Mom, you don't understand. Mystery makes history."

"*Mystery makes history?* Are you insane? What if you fly to London and Mr. Mystery isn't there? Where are you even going to stay?"

"Elliott said he'd text me when I land."

"He'll *text you when you land?* You *are* insane! I don't have the energy for this. You're not going."

"Mom, I've thought it through. Worst-case scenario is he ditches me. I'll just book a return ticket and I'll have wasted my *Price Is Right* money. But the best-case scenario is maybe he'll become my mentor."

"No. The worst-case is he *doesn't* ditch you, and once you're with him, you don't *know* what he pressures you to do, you don't *know* where he takes you, you don't *know* what kind of people he hangs out with—"

"Mom, listen—"

"No, *you listen!* Look at yourself. You met some guy and he told you to meet him in London the next day—and you said yes? Have we taught you nothing? Where is your common sense? Did you ever stop and ask yourself why Elliott never stays put in any one city? Why does he buy his plane ticket only a few hours in advance? What is he running away from? And why does he want a nineteen-year-old to come with him? What's his agenda?"

I didn't have an answer. But something inside me said it didn't matter. "Mom, I won this money. It's my decision. I'm going."

Her face flashed red. "We'll talk in the morning."

Late that night, through my bedroom walls, I could hear my mom crying on the phone to my grandma. "I don't know what to do with him anymore," my mom said. "He's out of control."

The next morning I found her in the kitchen. I showed her my laptop and told her, if I was going to make it to London, I had to buy my ticket in the next two hours. The time pressure didn't persuade her.

Our talk from the night before played out again, and as happens in many Persian families, it was only a matter of time before our one-on-one discussion turned into a circus: my sisters Talia and Briana appeared in their pajamas and immediately started arguing for both sides, yelling over each other; my dad walked in completely confused and started shouting, "WHO IS ELLIOTT? *WHO IS ELLIOTT?*"; the doorbell rang and it was my grandma, holding a Tupperware of peeled cucumbers, asking if we'd made a decision.

Fifteen minutes before the cutoff, my mom still hadn't budged. I told her that as much as I loved her, I had to make this decision for myself.

Right as she began to respond, my grandma cut her off.

"Enough," she said. "He's a good kid. Let him go."

The kitchen fell silent.

My mom reached for my laptop. When I looked at the screen, she was helping me book my ticket.

CHAPTER ELEVEN

Bite Off More Than You Can Chew

ONE DAY LATER, ROOFTOP IN LONDON

I didn't think places like this actually existed. There were dozens—no, hundreds—of tall, beautiful women in bikinis, with the kind of curves that melt the mind of a kid who can't even get into a frat party. They were shoulder to shoulder in the swimming pool, overflowing onto the deck, bathing in the bright summer sun. All I heard were the sounds of giggling and splashing and popping champagne bottles. Elliott reclined in a pool chair to my right, his hair dripping wet from a recent dip. Austin sat beside him, strumming a guitar.

"So," I said to Elliott, "this is what it's like being an entrepreneur?"

"Not in the slightest," he replied.

He told me he barely knew what the word "entrepreneur" meant when he started college. The concept first clicked during his freshman year. Elliott was walking down his dorm room hall when he saw steam creeping out from under a doorway. He stumbled in and saw that his friend had converted his room into a makeshift T-shirt factory.

"What are you doing?" Elliott asked.

His friend explained how screen printing worked.

"Cool," Elliott said. "Who do you work for?"

"Nobody."

"What do you mean 'nobody'? What company hires you?"

"No company."

"You can't just work for nobody. Then who pays you?"

"The people I sell the shirts to pay me."

"I literally don't understand. You don't have a boss or an office? How can you—"

"Dude, it's called being an entrepreneur. You can do that."

It seemed so simple: here's this kid, he made a T-shirt, and then somebody bought it for twenty bucks. Plus, no boss? To Elliott, that was a dream. But he didn't have any ideas of his own, so Elliott figured he should just make T-shirts too.

He asked his friend if they could partner, and boxes of unsold T-shirts later, they gave up. The following year, they created a marketing consulting company for stores neighboring their campus. After nine months of pitching every shop, no one hired them.

When he went back home to Washington, D.C., for the summer, he learned that his dad had started an email newsletter on local real estate. "Why don't I sell ads for it?" Elliott wondered. His dad said no. At the time, Elliott was just a college kid with two failed businesses to his name. But after some convincing, his dad finally gave in and Elliott got to work. He picked up the local newspaper, turned to the real estate section, saw which companies were buying ads, and called the first one.

"Hi! I'd like to sell you some advertising. Who should I talk to?"

"Sorry, we're not interested." *Click.*

He dialed the next one. "Hi, who buys your advertising?"

"Oh, our marketing director."

"Oh, great! I'd love to talk to them."

"Sorry, not interested." *Click.*

Elliott called another. "Hi, who's your marketing director?"

"Sarah Smith."

"Oh, can I talk to her?"

"No." *Click.* Elliott made a note to call her back.

A week later, he called again in his most professional voice and said, "Hello, this is Elliott Bisnow for Sarah Smith, please."

"One second," and he was patched right through.

After three weeks of cold calls, Elliott finally booked his first sales meeting at the D.C. office of Jones Lang LaSalle, a large real estate firm. Elliott had once heard that if you present three pricing options and make the first option too expensive and the third unappealing, people often choose the middle one. So he made a gold, silver, and bronze package, with silver being ten ads for $6,000. There was no science behind his pricing. It just sounded right.

Elliott went to the meeting and made his pitch. Sure enough, the man said, "We'd like to go with . . . the silver package."

Now Elliot had no idea what to do.

"Okay, great," Elliott said, trying to sound professional. "So, just to make sure, how do *you* most feel comfortable with the follow-up? What do *you* like to see when you're a new client of someone?"

"Well, they send me an insertion order."

"Absolutely," Elliott said. He wrote down *send insertion order* and Googled it when he got home.

Elliott hit the phones every day that summer, selling thirty thousand dollars' worth of ads. He made 20 percent commission, which put $6,000 in his pocket. After returning to college for his junior year, he woke up at five o'clock every morning to sell ads. Through sheer practice, he became a cold-calling expert. He made twenty-thousand-dollar sales, fifty-thousand-dollar sales, and a few hundred-thousand-dollar sales. He took a semester off from school, then another, eventually dropping out. During the early years of his company, Bisnow Media, Elliott went on to sell a million dollars' worth of ads.

"It's not rocket science," Elliott told me, sitting up in his pool chair. "And it's not as complicated as all those business books make it seem, huh?"

I nodded, then admitted to Elliott that sometimes when I cold-called someone, I'd get so nervous I'd forget what to say.

"It's because you're overthinking it," he said. "Just tell yourself you're calling your friend, dial the number, and start talking right away. The best cure for nervousness is immediate action."

Immediate action was at the core of Elliott's life. That, plus relentless hard work, added up over time. Just ten years after Elliott sold his first ad, he and his dad would sell Bisnow Media to a private equity firm for fifty million dollars in cash.

"Wait," I said to Elliott, shading my eyes from the sun, "if you were spending all your time cold-calling, how did you have time to start Summit?"

"It just started as a side project," he said.

After dropping out of school, Elliott didn't know any people his age in the business world. He wanted not only to make new friends, but also to create relationships with people he could learn from. So Elliott cold-called some young entrepreneurs he'd read about in a magazine and asked, "What if we get a bunch of us together and just hang out for a weekend?"

He rallied the founders of CollegeHumor, TOMS Shoes, Thrillist, and more than a dozen other entrepreneurs, and they all went skiing for a weekend on Elliott's dime. Elliott even paid for their flights. Of course, he didn't actually have that kind of money, so he put the $30,000 cost of the trip on a credit card and gave himself until the end of the month to pay it off.

He then did what he knew best. Elliott cold-called companies and asked if they wanted to sponsor a conference of twenty of the greatest young entrepreneurs in America—and they said yes.

"My mom helped me book the cabin, I rented a few cars, and once everyone was there, it kind of took care of itself," Elliott said. "I remember asking my mom, 'What should I get for these people? Like, apples or granola bars? What kind of granola bars? How do you even get granola bars?' I had no idea what I was doing. Ever since then, I've lived my life by one motto: Bite off more than you can chew. You can figure out how to chew later."

Elliott fanned his face with a cocktail menu and looked around the pool deck. "It's a bit too hot here."

He took out his iPhone, opened the weather app, and began flicking through major cities in Europe.

"Ninety-one degrees in Paris? Nope. Eighty-seven in Berlin? Nope. Eighty-five in Madrid? Nope." Elliott reclined in his chair, chin tilted high, flicking through cities as if he were Zeus on Mount Olympus.

"Ah, yes," he said. "*Barcelona*: seventy-one and sunny."

He opened another app, bought three plane tickets, and we were out the door.

CHAPTER TWELVE

That's How You Do Business

EIGHT HOURS LATER, NIGHTCLUB IN BARCELONA

Music blared as seven waitresses paraded toward us, fire-crackers in one hand, giant bottles of vodka in the other. Seven bottles, six of us. Whenever someone handed Elliott a shot, he'd smile, say "Cheers," and as everyone downed their drinks, he'd pour his into a potted plant on his left.

Our plane had landed three hours earlier. In the hotel lobby, Elliott had bumped into a Peruvian media mogul he knew who invited us to a party at the hotel's nightclub. When we arrived at his table, Elliott had me sit next to the media mogul and tell the *Price Is Right* story. As I said it, the man's eyes wandered. Elliott then jumped in and guided the story, interjecting funny details I forgot to include, and by the end we were all laughing and the man asked for my email address to stay in touch.

Then Elliott pointed to another guy at the table. "Alex, tell him the story."

I did, and once I finished, Elliott pointed to someone else. "Now tell him."

He continued pointing. "Tell it again. Tell it again."

Elliott started pointing to complete strangers. The more uncomfortable the situation, the better I became. Each repetition wore down The Flinch. At a certain point, I could barely feel it.

"This is what you don't understand," Elliott told me. "You probably think everyone loves your story because you were on a game show. But *what* your story is about isn't as important as *how* you tell it."

It was now two hours past midnight. I was watching Elliott mingle with the other people at our table. In my business classes we were taught to be professional with new contacts. Exchange business cards, email rather than text. Elliott did the opposite.

But this wasn't a skill he was born with, he told me. As we stepped out to the balcony of the nightclub, Elliott admitted that he didn't have many friends growing up. He was short and chubby, and at school he felt invisible. Bullies called him "midget." They pronounced his last name as *big-nose* instead of *bis-now*. The one place he felt safe was on the tennis court. Elliott decided to leave high school during junior year and enroll at a tennis academy. When he got to college, his social life wasn't much better. Most people didn't want to hang out with him or invite him to parties. He eventually got a girlfriend, but she soon broke up with him because she thought it was weird that he woke up so early to make cold calls. When Elliott left college, his social awkwardness stayed with him. He collected so many business cards at networking events that he had to use shoeboxes to store them all. But one night around that time, Elliott learned his lesson.

He put on a suit and tie and went to meet a potential advertising client at a steakhouse. Elliott was nervous. This was his first time taking a meeting outside of an office. When Elliott greeted the client, the man looked at him and shook his head.

"Elliott, take off your jacket. Take it off. Now take off your tie. Roll up your sleeves. Grab a seat."

Elliott had reserved a table in the corner. The client said they weren't sitting there. He led Elliott to the bar.

"Ma'am, we'd like two orders of cheesy fries and a beer."

"I thought we're having a business meeting," Elliott said.

"Relax. So, tell me about yourself."

They exchanged stories, joked around, and Elliott realized they actually had a lot in common. After an hour of getting to know each other, the man put down his drink and said, "All right, what do you want to sell me?"

"Well," Elliott said, "I'd love you to do this, this, and this, at this price."

"Well, I'd like to do it at this price, and I'd like to do it like this. Will that work?"

"Could we change this a little?"

"Absolutely," the man said. "Does that sound good?"

"Sounds great."

They shook hands and closed a sixteen-thousand-dollar deal. They hung out for another hour, and then as they were getting up from the bar, the man looked at Elliott and said, "Kid, *that's* how you do business."

———

ELLIOTT AND I LEFT the nightclub and headed to our room.

"I didn't think you'd actually come," Elliott said as we stepped down the hallway.

"What do you mean?"

"When I said you should come with us to Europe, you hesitated. I'm surprised you actually came. Why'd you do it?"

"I just thought about it logically," I said. "The best-case scenario was that I would have a great learning experience with you. The worst-case scenario was that I would lose some money, which would've hurt, but life would go on, you know?"

Elliott stopped walking. He looked me in the eyes, but didn't say a word.

Then he just continued moving.

Minutes later, Austin joined us in the room and we got ready to sleep. Elliott was in one bed, Austin in the other, and I was on a rollaway tucked next to the bathroom sink. I hit the lights. A bit later, I heard Elliott's voice whispering.

"Alex, you awake?"

I was exhausted and not in the mood to talk, so I stayed quiet. Thirty seconds later, I heard him whispering to the other side of the room.

"Austin?" Elliott said, with a smile I could hear through the dark.

There was a rustle in the sheets.

"Austin . . . he's one of us."

CHAPTER THIRTEEN

Exponential Life

"Tell him the Hamptons story," Austin said, egging Elliott on. We were having lunch the following afternoon at a sidewalk café along Barcelona's La Rambla, and surprisingly, feeling extremely well rested. Elliott had insisted we all get a full eight hours of sleep, do yoga in the morning, and get a few hours of work done before leaving the hotel. He didn't drink or smoke, and he took conference calls while we walked the streets. His life was a lot more balanced behind the scenes than he made it seem.

"Oh, man, the Hamptons story?" Elliott said. "Alex, you're going to love this one."

A year after he left college, Elliott had heard about a tennis pro-am in the Hamptons. To play, nonprofessionals like Elliott had to donate $4,000 to charity. Elliott knew a wealthy individual from Washington, D.C., flying there on a private jet and wanted to go with him.

"Even though I didn't have much money," Elliott said, "I decided to make the donation and play in the pro-am, because I thought, 'If I do that, then I'll be a baller! And then I'll fly on the private plane, get to the Hamptons, be in the tournament, everyone will think I'm super legit, and then I'll take it from there.'"

Over the course of the three-day tournament, people he met asked what he planned to do for the rest of the week. Elliott said he planned on staying in the Hamptons—which he actually hadn't—but didn't have a place to stay, prompting those he was talking with to say, "Oh, you should stay with me!" And Elliott innocently replied, "Gosh, I'd love to stay with you! That's so kind. Thank you for offering."

By the end of his trip, one guy loaned Elliott his Aston Martin to drive around, he was sleeping in mansions, and watching Yankees games on TV with one of the owners of the team. "I was backpacking through the Hamptons," Elliott told me, "and I was just *in it*. It turned into a three-week adventure."

At the tournament, he met a Goldman Sachs executive who said he might be able to get his firm to sponsor the second Summit event. Elliott told him Goldman didn't even have to pay as long as Elliott could put the firm's logo on the "sponsors" page of the event website. Elliott then called other companies and said, "Look, it's almost impossible to get to be a sponsor of Summit right now. We're working with *very few* companies, and our most recent client is Goldman Sachs, so if you want to be serious, let's be serious. We're only working with the best." It was another example of Borrowed Credibility. That Goldman Sachs relationship enabled Elliott to lock in other sponsors, which led to a lot of the eventual success of Summit.

"The point of this story is less about throwing money around and more about personal investing," Elliott told me. "You have to make a calculated judgment that the amount of money you're going to put in is going to either pay off way bigger in the long term or enough in the short term to offset your costs. Aside from the money you live on, the rest is your money to play the game."

As our lunch continued, one word kept coming back to me: "momentum." How did Summit go from this small ski trip to being called "a gift to the United States" by President Clinton? I felt I was missing a piece of the puzzle, so I pressed Elliott about Summit's early days.

Elliott said that a few years after his first Summit, he read Tim Ferriss' *The 4-Hour Workweek*, sold all of his possessions, left day-to-day operations of Bisnow Media, and traveled the world, living between Nicaragua, Tel Aviv, and Amsterdam. Around that time, he flew home to see his parents in D.C. and went to a party where he met a man named Yosi Sergant, the cocreator of the Obama "HOPE" campaign with Shepard Fairey. The Obama administration had tasked Yosi with inviting young entrepreneurs to the White House, and when Elliott told Yosi about Summit, Yosi asked if he would host an event at the White House. Elliott didn't know if he could pull it off or not, but he said yes anyway. He assumed he could just figure it out. Yosi called a week later.

"We're set for the event. It's on Friday."

"Which Friday?" Elliott asked.

"*Next* Friday."

"That's impossible, I'll be in—"

"And we need all of their Social Security numbers and names by Tuesday at noon. Bring thirty-five people."

"But how are we going to get people to say yes in just four days?"

"Just tell them: *When the White House calls, you answer.*"

So Elliott started calling people he had met planning earlier Summit events and they connected him with other entrepreneurs, from the cofounder of Twitter to the CEO of Zappos. Elliott called them up using his most official-sounding voice: "Hello, this is Elliott Bisnow from Summit Series. I have a mandate from the White

House. I'm organizing a group on behalf of the Executive Office of the President and we'd like to have so and so there."

Yosi insisted that the founders of Method, the ecofriendly soaps, be at the event. So Elliott called their office.

"Hello, it's Elliott Bisnow for Eric Ryan and Adam Lowry. I need to speak to their assistant immediately."

He got through. "How can I help you?"

"I'm calling on behalf of the president *of the United States of America*. The presence of Mr. Ryan and Mr. Lowry has been requested at the White House next Friday."

"Well, that's very gracious of you, but that's impossible. They're doing a huge paid speaking engagement next Friday."

"Ma'am," Elliott said, lowering his voice, "when the White House calls, *you answer*." And just like that, he got them to cancel their paid speaking gig.

A few days before the event, Elliott found out that Yosi wasn't actually planning as high-level an event as he'd assumed. To avoid looking like a fool in front of his new entrepreneur friends, Elliott cold-called the White House offices, spreading a whisper campaign among the senior administration that they weren't invited to this "exclusive" event—so they would reflexively demand to be there. Elliott told them, "I don't know if you've heard, but *all* the leading young entrepreneurs *in America* are coming to the White House, and everybody who's anybody was invited."

And it worked. The people who put together the stimulus package, the staff of the National Economic Council, the environmental team—they all showed up. It reached the point that Rahm Emanuel, Obama's chief of staff, called Yosi screaming about why he wasn't invited.

The event went so well that word began spreading about Summit, and eventually the Clinton Foundation called Elliott and asked him to host a fundraiser. Later, the Summit team planned another event in D.C., this time with 750 people. The next one took place on a cruise ship in the Caribbean with a thousand people. The events continued swelling in popularity, the following one at a ski resort in Lake Tahoe. Now Elliott was buying a private mountain in Eden, Utah, to make it the home of the Summit community.

"I could've told Yosi, 'I don't think we can pull off the event,' or, 'Let's do it in a month,'" Elliott told me. "At the end of the day, Yosi said he wanted it on Friday, and we said yes. I've learned that you have to go for it, even if there's a chance you'll fail. The planets are never going to perfectly align. When you see an opportunity, it's up to you to jump."

FOUR DAYS LATER, NEW YORK CITY

"What I'm about to tell you," Elliott told me, "ninety-nine percent of people in the world will never understand."

For the first time all week, it was just the two of us. Elliott had told Austin he wanted to talk to me one-on-one. We were standing on a rooftop lounge during sunset, looking out at the Manhattan skyline.

"You see, most people live a *linear life*," he continued. "They go to college, get an internship, graduate, land a job, get a promotion, save up for a vacation each year, work toward their next promotion, and they just do that their whole lives. Their lives move step by step, slowly and predictably.

"But successful people don't buy into that model. They opt into an *exponential life*. Rather than going step by step, they skip steps. People say that you first need to 'pay your dues' and get years of experience before you can go out on your own and get what you truly want. Society feeds us this lie that you need to do x, y, and z before you can achieve your dream. It's bullshit. The only person whose permission you need to live an exponential life is your own.

"Sometimes an exponential life lands in your lap, like with a child prodigy. But most of the time, for people like you and me, we have to seize it for ourselves. If you actually want to make a difference in the world, if you want to live a life of inspiration, adventure, and wild success—you need to grab on to that exponential life—and hold on to it with all you've got."

I looked at him, nodding my head, mesmerized.

"You want that?" he asked.

Every fiber in my body pulsed with *yes*.

But Elliott didn't wait for my answer. "All right, let's get to the point," he said. "You're making a huge mistake."

"What?"

"You're not going to stay nineteen forever. You can't live off game show money the rest of your life. You need to stop focusing all your time on getting these silly interviews. There needs to be a point in your life where you step it up. I think you're ready. Quit your mission and come work for me."

I didn't respond.

"Look," he said. "The mission is nice and all, and I'm not trying to insult it, but it's not a career. It brought you to this point—congratulations, you got what you wanted. You were lost and now you have a sense of direction. It's time for you to go to the next level. There's no money in writing. The money is in business. And I'm willing to give you a fastpass. Skip the line and join me at the front. It's time for you to get in the game."

"Can I have some time to think about—"

"What is there to think about? I'll pay you more than you'd ever want. I'll teach you more than you'd ever need to know. And I'll take you more places than you ever thought existed."

"That's seriously amazing," I said, measuring my words, "but the mission is really important to me and—"

"Fine. Email me the list of people you want to interview. I'll get you all of them, we can get a ghostwriter to put it together, and you can start working for me next week."

Elliott waited for my response, but no words came to me.

"If you don't take this," he said, "you're making the biggest mistake of your life. Tell me another time someone will offer you an opportunity like this. And you don't have to climb up the ladder. I'll take you under my wing and bring you to the top. Everything you dreamed about in your dorm room, I'll give you right now. Stop chasing interviews, ditch the mission, and work with me. What do you say?"

CHAPTER FOURTEEN

The Avoidance List

ONE DAY LATER, EDEN, UTAH

ields of yellow grass and old wooden shacks flicked by the window of my rental car. Elliott lived in a town called Eden: population, six hundred. If I accepted his offer, this would be my new home, an hour north of Salt Lake City off a one-lane road.

I'm not a wooden shack kind of guy . . .

But I'd be crazy to say no to him. Working with him would change everything . . .

It was Friday and Elliott wanted an answer by the end of the weekend.

Driving farther, I turned a corner, pulled into a long driveway, and that's when I saw it—a massive, mansion-sized log cabin. It sat beside a glistening lake, backdropped by thick evergreen trees and a towering mountain range. The front lawn was the size of a football field. *This* was Elliott's house.

We'd taken separate flights from New York that morning. I walked into his home and found Elliott in the vast living room.

"This house is unreal," I said.

Elliott grinned. "Just wait until you see what we build on the mountain."

He explained this was just a temporary home where he and his dozen employees lived and held Summit events. This weekend, he was hosting a hundred attendees who were housed in smaller cabins a few miles away. Elliott was still in the process of buying Powder Mountain, which was ten miles to the north. On its backside he was building his entrepreneurial utopia.

"Grab some food and make yourself at home," Elliott said, and before I responded he was already gone, greeting another guest.

I made my way to the kitchen and was overcome by aromas so tantalizing they made me never want to set foot again in my college dining hall. Three private chefs were setting out overflowing trays of scrambled eggs, fried eggs, poached eggs, sizzling bacon, stacks of fluffy blueberry pancakes, rows of caramel French toast; giant bowls of chia pudding, berry parfait, and smashed avocado drizzled with olive oil and Himalayan salt; there was a long counter covered in mounds of bagels and breads and frosted homemade cinnamon rolls; a whole other counter had freshly cut fruits and vegetables that were grown on the farm next door. *Hello, Eden.* I filled my plate to the brim and took a seat next to a man eating alone.

He had long hair and tattoos running up his arms. Within minutes, we were talking as if we'd known each other for years. The man told me stories about surfing in shark-infested waters and we spoke for the rest of the hour. We exchanged info and agreed to meet again in LA. I later found out he was the lead singer of Incubus, the multiplatinum rock band.

Another person joined our table, a former host of MTV's *TRL*.

Then another pulled up a seat, one of Barack Obama's economic advisers. *This was me just trying to eat some breakfast.*

I spotted Elliott looking down at us from a railing on the cabin's second floor. He pointed at me and yelled, "There's my favorite college dropout!"

I cringed—my grandma's voice echoed in my head. *Jooneh man.*

My mood later bounced back when I stepped outside and spotted a chalkboard listing the day's activities. There was yoga, hiking, horseback riding, mountain biking, volleyball, Ultimate Frisbee, meditation, ATVing, and skydiving. I could attend a survival course with a wilderness expert or a writing workshop with a National Poetry Slam champion. I dashed over to the volleyball game and one of the players on my team was the neuroscientist whose TED Talk I'd watched in biology class a year earlier. Then I hopped on a trampoline and the woman who joined me was Miss USA 2009. I went over to the meditation circle and sitting to my left was a former NFL player, to my right a Native American shaman. I kept running around all afternoon feeling like Harry Potter on his first day at Hogwarts.

Whenever Elliott saw I wasn't talking to someone, he'd put his arm around me and introduce me to someone else. I was in a pinball machine of inspiration, bouncing off the bumpers, scoring a thousand points a minute.

Everything about this place just seemed to be *more.* The people's energy was more vibrant, their laughs more contagious, their careers more interesting, their stories more exhilarating. Even the sky seemed bluer here. When I'd been lying on my dorm room bed, I felt I was suffocating. Here, I could breathe.

As the sun slowly set, we went inside for dinner where the living room had been transformed into a five-star dining room. This wasn't typical luxury—it was more like if the Ritz-Carlton was run by Paul Bunyan. Sparkling wineglasses were placed beside rustic mason jars. Hundreds of shimmering candles lined long picnic tables. Above my head hung a magnificent chandelier that lit up the moose head and black bear hide on the wall. I took a seat across from a woman who seemed to jump between three conversations at once. Her enthusiasm was so electric I didn't realize I was staring.

"Hey, you," she said. "Miki Agrawal."

She gave me a fist pound and then pointed to the men seated beside us. "This is my boy Jesse, this is my boy Ben, and this is my boyfriend Andrew." I introduced myself and Miki sped on.

"Alex, want to hear something crazy? I met Jesse playing pickup soccer in Central Park *ten years ago*. He was selling textbooks over the phone at the time, twenty-five cents a pop. I said he's smarter than that and yelled at him to get his shit together. We hung out for a bit, but I literally haven't seen Jesse since. Today I found out . . . he's now an executive at Nike."

Miki gleamed as if she'd done it herself.

"Ben, you have to tell Alex your story!" In the time it took Ben to put down his wineglass, Miki was already saying it herself. "It's crazy—Ben and his boys were in college, felt like they were in a slump, so they made a list of a hundred things they want to do before they die. They bought a van, traveled the country, and crossed things off the list—*and* every time they did, they also helped a stranger reach one of their dreams too. Ben, come on! Tell Alex some of the things you did!"

Ben told stories about playing basketball with President Obama, streaking at a professional soccer game, helping deliver a baby, and going to Las Vegas and betting $250,000 on black. These adventures went on for years and became the MTV reality show *The Buried Life*, which then led to a bestselling book. The more Ben went on about how fulfilling it was to chase his dreams, the more I thought about how Elliott was asking me to give up my own.

"I was pretty much the opposite of Ben out of college," Miki said. "I worked on Wall Street and hated it."

"What changed?" I asked.

"September eleventh," she said.

Miki had a breakfast meeting scheduled at the World Trade Center courtyard at the time the North Tower was hit. "In my entire life," she said, "that was the only morning I slept through my alarm and missed a meeting."

Among the thousands who were tragically killed that day were two of Miki's coworkers.

"It hit me that you never know when your life will be over," she said. "And I felt I would be an idiot to waste my days living out someone else's life rather than living my own."

I felt like my body was the rope of a tug-of-war. Elliott's offer was yanking on one side, Miki and Ben the other.

Miki said that after that realization she quit her job and chased every interest she had. She worked her way onto a professional soccer team, wrote a movie script, and then opened an organic, gluten-free pizzeria in New York's West Village. She was now starting a women's underwear line called THINX and writing a book called *Do Cool Shit*.

"Alex! Your turn!" Miki said. "Story! Go, go, go!"

As I told them the *Price Is Right* story, they laughed and cheered and threw me high fives. Miki asked what I had to do next for the mission and I said I was searching for a literary agent, so I could land a book deal and get to Bill Gates.

"So far," I said, "every agent I've reached out to has said no."

"Dude, I'll introduce you to my agent," Ben said.

"Talk to mine too!" Miki said. "She'll love you!"

"Are you kidding? That would be amaz—"

The ding of a fork against a glass cut through the air.

Elliott was at the front of the room, making a toast.

"Here at Summit," he said, "we have a little tradition. We like to take a moment during dinner to give thanks—for our chefs, for the food, and most of all, for each and every one of you. Welcome to Eden!"

We clinked glasses and the room erupted in cheers. Elliott continued and said he wanted to thank one person in particular at dinner: Tim Ferriss.

Elliott pointed his glass toward Ferriss, who I realized was sitting a few tables behind me, and said that Tim was the first person to teach him that he didn't have to sit behind a desk all day to succeed. He could work while traveling, adventuring, and expanding his mind. "Tim," Elliott said, "showed me how to reimagine my life."

A hundred pairs of eyes turned to Ferriss, bathing him in a collective spotlight.

"To Tim!" Elliott shouted.

"*To Tim!*" we roared back.

"And just as Tim mentored me and holds a special place in my heart," Elliott continued, "there is someone else here who is beginning to hold a similar spot. Just as I'd cold-emailed Tim when I was starting out, this someone cold-emailed me."

I began to feel heat rising in my face. Elliott told the *Price Is Right* story better than I ever could. Then he pointed his glass at me.

"That's the kind of creativity we embrace here at Summit. That's the kind of energy we empower here. That's why I've taken Alex Banayan under my wing, and that's why I'm proud to welcome him as the newest member of our community. To Alex!"

———

IF ON FRIDAY I FELT like a pinball, on Saturday I was a magnet.

"Are you the kid Elliott was talking about last night?"

"Are you the one who hacked The Price Is Right?*"*

"How long have you known Elliott?"

"Are you two related?"

"What's the project you're working on?"

"What can I do to help?"

Elliott not only brought me into a new world, he kicked down the doors.

This is what I've always wanted, I thought. *If I work with Elliott, I'll never have to leave. All these people are coming to me, gushing to help with the mission . . .*

But if I accept his offer, there will be no mission . . .

On Sunday morning, I sat alone at the breakfast table, too conflicted to eat. Elliott's words from New York replayed in my mind. *If you don't take this, you're making the biggest mistake of your life.*

The more I reflected on his offer, the more I felt the threat underneath it. Something about his tone and the sharp look he had in his eyes told me: "If you say no, we're over."

No more Eden. No more mentor.

In a few hours, I had to leave to catch my flight home. And I still didn't know what I would tell him.

"Rough morning?" An attendee pulled up a chair beside me, cradling a cup of coffee.

"Uh, sort of," I said.

The man was tall and had a gentle face. For reasons that will become clear later, I'll use a pseudonym for him and call him Dan Babcock.

I must've been desperate to get the thoughts off my chest, because I soon found myself confiding in Dan about my internal tug-of-war.

"What do you think I should do?"

"I don't think anyone can tell you what you should do," Dan said. "It's a hard decision. The only person who knows the right answer is you. But maybe I can share something that might help."

Dan reached for his notebook, ripped out two sheets of paper, and handed them to me.

"I worked for Warren Buffett for seven years," he said, "and out of everything he's taught me, this was his greatest piece of advice."

I pulled a pen out of my pocket.

"On the first sheet of paper," Dan said, "write a list of twenty-five things you want to accomplish in the next twelve months."

I wrote things related to my family, health, working with Elliott, working on the mission, places I wanted to travel, and books I wanted to read.

"If you could only do five of those things in the next three months," Dan said, "which would you choose?"

I circled them. Dan told me to copy those five things onto the second sheet of paper, and then cross them off the first.

"You now have two lists," he said. "On top of the list of five, write: 'The Priority List.'"

I scribbled it across.

"All right," he said. "Now over the list of twenty, write: 'The Avoidance List.'"

"Huh?"

"That's Mr. Buffett's secret," Dan said. "The key to accomplishing your top five priorities is to avoid the other twenty."

I looked at my list of five. Then at my list of twenty.

"I see your point," I said. "But there are things on that Avoidance List that I really want to do."

"You have a choice," Dan said. "You can be good at those twenty-five things or you can be world-class at the five. Most people have so many things they want to do that they never do a single thing well. If I've learned one thing from Mr. Buffett, it's that the Avoidance List is the secret to being world-class.

"Success," he added, "is a result of prioritizing your desires."

———

EACH SHIRT I PACKED IN my duffel bag reminded me of a day in Barcelona; every pair of pants, a night in New York. I got in my rental car, headed back to Elliott's cabin, and found him by the front door, chatting with one of his guests. Elliott finished his conversation and came over.

"Enjoy the weekend?" he asked.

"It was incredible," I said. "I can't thank you enough. And . . . and I think I have my answer."

A wide smile spread across his face.

"I love Summit," I said. "And I've never had a mentor like you in my entire life. But at the same time, I don't think I can live with myself doing two things half-assed. I need to do one thing right. And it has to be the mission."

Elliott's jaw clenched. He slowly lowered his head, as if trying to suppress his anger.

"You're making a huge mistake," he said.

But then he stopped himself before saying anything else. He took a heavy breath and let his shoulders deflate.

"If that's what you have to do," he said, "then that's your decision—and I respect you even more for making it."

He put his hand on my shoulder.

"And just know," he added, "you always have a home here. I love you, man."

CHAPTER FIFTEEN

You Can't Out-Amazon Amazon

The following day, I returned to the storage closet feeling completely renewed. I fixed my gaze on the white sheet of paper on the wall. Five words were scrawled across the top, and at this point in my life, no words were more important: NO AGENT, NO BILL GATES.

Without a literary agent, I couldn't get a publishing deal. And without a deal, I couldn't get to Gates. From the day I'd started this journey, I'd felt that Bill Gates' advice would be my Holy Grail, so in my eyes, the mission wouldn't be complete without him.

I sat at my desk, checked my email, and of course, there was another rejection. I uncapped my pen and drew a line through the agent's name on my list. There were now lines through nineteen of the twenty names.

I looked at the tower of books on my desk about the publishing process. I'd followed every word those books prescribed. I did everything the bestselling authors I'd spoken to advised me to do.

Why isn't this working?

This last rejection, though, was different from the rest. It didn't sting as much. As I drew a line through that agent's name, I felt as if I was drawing a line through the idea of this list altogether. I didn't need it anymore. Now I had Miki and Ben.

I called Miki to see if her offer still stood.

"Are you kidding?" she said. "Of course! My agent will love you. Come to New York!"

"When should I—"

"Book your ticket right now. And don't even think about wasting money on a hotel. You're staying in the extra bedroom in my apartment."

When I called Ben, he also said he'd set up a meeting for me with his agent.

I bought a plane ticket to New York, and the next day, right before heading out, I ripped the list of agents off the storage closet wall so I could drop it in the trash. I don't know why, but something within me said otherwise, so I folded the list and stuffed it in my pocket.

After arriving at JFK airport, I jumped in a cab and went straight to Miki's gluten-free pizzeria in the West Village. As soon as I put my duffel bag in the back room, Miki sat me down and got to the point.

"Which agents have you talked to so far?"

Now I knew why I hadn't thrown away the list. I pulled it out of my pocket. Miki pointed to the name at the top. "Why is this the only one not crossed off?"

"Well, that's the agent I wanted the most. She's repped twenty-three books that became *New York Times* bestsellers. She's headquartered in San Francisco, gets huge deals with major publishers, and—"

"I get it, I get it. But why isn't she crossed off?"

"I spoke to one of the authors she represents, and when I asked him for an introduction, he said to not even bother reaching out. This agent didn't represent him on his first book, she didn't represent Tim Ferriss on his first book, and if I can't even get a meeting with smaller agents, then who am I kidding? I'm optimistic, but I'm not delusional . . ."

"We don't have time for failure," Miki said.

She grabbed my arm and pulled me toward the door.

"Let's go, let's go, let's go!" she said. "There's an hour before the dinner rush."

Miki yanked me through the Manhattan streets as she wove around pedestrians, running across intersections, leaping in front of honking cars. When we got to her agent's office building, Miki swung open the front door, sped past the front desk and down a hallway. An assistant with a comb-over jumped up and flailed an arm in the air. "Miki! Wait! You don't have an appointment!"

Miki practically kicked down her agent's door, pushed me in, and I saw her agent, sitting at a cluttered desk, phone to her ear. Her face turned white. Papers were scattered around the room. Books were piled on the floor.

"Drop what you're doing," Miki told her. "I need ten minutes."

The agent mumbled into the phone and put it down.

"Alex, take a seat," Miki said, pointing to a couch. "Tell her about your book."

I made my pitch, spitting out every fact, statistic, and marketing idea I could, exactly like the authors I'd spoken to advised me. I spoke with all the passion I had, and by the end of the meeting, Miki told her agent that she *had* to work with me and her agent nodded.

"This all sounds great!" she said. "Alex, send me your proposal. I'll read it and get back to you as soon as I can."

I walked out of the office building, glowing. The New York City sidewalk was just as loud as ever, but for a moment, the noise seemed to fade away.

"Little bro, let's roll!" Miki hollered. She was already halfway down the block, speeding away. I ran to catch up.

"I can't thank you enough," I said, trailing behind her.

"Don't think of it," she said. "When I was younger, a group of thirty-year-old entrepreneurs took me under their wing and did the same for me. This is how the world works. It's the circle of life."

———

A DAY LATER, THE CIRCLE kept on giving. I was escorted across the shimmering tile floors of William Morris Endeavor, one of the most powerful talent agencies in the world. I felt like everybody I passed in the halls knew that Ben had set up this meeting for me. Ben's book had hit the *New York Times* bestseller list a few months prior, so there were no doors that needed kicking down.

Ben's agent stood up from her desk and gave me a warm welcome. Her office was large and had sweeping views of the skyline. We sat on her couch, I made my pitch, and because my meeting with Miki's agent had gone so well, I doubled down on my approach: I laid out even more statistics, spit out even more facts, and focused even more on marketing ideas. I spoke with Ben's agent for more than an hour, and at the end, she too asked me to send her my proposal. I felt the meeting couldn't have gone better.

The next day, I flew back to LA feeling triumphant. When I stepped back into the storage closet, I saw the gigantic tower of books on my desk and wanted to kiss it the way a hockey player kisses the Stanley Cup.

Over the course of a week, I sent follow-up emails to both Ben's and Miki's agents. There was no response from Miki's, but a few days later, Ben's called.

"Alex, I loved meeting you. And I think you're great. But . . ."

There's always a *but*.

". . . but I don't think we're a fit. Though, I know someone here who might be."

She introduced me to one of her colleagues at William Morris. I got on the phone with her coworker, made my pitch, and for some reason, right on the spot, she said *yes*. I put the call on mute as I cheered out loud. I felt as if the brick wall that had blocked my path to Bill Gates was blasted by dynamite.

And the dynamite wouldn't stop detonating. The very next day, *another* author I knew introduced me to *another* agent at William Morris who *also* said yes on the spot.

I booked a plane ticket to fly back to New York to meet the two William Morris agents in person. I didn't understand why Miki's agent hadn't replied yet, because that seemed like a guaranteed yes too. Either way, now it was *my* turn to decide.

I walked off the subway in New York a few days later. As I felt the warm summer sun on my face, I reached into my pocket to check my phone. There was an email from one of the William Morris agents, sent on behalf of both of them. It effectively said: Dear Alex, We regret to inform you that we have to rescind our offers.

Apparently, both agents were brand-new, and because they both extended me offers, they met with their boss about how to handle the situation. The verdict was for both of them to drop me altogether—their boss decided I wasn't worth the time.

It felt like the sidewalk was pulled from under me. Never in my life had I felt so worthless. In that instant, it hit me that if I wasn't good enough for the nineteen agents on my list, and if I wasn't good enough for the two agents who were just getting started, Miki's agent never planned on signing me either. She was only nice to me in the meeting to please *Miki*, not because she wanted to work with me. I was nothing. I was nobody. I wasn't even worth a response.

I went to Miki's apartment, completely gutted. I pulled out my list of agents and saw those five words at the top, glaring back at me: NO AGENT, NO BILL GATES. I crumpled the paper in my fist and threw it at the wall.

An hour later, I was still slumped on the couch when my phone rang. But I wasn't in the mood to answer. I glanced at the screen and saw it was my friend Brandon. I picked up and began to vent, telling him everything that happened.

"I'm so sorry, man," he said. "What do you think you're going to do?"

"There's nothing else I *can* do. I did everything those authors told me to. I followed everything the books I read said. There's nothing I've left out."

Brandon was quiet. Then he said, "Well, maybe you could try a different approach. I read a story a long time ago, and I don't even remember where I read it, so who knows if it's true, but the lesson is important."

"I know you're trying to help, but I'm not in the mood to hear about another one of your books."

"You need to hear this one."

I groaned.

"Just give me a second," Brandon said. "So, the story takes place around the year two thousand. The Internet was booming and Amazon was killing the e-commerce competition. In the beginning, Walmart's executives hadn't thought much of it, but then Amazon's growth started eating at their revenue. Walmart's executives panicked. They called emergency meetings. They hired people, fired people, and filled buildings with more and more engineers, pouring all the money they could into their website. Nothing helped. So they focused even harder on being more like Amazon. They copied Amazon's strategies, tried to replicate their technology, and spent even more money. But still, nothing changed."

"Bro, what does this have to do with me?"

"Damn it, just listen," Brandon said. "So one day, a new Walmart executive walked into the office. She looked around and noticed what was going on. The next day she hung a banner across the office. Soon after, Walmart's market share skyrocketed. The banner simply said: YOU CAN'T OUT-AMAZON AMAZON."

Brandon paused to let the story sink in.

"Don't you get it?" he said. "*You're* Walmart."

"What?"

"Ever since you started looking for an agent, all you've done is copy *other people's* strategies. You've been pitching these agents as if you have the same strengths Tim Ferriss has, but you don't have the platform he has. You don't have the credibility he has. Your circumstances are completely different. *You can't out-Ferriss Tim Ferriss.*"

Shit . . . he's right.

Ever since I'd been on my dorm room bed, I'd been obsessed with studying the paths of successful people, and while that's a good approach to learning, I couldn't solve every problem that way. I couldn't copy and paste other people's playbooks and expect it to work exactly the same for me. Their playbook worked for them because it was *their* playbook. It played to *their* strengths and *their* circumstances. Not once had I ever looked within myself and wondered about my strengths or my circumstances. What did it mean to out-Alex someone? While there's a time for studying what's worked for other people, there are moments when you have to go all in on what makes you unique. And in order to do that, you have to know what makes you, you.

Late that night, I couldn't sleep. I kept tossing under the covers, thinking about the story Brandon had told me.

You can't out-Amazon Amazon . . .

The hours crept by. Nothing I did would quiet my mind. At about three in the morning, I climbed out of bed and walked to the corner of the room. I found my crumpled list of agents. I opened it and stared at the name at the top of the list: the agent in San Francisco.

Screw it. I have nothing to lose.

I grabbed my laptop and began writing her an email. But instead of saying the same thing I did to all the other agents, I just wrote about why I believed in the mission. I told her I was sick of the publishing industry and tired of playing games. I told her my story and then, for paragraph after paragraph, told her how I thought the two of us could change the world together. In the subject line, I wrote "my 3 a.m. stream of consciousness," and as I reread the email, it felt like a teenage love letter, but I sent it anyway.

I didn't expect a response. A day later, she replied.

"Call me."

I did, and she offered to be my agent on the spot.

CHAPTER SIXTEEN

No One Ever Asks

pulled my duffel bag out of Miki's closet and began packing.

"Wait, wait, wait!" Miki said. "Where are you going? You can't go now."

"My flight home leaves in a few hours," I said.

"That's impossible. You have to change your flight. You can't miss Agrapalooza!"

Agrapalooza was Miki's summer camp–themed costume party, which she was hosting at a friend's house in New Jersey.

"I'd love to," I said, "but I don't think I should." After talking with my literary agent, I learned I had to completely rewrite my book proposal, and I wanted to finish it as quickly as possible.

"Little bro, you're changing your flight. End of discussion."

"But . . . Miki, Miki . . ."

The following morning, I woke up on a couch at Miki's friend's house, the New Jersey sun flooding through the windows. On the other side of the room, I saw Miki talking to a man with a shaved head and a navy-blue Zappos T-shirt. I picked the crust out of my eyes. It was like seeing Santa on Christmas morning. Standing ten feet away from me, talking to Miki, was the CEO of Zappos, Tony Hsieh.

Deep breaths . . . deep breaths . . .

Elliott had taught me you can either be someone's friend or a fan, but never both. So I tried to play it cool, thinking of ways to introduce myself. But I thought so much about what to say I ended up saying nothing at all.

I headed out through the sliding glass doors. The backyard was so big a golf cart was parked to help people get around. As the party began, I stumbled my way through the three-legged race, then got second place in the egg toss. Before the next game, a few of us headed to the patio to grab some food. We were standing under a large orange umbrella when Tony Hsieh passed by. No one, especially myself, could help but sneak a glance.

A few minutes later, Tony approached again, but this time he stopped and joined us. He had a clipboard in one hand, a purple marker in the other.

"What's your wish?" Tony said to the guy on my right.

"Huh?" the guy said.

Tony flashed his clipboard: WISHES LIST was written across the top.

"You didn't hear?" Tony said. "Today I'm a magical fairy."

He said it with such a straight face it took a few moments to realize this was just his sense of humor. Miki later explained to me that Tony's face always looks like it's made of stone, his eyes of glass. He has a permanent, uncrackable poker face.

"I want to teleport," the guy said.

"Okay," Tony replied. "You'll be teleporting eighty-five percent of the way there."

He pointed to the bottom of the clipboard: "15 PERCENT COMMIS-
SION WILL BE TAKEN ON ALL WISHES UPON GRANTING."

"I'm less a magical fairy," Tony said, "and more a 'wish broker.'
Hey, a fairy's gotta make a living too."

He turned and asked for my wish. I tried to think of something
funny, hoping it would get him to like me. Though a part of me
wanted to tell him the first thing that came to mind. *But I can't ask
for that . . . He'll think I'm obnoxious. And what if Miki gets mad? And—*
Thankfully, I realized what was going on. This was The Flinch dis-
guised as "logic." I gave myself a mental slap and forced myself to
spit it out.

"I want to be CEO of Zappos for a day."

Tony didn't respond. He didn't write my wish on his clipboard.
He just stared at me.

"Uh, you know," I said, trying to explain myself, "like, I follow
you around, see what a day in your life is like."

"Oh. You want to shadow me?"

I nodded. Tony took a moment to think.

"Okay . . . sure," he said. "When do you want to do it?"

"Well, it's my twentieth birthday in a couple weeks, so how
about then?"

"Cool. And since it's your birthday, we can do it for two days."

———

IT WAS A FEW HOURS after dinner and the costume dance party was
about to start. I was passing through the kitchen when I saw Tony,
dressed as a teddy bear, deep in conversation with Aasif Mandvi,
the "Senior Middle East Correspondent" on *The Daily Show with Jon
Stewart*, who was dressed as a hillbilly. I overheard Aasif saying he
was writing a book. He was asking Tony for marketing advice and
I stepped over to join them.

"Well, there are a lot of tactics you can use," Tony told him. "But
I can't tell you which ones would be most effective until I know

what your motivations are for writing the book. What are your end goals?"

Aasif's forehead furrowed.

"Most people never take the time to ask themselves why they're doing what they're doing," Tony said. "And even when they do, most people lie to themselves.

"Like for *Delivering Happiness*, I'm aware that deep down, there was definitely some vanity and ego at play. It's nice to go to your mom and dad and tell them your book is number one on the *New York Times* bestseller list. So that was one motivation. Another was..."

I couldn't tell if I was more shocked or confused hearing that. I'd always thought "vanity" and "ego" were bad. I never would've used them to describe myself. But Tony did, without any shame or hesitation. His face was as emotionless as ever.

"Ego isn't particularly healthy," Tony continued, "but what's worse is having it and lying to yourself that you don't. Before you start thinking about marketing tactics, become self-aware of what's motivating you below the surface. Don't judge the motivations as 'good' or 'bad.' Just ask yourself why you're doing what you're doing. Choosing the right tactics becomes easy once you know your end goal."

Tony explained that just because there was some vanity in wanting to write a bestseller, it didn't diminish his other motivations of wanting to inspire young entrepreneurs or teaching people how to create a strong company culture. Those desires coexisted.

As the conversation went on and more people gathered in the kitchen to listen, I took a second to mentally step back to appreciate what was going on—here I was, dressed as Rango the chameleon-cowboy, with a tail sticking out of me and a cowboy hat on my head, listening to a teddy bear tell a hillbilly how to launch a book.

"The first three months after your launch are the most important," Tony said. "Because one of my end goals was for my book to become a bestseller, I spoke everywhere I could during those months: business conferences, college classes, wherever. I bought an RV, wrapped it with an image of the book cover, and spent three months living on the road.

"Those three months were some of the most exhausting of my life," he said, his voice deflating. "I was speaking all day and traveling all night. I was doing everything I could to spread the seeds. But even then, I couldn't be everywhere at once. So I sent boxes of books to events and conferences, hoping the message would reach people.

"Honestly," he added, "I have no idea if those books were ever read. I don't even know if that made a difference."

I have to tell him . . .

But the spirit of Elliott was hanging over my shoulder: *Don't be an idiot. If you tell him, he'll always see you as a fan.*

In that moment, though, I knew I had to be myself.

"Tony," I said, "during my freshman year of college, I was a volunteer at one of those business conferences you'd sent boxes of books to. I'd never heard your name before, and I didn't even know what Zappos was, but the event coordinators were handing out your book, so I took one home. A few months later, when I was going through one of the toughest times in my life, I picked up your book and couldn't put it down. I read the whole thing that weekend. Reading about how you chased your dream, well, it made me feel like mine was possible.

"If you didn't send those books to that business conference," I continued, my voice shaking, "I wouldn't be doing what I do today. Tony, your book changed my life."

Everyone in the kitchen froze.

Tony was just looking at me, silently. But the softening of his face, and the welling of his eyes, told me more than any words could've said.

TWO WEEKS LATER, DOWNTOWN LAS VEGAS

I ripped open a UPS box and pulled out a navy-blue Zappos shirt. To anyone else, it was just a piece of fabric. But to me, it was Superman's cape.

I'd just woken up in a unit in Tony's apartment building, where he'd arranged for me to stay. I slid the shirt over my head, grabbed my backpack, and headed downstairs, where a Zappos company car was waiting. The car curved along the road, and ten minutes later, we pulled up to Zappos headquarters.

As I stepped through the doors, I saw a popcorn machine on the reception desk, a Dance Dance Revolution arcade game by the couch, and hundreds of cut-off neckties stapled to the walls. An assistant escorted me down a hallway to the work area where the desks were decorated even more wildly than the lobby. One aisle was covered in an avalanche of birthday streamers; another with flashing Christmas lights; a third had a ten-foot inflatable pirate. Sitting at a cluttered desk, in a rain forest–themed section, was Tony. He was hunched in front of his laptop. When he saw me, he motioned for me to grab a chair.

I said good morning. Tony's assistant leaned over to me and whispered, "You're about five hours late. He's been up since four."

Tony shut his laptop, stood up, and motioned for me to follow. We moved down the carpeted hallway to our first meeting. I trailed a few feet behind the methodical steps of his black leather shoes. I could feel how timid my steps were. Despite how nice Tony had been, I still felt I didn't deserve to be there. A part of me was scared that if I did even the smallest thing wrong, he'd send me home.

We got to the conference room. I spotted a chair in the back and moved toward it. Tony saw me, shooed away the seat, and pointed to the spot next to him. When we went to another conference room for our next meeting, Tony motioned for me to sit next to him again. He did it again in the meeting after that. By our fourth meeting in the afternoon, I sat next to him, without him having to point.

After our lunch meeting with a corporate distributor, Tony exited into the hallway with me behind him. He turned his head back over his shoulder and asked, "What'd you think?" I stumbled out an answer. He didn't respond. He just listened, nodding. After our next meeting, again he cranked his neck back and asked, "What'd you think?" Tony asked for my opinion again, then again.

The light outside the windows began to darken. The office emptied. As we walked out of the final meeting, Tony again asked what I thought. But he didn't have to crank his head back this time. I was no longer behind him—I was walking beside him.

The next morning, I threw on another Zappos T-shirt and went downstairs where Tony's driver was waiting for me. We headed across town to a two-thousand-person auditorium where Tony was preparing for a company-wide meeting. He'd already been there for two hours.

I arrived at the auditorium and stayed backstage all morning watching Tony rehearse. The presentation was a cross between a corporate keynote speech and a high school pep rally. Hours later, the lights dimmed and the curtains opened. Tony's dad and I sat together in the front row, watching it all unfold.

As the day came to an end, I was heading out of the auditorium when a Zappos employee stopped me by the door. He said he saw me shadowing Tony the prior afternoon. The guy told me that he'd worked at Zappos for a few years and one of his biggest dreams was to shadow Tony. He asked how I got so lucky.

The look in his eyes wasn't new. I'd noticed a few other Zappos employees looking at me the same way the day before, as though they wanted to be in the position I was in.

Later that evening, I went over to Tony and said goodbye, thanking him again for the past two days.

"And, I know this might sound weird," I said, "but why don't you let your employees shadow you?"

Tony looked at me blankly and said, "I'd be happy to—but no one ever asks."

CHAPTER SEVENTEEN

It's All Gray

TWO WEEKS LATER, THE STORAGE CLOSET

kept pacing, glancing at my phone on the desk. I knew I should call. But I couldn't. A memory kept flashing in my mind.

"You going to drop out?" Elliott had asked.

"What?"

"You heard what I said."

He was the last person I wanted to talk to about this. But I also felt he was the only person I could talk to. I reached for my phone.

"Hey, guy. What's going on?"

"Elliott, I need your help."

I told him my literary agent said the ideal time to pitch publishers was next month, which meant I needed to finish rewriting my book proposal by then. But my junior year of college began in a week.

"So what's the problem?" Elliott asked.

"I know if I go back to USC this semester, homework and tests will pile up and I won't finish rewriting the proposal in time. So, I guess I know what I need to do, but the last thing I want is to look my parents in the eye and tell them I'm dropping out of school."

"Whoa, whoa, whoa. You are *not* dropping out of school."

Wait—*what?*

"No one smart *actually* drops out of school," he went on. "It's a myth. Bill Gates and Mark Zuckerberg didn't drop out the way you think they did. Do some research. You'll see what I'm talking about."

When we got off the phone, I ran my finger across my shelf and plucked out a book I hadn't opened yet: *The Facebook Effect,* the authorized account of the company's early days. And there it was, on page fifty-two.

The summer before Mark Zuckerberg's junior year of college, he was in Palo Alto working on a couple side projects, one of which was a website called TheFacebook. It had launched seven months earlier. Later that summer, Zuckerberg pulled his mentor Sean Parker aside and asked for advice.

"Do you think this thing is really going to last?" Zuckerberg asked. "Is it a fad? Is it going to go away?"

Even when Facebook had nearly 200,000 users, Zuckerberg had doubts about its future. I sensed I was onto something, but I wasn't sure what.

I took out my laptop to dig deeper. After spending hours on YouTube watching interviews of Zuckerberg, I finally found one that shed more light. Weeks before his junior year, Zuckerberg met with venture capitalist Peter Thiel to raise money for Facebook. When Thiel asked if he was going to drop out of school, Zuckerberg said no. He planned to head back for his junior year.

Right before classes began, Zuckerberg's cofounder and classmate Dustin Moskovitz figured out a more practical approach.

"You know," Moskovitz said to him, "we're getting to have a lot of users, we have an increasing number of servers, we have no operations guy—this is really hard. I don't think we can do this and take a full course load. Why don't we take one term off and just try to get it under control, so that way we can go back for spring semester?"

So *that's* what Elliott was talking about.

Ever since I'd watched *The Social Network*, I'd thought of Zuckerberg as a rebel who dropped out of school, threw his middle finger to the sky, and never looked back. The film never showed Zuckerberg doubting Facebook's future. It never showed him cautiously debating taking one semester off.

For years I'd seen headlines that read "Dropout Mark Zuckerberg" and naturally assumed his decision to leave college was clearcut. Headlines and movies make things seem black and white. But now I was realizing: the truth is never black and white. It's gray. It's all gray.

If you want the whole story, you have to dig deeper. You can't rely on headlines or tweets. Gray doesn't fit in 140 characters.

I grabbed a book on Bill Gates, and on page ninety-three, there it was again.

Gates didn't impulsively drop out of college either. He took just one semester off during junior year to work full-time on Microsoft. And when momentum for the company didn't fully pick up, Gates *went back* to college. Again, no one talks about that. It wasn't until the following year that Gates took another semester off, and then another, as Microsoft grew.

Maybe the hardest part about taking a risk isn't *whether* to take it, it's *when* to take it. It's never clear how much momentum is enough to justify leaving school. It's never clear when it's the right time to quit your job. Big decisions are rarely clear when you're making them—they're only clear looking back. The best you can do is take one careful step at a time.

Although the idea of dropping out of USC altogether didn't

sit well with me, staying enrolled and taking one semester off sounded perfect. I drove to campus, spoke to my academic adviser, and she handed me a bright green form that said "USC Leave of Absence," which gave me a seven-year window to return to classes at any point.

I ran off to tell my parents the good news.

———

"A SEMESTER OFF?" my mom yelled. "Are you out of your mind?"

She was slicing tomatoes in the kitchen.

"Mom, it's not as big of a deal as you think."

"No, it's a *bigger* deal than you think. I know you. I've known you longer than you've known you. I know that once you walk away from school, you'll never go back."

"Mom, it's just a—"

"*No!* My son is not going to be a college dropout!"

"It doesn't say *dropout*," I said, waving the green form in the air. "It says *leave of absence.*"

She sliced harder into the tomato.

"Mom, you just have to trust me. Elliott told me—"

"I knew it! I knew Elliott was behind this!"

"This has nothing to do with Elliott. I love college, but—"

"Then why can't you stay?"

"Because I need to get this publishing deal. The moment I get one, I'll get to Bill Gates, and once he's in, the mission will hit its tipping point and everyone else I want to interview will be in. I have to make this happen."

"But what if you can't make it happen? Or worse: what if you don't *realize* you can't make it happen? What if you try to get the book deal and you don't get it, so you try again, and again—and it's not until years later that you finally call it quits and decide to go back to school—and then they won't let you back in?"

I explained to her the seven-year window.

My mom stared at me with gritted teeth, then stormed off.

I went to my room and slammed the door. But as soon as I collapsed on the bed, a voice within me wondered . . . *what if Mom is right?*

Normally when my mom and I argued like this, I would call my grandma. But now that was the last thing I could do. My insides knotted as I thought about it. *Jooneh man.*

I'd sworn on my grandma's life I wouldn't drop out. How could I break that promise?

But staying true to that promise wouldn't be staying true to myself. When I'd said those words, I didn't know where my life would lead.

The advice I got at Summit from Dan Babcock came to mind: *Success is a result of prioritizing your desires.*

But how could I prioritize this?

Family of course comes first, but at what point do I stop living for others and start living for myself?

The tension pulled at me. I called Elliott that night filled with fear and confusion, but his voice couldn't have been more matter-of-fact.

"I went through that same stuff with my parents," he said. "But then I realized: Why the hell is school supposed to be one-size-fits-all? There's a line from a Kanye song I heard years ago:

Told 'em I finished school and I started my own business

They say "Oh you graduated?"

No, I decided I was finished.

"You did school," Elliott said. "Now it's time for you to do you. It's time for you to finish."

===

EVERY DAY FOR THE NEXT WEEK, I sat in the living room with my mom and dad, trying to make them comfortable with my decision. I was now down to the final day to submit the leave-of-absence form. There were three hours until the deadline. I'd signed the form and was in my room, getting ready to drive to campus to hand it in.

The more I looked at the green form on my bed, the more I felt fear pulsing through my veins. As much as Elliott's guidance had helped, twenty minutes on the phone with him was nothing compared to twenty years of living with my mom. A part of me felt she might be right—maybe ten years from now I would end up delusional, without a publishing deal, and without a college degree. Although I knew I had a seven-year window, and Elliott had told me not to worry, I still felt I might be making the biggest mistake of my life.

As I tied my shoes, the doorbell rang. I slipped the green form in my pocket, grabbed my car keys, and headed for the door. I twisted the knob and pulled it open.

It was my grandma.

She was standing on the steps, trembling, tears streaming down her face.

STEP 4

TRUDGE THROUGH THE MUD

CHAPTER EIGHTEEN

Hallelujah!

I locked myself in the storage closet and rewrote the book proposal as fast as I could. I didn't talk to my friends. I didn't see my family. I slept just three or four hours a night. When I would close my eyes, one image kept coming back to me as if it had been chiseled into the insides of my eyelids—my grandma, tears streaming down her face.

Qi Lu had told me he'd slept only a couple hours a night while creating Yahoo Shopping and I'd wondered how it was possible. Now I knew.

My agent had told me rewriting the proposal would take thirty days. I finished in eight. When your back is against the wall, you learn what you're capable of. I emailed her the 140-page document, prayed she could work her magic, and then, just eleven days after I'd turned in the leave-of-absence form—I got the publishing deal.

I IMMEDIATELY SHARED THE NEWS with my parents. Even my dad, who celebrated every possible occasion, couldn't crack more than a smile. I could tell he was still shaken by my leaving school. I needed to talk to someone who I knew would be as excited as I was. I called Elliott.

"You didn't," he said. "No way. You're lying."

"It really happened."

"Holy . . . shit. You did it! It worked! *BRO, YOU ARE A SUPER-STAR!*"

I'd never heard Elliott talk to me like this before.

"This is nuts!" he went on. "So what are you going to do next?"

"Now it's time to get my interview with Bill Gates."

"That's insane! How much time do you think you'll get with him? Are you going to do it at his office? Or can you do it at his home? Is it just going to be you two, one-on-one? Or will you be in a room with a dozen PR guys?"

"Dude, I still haven't told his Chief of Staff the news."

"Stop," Elliott said. "That email has to be . . . *perfect.*"

We spent the next hour on the phone drafting it. I didn't write a direct ask because I assumed it was abundantly clear why I was reaching out. Before hitting send, I thought about how just two years earlier I was on my dorm room bed, fantasizing what it would be like to learn from Bill Gates. It was finally coming together.

A day later, the Chief of Staff's reply popped up on my screen. I felt as though a gospel choir had stepped into the storage closet singing *Hallelujah!* I wanted to call Elliott so we could read the response together. But I couldn't wait. I clicked it open:

Well, that's fantastic news. Congratulations!

I hit the down arrow, searching for the rest of his message. But that was it.

Clearly my email strategy didn't work, but I wasn't deterred.

I emailed the Chief of Staff again.

A week passed. No response.

I told myself he must not have seen my message, so I sent a third email.

Another week passed. There was still no answer.

I began to come to terms with what his silence meant. The answer was no. And not only was it no, but now the Chief of Staff wasn't talking to me.

The choir stopped singing, gathered their things, and slipped out the door.

———

I'D GUARANTEED MY PUBLISHER I'D get Bill Gates; now I had no Bill Gates. What would my agent say? And how would I explain this to my parents, after I'd sworn Gates would be a done deal if I took a leave of absence? I'd disappointed my family, let down my agent, and lied to my publisher: the asshole-trifecta.

I frantically thought through my options in the storage closet. *All right . . . If I can't get Bill Gates . . . I'll get Bill Clinton. Elliott has an in with him. And if I can't get Clinton, I'll get Warren Buffett. Dan can help with that. Plus, Buffett is best friends with Gates, so if I interview Buffett, he can get me to Gates. I don't even need the Chief of Staff!*

While I had sent interview requests to most of these people before, I didn't know what I was doing back then. Now I felt a bit more experienced. And the more I dreamed up next steps, the better I felt. *My friend from Summit works for Oprah—so I have an in there. Another friend from Summit worked for Zuckerberg—maybe she can get me to him. And Elliott is friends with Lady Gaga's manager—so I'm definitely golden there.*

I downloaded photos of Lady Gaga, Warren Buffett, Bill Clinton, Oprah Winfrey, and Mark Zuckerberg, pasted them on a single page, and printed a dozen copies. I taped the pictures by my desk, on the walls, above my bed, and on my car's dashboard.

Only in hindsight can I see the change that was overtaking me. I'd left school and felt completely on my own. And I had sold everyone around me on a dream that was now falling apart. I was so terrified of being seen as a liar, so ashamed of being seen as a failure, that I became desperate to do whatever it took to save face. Ironically, that desperation fueled me to lie and fail even more.

"The momentum couldn't be stronger!" I told Elliott over the phone. "I'm sure Bill Gates' Chief of Staff will get back to me any day now. Anyway, now that things are going so well, it's the perfect time to get the rest of the interviews. Could you introduce me to Lady Gaga's manager? And didn't you say you knew Buffett's grandson? And Clinton's assistant?"

I felt horrible about misleading Elliott, but an hour later I felt a lot better when I saw an introduction to Lady Gaga's manager in my inbox. I asked for the interview, the manager replied back, and the answer was no.

Elliott contacted Bill Clinton's office.

Another no.

Elliott introduced me to Warren Buffett's grandson.

Dead end.

A friend from Summit took me to a party where I met Buffett's son.

No help.

Another friend from Summit introduced me to one of Buffett's business partners.

Again the answer was no.

A third friend from Summit introduced me to Oprah's PR team. When I explained the mission to them, they loved it and told me to write a letter addressed to Oprah. They passed it along to the first level in her PR chain and it was approved. The second and third level approved it too. Finally, it made it to Oprah's desk and . . . her answer was no.

My fear of failure had its hands around my neck, cutting off circulation to my brain. The only thing keeping me from suffocating was knowing I still had an ace up my sleeve.

It was time to call Dan.

Dan seemed like the obvious route for me to get to Warren Buffett. After the breakfast at Summit where Dan shared the Avoidance List, we became friends and talked on the phone every week. But anytime Buffett's name came up in conversation, Dan seemed to get uneasy. I figured he was extremely protective of his former boss. I had decided going through Elliott to get to Buffett would be easier, but now Dan was my only hope.

Instead of being transparent about what I wanted, I called Dan and said, "I miss you, man! When are we hanging out?" He suggested I come to San Francisco for the weekend and stay with him on his boat. I jumped on the offer.

A few nights later, I landed in San Francisco and my cab pulled up to a fog-shrouded marina where Dan docked the boat he lived on. Before I even put my bags down, Dan wrapped me in a giant bear hug. He threw my duffel bag inside and whisked me off to a lavish dinner on the San Francisco Bay, followed by live music at his favorite café. The next morning, we played Frisbee at a sloping, grassy park. Over the two days, Dan took me around the city, treating me like family.

Throughout our time together, I never brought up Buffett. I hoped the more Dan and I bonded, the likelier it would be that he'd agree to make the introduction. I felt like a salesman plotting an ask with a new client. Except this was my friend, so I felt terrible.

And now I was running out of time. As I woke up on my final day in San Francisco, I checked my watch—two hours until I had to leave for the airport. I headed out to the deck where Dan and his girlfriend were lounging, looking out at the Golden Gate Bridge, coffee mugs in their hands.

After talking to them for a while, I glanced at my watch once more—thirty minutes until I had to leave. I still hadn't asked Dan for the introduction.

"Dan, can you look this over?"

I took out my laptop and passed it to him. Dan's eyes narrowed as he realized that on the screen was a letter I'd drafted to Warren Buffett. Dan read it, then looked back up a minute later.

"Alex," he said, "this is . . . fantastic. Mr. Buffett will love it."

I remained quiet, hoping Dan would fill the silence by offering to call Buffett and push this through.

"And you know what?" Dan said.

I edged forward.

"You should print two copies!" he said. "Mail one to his office and one to his home!"

Dan's girlfriend put down her mug and reached for the laptop. "Let me read it," she said. After she finished, she looked at Dan.

"Honey, this is wonderful. Why don't you just email this to Warren directly?"

"That would be life-changing," I said.

Dan's eyes darted from the laptop to his girlfriend to me.

He stayed silent, and then a moment later said, "You got it, Alex. Email me the letter and I'll pass it along."

Dan's girlfriend kissed him on the cheek.

"And if that doesn't work," he added, "I'll fly to Omaha with you and talk to Mr. Buffett myself! We're going to make this happen, Alex. You'll have this interview in no time."

CHAPTER NINETEEN

Grandpa Warren

B efore I left the boat, Dan pointed out that if I sent Buffett the letter and he immediately said yes, I wouldn't be prepared for the interview. So I decided to hold off on sending it and went back home to do my research.

I already knew what a lot of people know about Buffett: that he's the most successful investor in history and the second richest man in America, yet he's not someone who lives in New York with a big office on Wall Street. Buffett was born in Omaha, Nebraska, and still runs his company, Berkshire Hathaway, from there to this day. I once saw on TV that tens of thousands of people from around the world make an annual pilgrimage to Omaha for the Berkshire Hathaway shareholders meeting. These people revered him, even loved him, which is why when I got to the storage closet and stared at Buffett's face on the cover of an eight-hundred-page biography, I felt like I was about to join the extended family.

Looking closer at his soft wrinkles and bushy eyebrows, I couldn't help but feel a sense of warmth. Buffett's eyes seemed to twinkle with a Midwestern charm. The more I stared at his image, the more I felt like the picture was moving and coming to life— Buffett was smiling at me, winking, and waving a hand, saying, *"Alex, come on in!"*

I laid the book on my desk and happily began turning the pages. Now that I knew Dan would help me get the interview, the pressure was off. I was having so much fun reading I barely noticed the hours pass. Never before had I felt like this about learning. In college, I had all these tests and assignments, and reading felt like taking medicine. Now it was like drinking wine. I read his biography during the day, listened to audiobooks about him in the evening, and watched YouTube videos of him late into the night, taking in his every gem.

> "I tell college students, when you get to be my age, you will be successful if the people who you hope to have love you, do love you."

> "No matter how great the talent or effort, some things just take time. You can't produce a baby in one month by getting nine women pregnant."

> "I insist on a lot of time being spent, almost every day, to just sit and think. That is very uncommon in American business . . . So I do more reading and thinking, and make fewer impulse decisions than most people in business."

I'd never known much about finance and hadn't thought I had a passion for it, but there was something about the way Buffett explained it that completely drew me in.

"I will tell you the secret to getting rich on Wall Street. You try to be greedy when others are fearful. And you try to be fearful when others are greedy."

"The stock market is a no-called-strike game. You don't have to swing at everything—you can wait for your pitch. The problem when you're a money manager is that your fans keep yelling, 'Swing, you bum!' "

"I try to buy stock in businesses that are so wonderful that an idiot can run them. Because sooner or later, one will."

As soon as I finished the eight-hundred-page biography, I cracked open another. I eventually had fifteen books about Buffett laid out on my desk and I still couldn't get enough. I learned everything I could about him, from his first business selling Juicy Fruit gum door-to-door at age six to the fact that Berkshire Hathaway was now the fifth most valuable company in the world, with investments in Coca-Cola, IBM, and American Express, and outright ownership of Heinz, GEICO, See's Candies, Duracell, Fruit of the Loom, and Dairy Queen. The more I reveled in Buffett's experiences and wisdom, the more I saw him as Grandpa Warren.

My favorite stories about him went back to when he was my age. I began to see some of my friends facing similar situations right in front of me. When my friends had problems, Grandpa Warren had answers.

———

I NEVER WOULD HAVE THOUGHT to put my friend Corwin and Warren Buffett in the same sentence. Corwin's passion for filmmaking had only grown stronger and his interests couldn't be farther from finance. But when he needed advice on how to get meetings with directors who wouldn't return his calls, I told him to do what Grandpa Warren did.

After Buffett finished undergrad at University of Nebraska in Lincoln, he was working as a stockbroker, which essentially means he was a stock salesman. Though nearly every time Buffett tried to get a meeting with a businessperson in Omaha, he was turned down. No one wanted to meet with a young guy with no credibility, trying to sell them stocks. So Buffett changed his approach—he began calling up businesspeople and made them feel he could save them money on their taxes. All of a sudden the businesspeople said, "Come on in!" And just like that, Buffett booked his meetings.

"This is the thing," I told Corwin. "Although people won't meet with you for the reason *you* want, that doesn't mean they won't meet *at all*. Just find another angle. Figure out what *they* need and use that as your way in."

My friend Andre wanted to break into the music industry. He didn't know if he should try to get a well-paying job at a music label or work directly under a big songwriter and perhaps not get paid anything. I told Andre it was a no-brainer.

When Buffett was working as a stockbroker, he decided he wanted to hone his skills and go to business school. He applied to Columbia University because he knew Benjamin Graham, the Wall Street legend known as the father of value investing, taught there. Buffett got into Columbia, took Graham's class, and eventually Graham became his mentor.

When Buffett was about to graduate, he decided not to take a high-paying corporate job, which most MBAs did, but to try to work directly for Graham instead. Buffett asked Graham for a job, but Graham said no. Buffett then offered to work *for free*. Graham still said no.

So Buffett went back to Omaha and worked as a stockbroker

again. But he continued writing letters to Graham, visiting him in New York, and in Buffett's own words, after two years of "pestering him," Graham finally gave him a job.

Buffett was married and had a child by this point, but he still flew to New York as soon as possible to begin working. Buffett didn't even ask if there was a salary. He worked at a desk outside of Graham's office, learning firsthand under the master. Two years later, when Graham retired and closed down his firm, Buffett moved back to Omaha to start his own fund. And when Graham's old clients were looking for a new place to invest their money, Graham referred them to Buffett.

Buffett is famous for being a long-term value investor and this story shows he treated his career the same way. He could've gotten a high-paying job right out of school and made far more money in the *short term*. But by offering to work for free under Graham, he set himself up to make much more in the *long term*. Instead of trying to get paid as much as possible in dollars, Buffett chose to get paid in mentorship, expertise, and connections.

"It's like what Elliott told me," I said. "One path leads to a linear life, the other an exponential."

Sometimes I had friends who didn't even have a problem. Ryan, who wanted to work in finance, just wanted to know how he could be more like Grandpa Warren. I said the answer was three words: read the footnotes.

After Buffett opened his own fund, a writer called one day and asked to interview him. The writer posed a tough question to Buffett about a public company. Buffett told him the answer was in an annual report he'd just read. The writer studied the report, but then called Buffett to complain there wasn't an answer.

"You didn't read carefully," Buffett said. "Look at footnote fourteen."

Sure enough, there it was.

The writer was dumbfounded.

"While this story is short," I told Ryan, "the lesson is huge, and I think it's one of the biggest keys to Buffett's success. When everyone else skims a report, Buffett is obsessively scouring the fine print, going above and beyond, studying every word, looking for clues. You don't have to be born a genius to read the footnotes—it's a choice. It's a choice to put in the hours, go the extra mile, and do the things others aren't willing to do. Reading the damn footnotes isn't just a task on Buffett's to-do list—it's his outlook on life."

It didn't take long for all my friends to fall in love with Grandpa Warren too. The more stories I shared, the closer I felt to him. Finally, I was ready to reach back out to Dan.

I rewrote my letter to Buffett and infused as many facts as I could about him, trying to show how much I cared. I emailed it to Dan for a final review. He said it was perfect.

When I asked Dan if I should print the letter or copy it down by hand, he said, "Both!" I did just that and FedExed one set to Buffett's office and another to his home. I emailed the letter again to Dan so he could forward it directly to Buffett.

Dan called two days later. "Your note is sitting in Mr. Buffett's personal inbox as we speak."

And, with those happy words, began the six most miserable months of my life.

CHAPTER TWENTY

The Motel 6

TWO WEEKS LATER, THE STORAGE CLOSET

From: Assistant to Warren Buffett
To: Alex Banayan
Subject: Letter to Mr. Buffett

Dear Mr. Banayan –

Attached is a written response from Mr. Buffett to your letter.

I clicked it open. The letter I'd mailed was staring back at me, with two lines of Buffett's loopy cursive in light blue ink at the bottom. He must have loved my letter so much he'd written his reply on the spot and told his secretary to scan it and email it to me right away. But because of the way it was scanned, I couldn't make out the words. So I emailed Buffett's assistant to ask what it said. I assumed it must have read something like: *"Alex, you probably spent months researching to write this letter! I must say, I'm impressed. I'd love to help your mission. Why don't you call my assistant and we can find some time to do the interview next week?"*

Five minutes later, his assistant replied:

> From: Assistant to Warren Buffett
> To: Alex Banayan
> Subject: Letter to Mr. Buffett
>
> It reads:
>
> Alex—All aspects of my life have been covered many times over. Too much on my plate to grant all the interviews requested.
>
> —WEB

He barely lifted a finger to write that rejection, but it felt like he swung his arm back and punched me in the throat.

I called Dan.

"I thought we were golden . . . I thought this was a done deal . . . What did I do wrong?"

"Alex, you have to understand, this is Warren Buffett we're talking about. He gets hundreds of requests a day. You shouldn't see this as a negative. The fact he sent you a handwritten response means he likes you. I know Mr. Buffett. I know he doesn't write responses to just anyone."

I asked what I should do next.

"You just have to be persistent," Dan said. "Colonel Sanders got rejected a thousand and nine times when he started KFC. This is just your first no. Mr. Buffett is testing you. He wants to see how bad you want it."

As soon as I got off the phone, I printed out ten quotes and plastered them across the storage closet walls.

"Persistence—it's a cliché, but it happens to work. The person who makes it is the person who keeps on going after everyone else has quit. This is more important than intelligence, pedigree, even connections. Be dogged! Keep hitting that door until you bust it down!"
—JERRY WEINTRAUB

"Energy and persistence conquer all things."
—BENJAMIN FRANKLIN

"The most certain way to succeed is always to try just one more time."
—THOMAS EDISON

"You just can't beat the person who never gives up."
—BABE RUTH

"My success is based on persistence, not luck."
—ESTÉE LAUDER

"It's not that I'm so smart, it's just that I stay with problems longer."
—ALBERT EINSTEIN

"We can do anything we want to do if we stick to it long enough."
—HELEN KELLER

"If you are going through hell, keep going."
—WINSTON CHURCHILL

"Nothing in the world can take the place of persistence."
—CALVIN COOLIDGE

Dan helped me write a second letter to Buffett and I sent it off. A week passed and there was no response. I emailed Buffett's assistant to see if it made it to his desk.

From: Assistant to Warren Buffett
To: Alex Banayan
Subject: RE: Letter to Mr. Buffett

Mr. Buffett got your second letter. However, his first response remains. I am sorry he can't help you . . .

POW.

When I'd interviewed Tim Ferriss, I also felt like I was getting punched, but compared to this, that was a third-grade playground scuffle.

Looking back, I can see that Buffett wasn't doing anything wrong. He didn't owe me anything. But I wasn't thinking clearly then. And on top of that, Dan kept reminding me: *persistence.*

My alarm blared the next morning at 5:00 a.m. I laced up my running shoes, stepped out onto the dark street, and blasted "Eye of the Tiger" through my headphones. I sprinted down the sidewalk, imagining Buffett at the end of each block. It was me versus him, I told myself, and I wanted to meet him more than he didn't want to meet me.

If this were a movie, this is where they'd show a montage of months passing as I'm running on the pavement, trees turning from green to orange, leaves falling, then snow piling. I read more books about Buffett, watched more interviews on YouTube, and listened to more audiobooks. There had to be something I was missing. Buffett found his answer on footnote fourteen. I was on footnote one thousand and fourteen.

Before I knew it, January arrived and USC's spring semester was about to start. Without hesitating, I took another semester off.

I researched Buffett even more, woke up even earlier, and ran even faster. As hard as it is to admit, I wasn't doing it just for Buffett anymore. I was doing it to prove to myself that they were *all* wrong—every girl who'd said she saw me as just a friend, every popular kid who'd made me feel invisible, every fraternity that'd turned me away.

I sent Buffett a third letter.

No response.

BOOM—jab to the jaw.

A fourth.

BAM—hook to the eye.

Sugar Ray had warned me about this. *"You've got to stay in the fight. It's going to get tough. You're going to hear no. But you've got to keep pushing."*

I called Buffett's assistant every Wednesday morning to ask if Buffett had a change of heart. The answer was always no.

I sent a fifth letter.

SNAP—a crack in my nose.

A sixth.

POP—I spat out a tooth.

I wrote a more detailed letter in February, hoping Buffett would see how much I wanted this.

From: Assistant to Warren Buffett
To: Alex Banayan
Subject: your letter to Warren Buffett

Alex,

Mr. Buffett read your February 5 letter. We are sorry but he just cannot do the interview. Requests have increased since our earlier reply and his schedule is more than full.

BAM BAM BAM. I was doubled over, coughing up blood.

By this point, I felt like the only person in my corner was Dan. His friendship was single-handedly keeping my hope alive.

"Why can't you just call Buffett yourself?" I asked him.

"Alex, do you trust me?"

"Of course I do."

"Then you have to trust that it's better that I teach you to fish, than if I get you the fish. Calling Mr. Buffett is easy. Learning how to get the yes on your own is what matters. You just need to get more creative in your next letter."

Dan told me about a friend of his who had wanted to meet Bill Clinton. After Clinton's staff said no, this friend purchased the domain AskBillClinton.com, wrote the former president a letter offering the domain as a gift, and Clinton's office arranged for a time for them to meet. Dan suggested I do the same for Buffett. So I bought AskWarrenBuffett.com, and then Corwin and I filmed a YouTube video that we put on the landing page. I wrote a letter to Buffett explaining he could use the website as a way to teach students all around the world.

> From: Assistant to Warren Buffett
> To: Alex Banayan
> Subject: RE: your letter to Warren Buffett
>
>
> Alex, sorry for the delay ... Attached is a handwritten reply from Mr. Buffett.

I knew it. *I knew it! Persistence!* Buffett hadn't sent me a handwritten response since that original letter. I knew Dan's advice would work. I opened the attachment:

Alex—my friends & I have discussed this basic idea for many years, in the end most advise—& I agree—not to do it & stick with the written word.

Warren E Buffett

I didn't know what to do.

"You know what you've been missing?" Dan told me. "You haven't spent enough time warming up the gatekeeper. You should send flowers to Mr. Buffett's assistant."

"Don't you think that's a bit much?" I asked.

"I've known her for years. She'll love it."

I felt uneasy, but ordered the flowers anyway, and attached a note thanking her for taking my calls and passing along my letters.

From: Assistant to Warren Buffett
To: Alex Banayan
Subject: thank you for the flowers

Alex,

Thanks for the beautiful flowers and your nice notes. I'm sorry I haven't kept in touch but unfortunately I'm up to my ears in annual meeting-related duties ... But the flowers really brightened my day and I wanted you to know how much I appreciate it.

I called Dan.

"You see? We're on the right track!" he said. "You know what you need next? You need to meet Mr. Buffett's assistant in person. She said she's busy, right? So write her a letter offering to come to her office and be her errand boy. You can stuff envelopes for her, fetch coffee, whatever she needs. Then once she gets to know you, you'll have the interview in no time. Oh, and attach the letter to a single shoe. Put the shoe in a nice package, and on the box write, 'Just trying to get my foot in the door!' "

"You're . . . kidding, right?"

"Not at all. Make sure you write the 'just trying to get my foot in the door' in big letters so she understands the joke."

"I . . . I really think the shoe is a bit much."

"No, the shoe is the best part. Trust me."

An uneasy feeling sank into me, but I felt I couldn't argue. Dan was my only lifeline. So I went to a Salvation Army store, bought a black leather shoe, wrote the note the way Dan said, and sent it.

> From: Assistant to Warren Buffett
> To: Alex Banayan
> Subject: (no subject)
>
> Hi Alex,
>
> You are sweet to offer but there isn't a need or even room for another person here. And while Mr. Buffett admires your persistence, his schedule is overbooked as it is and he just will not be able to meet with you. You are not the first (and won't be the last) to try but he never does it. I hope you will accept this no as I really can't respond to any more notes from you. The best way to help me for the next few months is to let me concentrate on my job and not be distracted. I hope you will understand.

———

"DAN, PLEASE, YOU'VE GOT TO help me. Can you *please* call Buffett yourself?"

"I can," Dan said, "but that wouldn't be being a good mentor to you, Alex. This is just your ninth no. You're not at the end of your rope yet."

I tried to think of more options and that's when it hit me: just as Elliott jumped on a plane to the Hamptons and trusted that serendipity would give him what he needed, what if I flew to Omaha and did the same? What if I bumped into Buffett in a grocery store or at his favorite restaurant?

Dan thought the idea was great. I began searching for a plane ticket and thought about how proud Elliott would be. This was everything he'd taught me. I called him, and after telling him my plan, there was silence.

"You're blowing it," Elliott said.

"What are you talking about? I'm working 24/7 on Buffett. I can't work any harder."

"That's my point. You need to understand that business is not target practice. It's not about obsessing over a bull's-eye. It's about putting as many balls in the air as possible and seeing which one hits. When was the last time you worked on getting Bill Gates?"

"Well, not for a few months."

"When was the last time you worked on Lady Gaga?"

"Not for a few months."

"When was the last time you worked on Buffett?"

"I've been working on Buffett every day!"

"That's my point! You need to start working on building a pipeline and getting other balls in the air. *Business is not target practice.*"

Elliott hung up.

I understood what he was saying, but it didn't sound right to me. Dan had taught me about the Avoidance List: *"Success is a result of prioritizing your desires."* Every business book I'd read said to persist; and Dan, who knew Buffett personally, said to go for it.

Just because Elliott was my mentor didn't mean he was always right.

I booked my ticket.

TWO DAYS LATER, OMAHA AIRPORT

The terminal was dead. It was past midnight and my duffel bag weighed heavily on my shoulder. Inside was my Kindle, as well as ten hardcover books on Buffett. If bringing the books would somehow make landing the interview even 1 percent more likely, it was worth it.

I trudged through the empty corridor, the silence broken only by the echo of my footsteps. A poster in front of me advertised the University of Nebraska. It had a giant version of Buffett's undergrad yearbook picture with "1951" captioned beneath. He was twenty-one at the time. As I looked at that picture of him, it looked like any other yearbook photo. He was just a human being. Why had I been killing myself the past six months, getting punched at every turn, just to ask a human being a few questions?

I exited the airport and a gust of wind shot through my coat. Snow fell from the sky. As I walked to the taxi line, every breath shot an icy pain through my lungs. A cab pulled to the curb. Its front bumper was missing. The interior smelled of three-month-old Big Macs.

"Is it always this cold?" I asked the driver as I climbed in.

"First time in Omaha, huh?"

"How'd you know?"

He laughed. "You're a *dummmmmmmmb* kid."

He grabbed a newspaper off the passenger seat, tossed it back, and it hit me in the face. The headline said tonight would be one of the worst snowstorms to hit Omaha in thirty years.

We curved along a desolate highway. Then the car began to shake. It sounded like semiautomatic guns were shooting from above. The snow had turned to hail, and twenty loud minutes later, we pulled into the driveway of a Motel 6. The lights in the lobby flickered.

After checking in, I headed to the elevator, where two women were leaning against a wall, their clothes barely covering their bodies. They both had three-inch-long nails and hair that was so long it brushed against their exposed waistlines. They stared at me, raising their eyebrows. My body tensed and I rapidly hit the elevator button.

The elevator opened and a smell struck me that was so strong, so vile, it could only have come from someone who hadn't bathed in weeks. There was a man in there with a pale face and bloodshot eyes. He staggered forward, one hand scratching his neck, the other extending toward me.

I got to my room and locked the deadbolt. It felt just as cold in the room as it did outside. The heater was broken. When I called the front desk to ask which restaurants and grocery stores were open, I was told everything was closed for the storm. I walked to the vending machine down the hall: also broken. I gave up, pouring myself a cup of tap water from the bathroom sink and eating a bag of airplane peanuts for dinner.

As I unpacked the Buffett books from my bag, it dawned on me ... *How am I going to bump into Buffett during the biggest storm in years?* What was I even doing here? I'd thought flying to Omaha would invigorate me, but as I looked around the empty room, it felt like every rejection Buffett had sent me was nailed to the walls. In that moment, I felt more alone than at any other point in my life.

I took out my phone and scrolled through Facebook. There was a picture of my friends Kevin and Andre laughing together, hanging out at a party that night; a photo of my sisters Talia and Briana, smiling, having dinner at my favorite restaurant; an entire album with more than a hundred pictures, uploaded by the girl I'd had a crush on since the first day of college. I scrolled through the photos. She was studying abroad in Australia. Seeing her smiling on the beach, under the warm sun, reminded me of how cold and miserable I was.

The worst part was I did this to myself. I chose this. I could've stayed in school. I could've been studying abroad and enjoying life. I left all that—for this?

I hurled my phone at the pillows and fell on the bed. The sheets were frigid. I rolled off and lay on the carpet, tucking my knees into my chest. I cradled on the floor, shivering, thinking about every rejection from the past six months.

As the thoughts swirled, I saw a cockroach crawl across the carpet, coming inches from my nose. It grew blurry as it moved toward a crack in the wall, and I felt a tear trickle down my cheek.

Sugar Ray had told me about the Hidden Reservoir, but I was no Sugar Ray. I had no Hidden Reservoir.

I was out.

CHAPTER TWENTY-ONE

Frog Kissing

left Omaha days later, empty-handed. For the next week, I didn't set foot in the storage closet. I didn't touch a book. I didn't send a single email. I just sat around, brewing in nothingness.

I was slumped on the couch and surfing through channels on the TV when I got a call from Stefan Weitz, the Inside Man who'd connected me to Qi Lu.

"You're not going to believe this," Stefan said, "but I just got you an interview with *Dean Kamen*."

"Dean . . . who . . . ?"

I continued flipping through the channels.

"Dean Kamen is my hero," Stefan said. "Do me a favor. Look him up and then give me a call when you've finished."

It wasn't until a few days later that I finally Googled "Dean Kamen." A picture popped up of him on a Segway. The caption said he'd invented it. I then read that he also created the Slingshot water purifier, drug infusion pump, insulin pump, surgical irrigation pump, and iBot electric wheelchair. I watched a TED Talk that had more than a million views in which Dean Kamen unveiled the bionic arm he invented. He had been awarded the National Medal of Technology, inducted into the National Inventors Hall of Fame, and had more than 400 patents to his name.

Then I came across two words that made me sit up in my chair: "frog kissing." It's a term Kamen coined to motivate his engineers, spun from the fairy tale of the princess and the frog. Think of a pond full of frogs. Each frog represents a different way to solve your problem. Kamen tells his engineers that if they keep kissing frogs, eventually one will turn into a prince. So even when you've kissed dozens of frogs—and all you have as a result is a nasty taste in your mouth—Kamen says to keep kissing them, and eventually, you'll find the prince.

But what if you've kissed all the frogs and there's still no prince?

Then I thought, *Well, if there's anyone who can tell me whether I should keep trying to get to Buffett, or whether I should call it quits, maybe it's Dean Kamen.*

TWO WEEKS LATER, MANCHESTER, NEW HAMPSHIRE

Large paintings of Albert Einstein covered the office. Tall oak shelves were packed with thick books. As I settled into a chair, Kamen sat across from me and sipped a dark cup of tea. He wore a denim shirt tucked into blue jeans. Although it was only three in the afternoon, his face looked like he'd been working for the past twenty hours.

"So," Kamen said, "what are we here to talk about?"

Part of me wanted to tell him exactly what happened with Buffett and ask for advice, but I stopped myself. This wasn't my personal therapy session. Instead I told Kamen why I'd started the mission, and when I finished, he let out a sad laugh.

"I've had a lot of young people come to me expecting that some-how I could give them insights on how to succeed," Kamen said. He lifted his gaze in thought. "Let's say there's a one-in-one-hundred chance you're going to get something right. If you're willing to do it more than a hundred times, you start to approach the probability that, eventually, you're going to get it right. Call it luck. Call it tenac-ity. You will eventually get it if you exhaust all your efforts."

"But I'm sure there's a point," I said, "and this is the phase I'm going through, where sometimes you go home and feel like you've kissed *all* the frogs. You've made out with the *whole* pond, yet there's *still* no prince."

Kamen leaned in.

"Let me make it uglier," he said. "You go home, you've kissed every frog, and you've got nothing but warts on your face. You're lying in bed thinking, 'I kissed every frog. I still don't have a solu-tion. And I don't even know where the next frog is.'

"But then," he continued, "you roll around in bed thinking, 'You got into this because it's a really big problem. You knew it would be hard. After all this time and effort, if you give up, it's because you're weak. You've lost your vision. You've lost your courage. Sooner or later there's going to be an answer. The only reason you're going to give up now is because you're a coward.'

"But then," Kamen went on, "you roll around in bed some more and think, 'Go ahead. Keep trying. You know why you're going to do that? You're stupid, you don't learn from your mistakes, you have a big ego, you're unwilling to change, you're recalcitrant, you're wast-ing your time, your resources, your energy, and your life. Anybody with half a brain would recognize it's time to move on.'"

"*How* do you decide?" I asked. "How do you decide when to keep fighting or when to cut your losses?"

"I will give you my ugliest, worst answer . . ." he replied.

I inched forward.

Kamen looked up, took a deep breath, then locked eyes on mine.

". . . I don't know."

I traveled thousands of miles to talk to one of the smartest people in the world and his answer is "I don't know"?

"That's the question that keeps me up at night," Kamen said softly. "That's the issue that bothers me most. Because if you keep going and you don't get the answer, then you keep going and you *still* don't get the answer, then finally you stop—"

"At *what point* do you stop?" I asked.

"Whenever you decide. By definition, you can't answer that question."

Kamen sensed my frustration.

"Look," he said, "I'm not here to give you a road map. I'm here to tell you: this is what you should expect to see. If I gave you the map Lewis and Clark made, it would be pretty easy to get from here to the West Coast. That's why everybody remembers the names Lewis and Clark and nobody remembers who read their map and took the trip the second time.

"If you don't think you can deal with this amount of uncertainty and failure," he continued, "then wait for Lewis and Clark to deliver the map and you can be one of those people who does a good job following their lead. But if you want to be one of those people who do what these innovators did, be prepared, like they did, to fail and get frostbite and have people not make it. If you're not prepared for that stuff, *that's okay*: don't do it. There is plenty of room in the world for other people. But if you do want to do it—if you want to go off and do really big things—be prepared for them to take way longer than you thought, cost way more than you expected, and be full of failures that are painful, embarrassing, and frustrating. If it's not going to kill you, keep trudging through the mud."

"Let's say I'm going through that mud," I said. "Could you at least give me a few tips or a checklist on how to find the right frogs to kiss?"

"Okay," Kamen said. "Here's a big one: it's better to prove it can't be done than to exhaust the infinite number of ways to fail."

He explained that when he's kissed a lot of frogs but hasn't made progress, he steps back and asks whether what he's doing is actually impossible. Does it contradict the laws of thermodynamics, Newtonian physics, or some other fundamental principle?

"It's good to know when you're wasting your time," Kamen said. "If you can convince yourself that a problem can't be solved, you can quit without feeling like a coward."

Reporters interview Buffett all the time. Of course it's possible.

"If you keep kissing frogs," he continued, "and you keep getting nothing but similar results, there needs to be a point where you say, 'I'm not going to count on luck. I'm not going to keep buying lottery tickets.' Although I always say 'tenacity is great' and 'don't be a coward'—brute force is just plain dumb.

"Sure, there may be billions of frogs, but sometimes I'll notice there are only ten different *kinds* of frogs. So that's a good second tip: you should kiss one of these, one of those—but don't try to kiss *every* possible frog. First figure out how many *kinds* of frogs there are and then see if you can kiss one of each kind."

Kamen went quiet and tapped his fingertips together.

"Restating the boundaries," he said, "is sometimes what gives you the insight to create an innovative solution."

He told me a story about the lack of science and technology education in American public schools. Most people claimed it was an education crisis, so they tried to solve it in the same old ways— updating curriculum, hiring more teachers—but nothing seemed to work. Kamen wondered what would happen if they asked the question differently. What if this wasn't an education crisis, but a culture crisis? As soon as he reframed the problem, new frogs appeared. Kamen decided to create a competition called FIRST, which treats scientists like celebrities and turns high school engineering into a sport. FIRST is now a phenomenon across the country, having impacted the lives of millions of students.

"Instead of getting frustrated by repeating the same old problem," Kamen said, "reframe the question in a new way that is amenable to a different kind of solution."

A different kind of solution . . .

I'd been focused on how to get Buffett to sit with me for a one-on-one interview. But what if I restated the problem? What if I just wanted Buffett to answer a few of my questions—no matter how or where he answered them?

When you put it that way, there's still one frog I haven't kissed . . .

CHAPTER TWENTY-TWO

The Shareholders Meeting

THREE WEEKS LATER, OMAHA, NEBRASKA

I t was so cold it felt like frozen needles were piercing my cheeks. The line to enter the arena stretched down the block, curving around the side. We'd been standing in line for three hours, since 4:00 a.m. Once again, it was me versus Omaha. But this time, I had backup.

I'd brought my boys.

There was Ryan: my numbers guy. Actually, it so happened my numbers guy wasn't too interested in calculations right now. He was bent over and shivering, a scarf wrapped around his head making him look like a mummy. I tried to energize him by asking the odds of Buffett answering my questions. He just mumbled, "I'm ... too ... cold ... to ... think ..."

There was Brandon, clutching a book under his nose and holding a phone above his head, using it as a flashlight. He hadn't moved for fifteen minutes. I couldn't tell if he was deep in the book or frozen stiff.

Of course, Kevin was the opposite of frozen stiff. He was jumping around and smiling while passing out granola bars, trying to keep our spirits high.

Andre had no time for granola bars. He was circling ChapStick on his lips and flirting with a woman a few spots behind us in line. The sun hadn't even risen yet and he was already trying to get a phone number.

And Corwin ... well, Corwin was so tired he didn't care how cold it was. He was lying down on the sidewalk and using a flannel jacket as a blanket, looking like he'd never gotten out of bed.

Okay, maybe we were less Navy SEALs and more *Dumb and Dumber*, but still, these were my boys.

A man in front of us turned around.

"How long have y'all been shareholders?"

None of us were shareholders, so I didn't know what to say. Thankfully, Corwin came to the rescue, pushing himself up from the sidewalk and pulling up his sagging pants. "Actually, sir," he said, pointing a finger in the air, "we were *personally* invited by Mr. Buffett's office."

I bit back my smile. While Corwin was right, he was leaving out 99 percent of the story.

Months earlier, Buffett's assistant had offered me passes to Berkshire Hathaway's annual shareholders meeting. She probably felt bad for me after all the rejections. Either way, it was extremely kind of her to offer. A pass to the annual meeting is like a ticket to the Buffett Super Bowl. Only shareholders or journalists can get in. At the time, I didn't see any benefit in going to just sit in the crowd, but after talking to Dean Kamen, I called her back and asked if the offer was still available.

"Sure, Alex. I'd be happy to send you a pass."

"Thank you! And, actually, do you think I could get a few more?"

"Of course. How many would you like?"

"Uh . . . six?"

"I, I suppose that's all right."

"Thank you so much. And just double-checking—during the Q and A portion of the event, people in the audience get to ask Mr. Buffett questions, right?"

"Alex, Alex . . . I know what you're thinking. Yes, people in the audience can ask Warren questions, but you should know that only thirty to forty people get that chance—and there will be *thirty thousand* people there. It's a lottery system. And it's completely random. So, as much as I love your optimism, I wouldn't get your hopes up."

Well, I was the king of hopes up.

Cheers erupted from the front of the line as the arena doors opened. Thousands of people began sprinting and shoving. Arms flailed, leather notebooks waved in the air; people shouted, "Pardon me! Pardon me!" It was like a business-casual Running of the Bulls.

My friends and I dove through the mob. Andre jumped down stairways, Corwin slid on railings, Kevin climbed over chairs, and we made it to the front, snagging six seats near the stage.

The arena was massive. I cranked my neck back, taking in the sight of the seats at the very top, which were at least six stories above me. I couldn't stop thinking that these thousands and thousands of empty seats were about to be filled by people also dying to ask Warren Buffett a question. Directly in front of me was a gigantic black stage, with towering dark curtains and three enormous screens above it. There was a table in the middle of the stage with only two chairs, which were about to be filled by Buffett and his vice chairman, Charlie Munger.

While I had come with high hopes, I hadn't come with a plan. I thought my friends and I could just figure something out when the time came. If there was one thing I'd learned on *The Price Is Right*, it's that there's always a way.

And now there was no time to waste.

I spotted a sign that read STATION 1. There was a line of people in front of it.

"Ryan," I shouted, "you're coming with me!"

At Station 1, a volunteer handed out pieces of gold paper that attendees dropped into a bucket. To the left of the bucket was a black microphone stand. Ryan and I jumped to the back of the line. When we got to the front, the volunteer offered us two lottery tickets.

"Actually, can I ask you a question instead?" This was our first time here, I told her, and I asked how the lottery worked.

She said I have to show my ID to get a ticket, and then I drop the ticket in the bucket. "Right before the meeting begins, we'll pull out the names," she explained. "It's a straight numbers game. I hope you're feeling lucky, because the odds are one in a thousand."

Ryan and I stepped aside and looked for Station 2. Even farther was Station 3. I saw tiny specks on the third level that I assumed were Stations 8, 9, 10, 11, and 12.

"Come on," I said, grabbing Ryan.

We ran to Station 2 and asked the volunteer for more information, hoping to piece together clues that would give us an edge. We got the same response.

Station 3.

Station 4.

Station 5.

I spoke to as many volunteers as I could, telling them the story of my six months of writing letters to Buffett and why my friends and I were here. All the volunteers repeated the same thing. That is, until one pulled me aside.

"You didn't hear this from me," she said, "but at last year's event, I noticed not all the stations are treated the same."

"What do you mean?"

She explained that the tickets aren't put into a single bucket.

They're pulled individually from the different stations, creating about a dozen *separate* lotteries. The stations closest to the stage had thousands of entries. But the stations in the nosebleed section? Probably just a few.

"That makes complete sense," Ryan said. "The kind of people who'd sit in the front are probably the same people dying to ask questions. And the people sitting in the shadows probably don't want any attention."

Ryan's face lit up as if all the processors in his brain were firing at once. His pupils narrowed as he scanned the arena. "Looks like there are three thousand people sitting there; a thousand sitting there; five hundred sitting there; a hundred there. And if we just . . ." He went silent, the numbers flashing in his eyes. Then suddenly he yelled, "Station 8!"

We sprinted back to the front of the arena, yelled for our friends to follow, and raced to the top floor. We made it to Station 8, got our lottery tickets, and placed them all in the bucket. About twenty minutes later, the volunteer started to pull the winners.

My throat tightened. My friends looked just as nervous as I was. Deep down, we all knew that this was my last hope to get Warren Buffett to answer my questions.

The volunteer announced the winners. Although we were told our odds were one in a thousand, out of the six of us—*four* got winning tickets.

———

THE ARENA LIGHTS DIMMED. My legs twitched with nervous energy as I analyzed the faces around me. There were rows of people wearing suits, hunched over notepads and laptops; then there were rows of people leaning back in their seats, muffins and coffees in their hands, ready to watch the Buffett Super Bowl. I'd met people in line who'd said the Berkshire Hathaway shareholders meeting was so important to them they had locked it on their calendars a year in advance. Some had been coming every year for decades.

The audience fell silent as the giant screens above the stage played an animated clip of Buffett and Munger as fictional judges on *Dancing with the Stars*. Buffett kept giving zeros to the contestants while Munger got bored and played Words with Friends on a phone. When the show's host asked them if they could do any better, Munger shot back, *"We thought you'd never ask!"* The cartoon billionaires leapt out of their chairs and danced to "Gangnam Style," the Korean pop song that went viral the summer before, and the arena erupted with laughter. "OP, OP, OP . . . OPPA GANGNAM STYLE!" blasted through the speakers, yet the music could barely be heard over the cheers.

Then a video played of Buffett on the set of *Breaking Bad*, but instead of doing a meth deal, Buffett and Walter White were dueling over peanut brittle, one of Buffett's favorite candies. That was followed by a clip of Buffett with Jon Stewart, and then a skit of Buffett with Arnold Schwarzenegger. Finally, the screen went black and I thought it was time for business. But no—disco balls dropped from the ceiling, red and blue lights lit the arena like a nightclub, and the song "Y.M.C.A." blared, except the letters had been replaced by "B.R.K.A.," the stock symbol for Berkshire Hathaway. The crowd sang along as if those were their favorite letters in the world. Then down the aisle came a parade of cheerleaders.

Buffett and Munger entered stage right, dancing and singing "B.R.K.A.!," which triggered a roar that shook the arena like a mini-earthquake. In the aisle to my left, in the midst of this chaos, was Corwin, grinding his hips and moving closer to the cheerleaders. One of them handed him a pom-pom, which he was now shaking over his head, B.R.K.A.-ing with her like it was the first night of their honeymoon.

Buffett sat at the table and leaned into a microphone. "Whew! I'm worn out!"

He started the meeting by announcing Berkshire's financials and introducing his board of directors, who were seated in the front row.

"All right," Buffett boomed. "We will now move on to questions."

I knew that the Q and A portion took up nearly the entire event. On Buffett and Munger's table were a few small piles of paper, two glasses of water, two cans of Cherry Coke, and a box of See's Candies peanut brittle. To the left of the stage was a table of three financial reporters from *Fortune*, CNBC, and the *New York Times*. To the right was a table of three financial analysts.

The Q and A went like this: a reporter asked about Berkshire's performance against the S&P index, then an analyst questioned the competitive advantage of one of Berkshire's subsidiaries. Buffett gave smooth answers, topped them off with a joke, ate some peanut brittle, and then said "Charlie?" to see if his partner had anything to say. Munger usually moved things along with a swift "Nothing to add." Then the spotlight shot on Station 1. A lottery winner from the audience asked about Buffett's biggest worry regarding Berkshire's performance.

The cycle continued. *Reporter, analyst, Station 2. Reporter, analyst, Station 3.* Ryan calculated we had about an hour before our first question. We all headed to the concession corridor to prepare.

"These are my top interview questions for Buffett," I said, pulling a sheet of paper from my pocket. "Andre, your ticket got pulled first, so you're asking the persuasion question. I'm going second, and Brandon, you're third. You're asking the fundraising question. Corwin, you're fourth and asking the value investing question. Guys, make sure when you—"

"Yo," Corwin blurted. "Anyone have an extra belt on them?"

I knew I shouldn't have asked, but I did anyway. "Why would anyone have an *extra* belt?"

He shrugged.

"Wait," I said. "You didn't forget a belt, did you?"

"Don't worry, man. I'll figure it out."

I tried not to dwell on how ridiculous we looked. In a sea of khaki pants and comb-overs, Andre had his shirt unbuttoned past his chest, Brandon and Kevin were in hoodies, and Corwin looked like he'd locked himself in an editing bay for the past three weeks. I was in my Tony Hsieh Zappos T-shirt, and for extra luck, the same underwear I had on for *The Price Is Right*.

The question I'd saved for myself was my favorite: the Avoidance List. I had called Dan a day earlier to tell him I'd be asking about it if I got a winning lottery ticket. Dan said it sounded great, but then for some reason he asked me not to mention his name.

We returned to our seats. After Buffett wrapped up his answer for Station 7, I handed Andre the white paper with the interview questions and he marched toward the Station 8 microphone. A reporter asked a question, then an analyst, and then the spotlight centered on Andre.

"Hi, my name is Andre and I'm from California," he said, his voice booming from hundreds of speakers, resounding around the arena. "During key events, like the Sanborn incident, when you were buying See's, or when you were buying Berkshire stock—you persuaded people to sell you their shares when they really didn't want to. What were your three keys in influencing people in those specific situations?"

"Yeah—" Buffett said, "I don't think—uh—you brought up Sanborn—and you brought up, uh, See's . . ."

When I'd originally written that question, it had sounded fine. But now when I heard Andre bellow "when they *really didn't want to*," it sounded less like a question and more like an accusation.

"The See's family—" Buffett continued, "there had been a death in the See's family . . ."

I listened to see where Buffett was going with this, but then I realized he was going nowhere. He was just spewing different facts about See's Candies and avoiding sharing any persuasion advice, which is what I actually wanted.

"Charlie probably remembers this better than I do," Buffett said, but then he continued for a bit more, and then moved on to the next question.

The See's and Sanborn incidents had taken place nearly forty years ago, so they were probably some of the last things Buffett expected to hear. It became painfully obvious to me that by packing the question with so many details, and unknowingly wording it to sound like an accusation, I'd caused it to backfire.

Thankfully, we still had three more questions.

The cycle continued and eventually it was my turn. The volunteer examined my ticket and then motioned me to the microphone.

I peered over the balcony in the darkness, looking down at the man whose picture had been taped above my desk for the past six months. After all it took to get to this point—plowing through thousands of pages, poring over hundreds of articles, agonizing on the phone for dozens of hours with Dan—I felt I had earned this moment.

"Okay," Buffett said, his voice coming from all directions. "Station 8."

The spotlight flashed on. It was so bright I could barely see the paper in my hands.

"Hi, my name is Alex"—my echo boomeranged back at me with such force it almost knocked me off balance—"and I'm from Los Angeles. Mr. Buffett, I've heard that one of your ways of focusing your energy is that you write down the twenty-five things you want to achieve, choose the top five, and then avoid the bottom twenty. I'm really curious how you came up with this, and what other methods you have for prioritizing your desires?"

"Well," Buffett replied, chuckling, "I'm actually *more* curious about how *you* came up with it!"

A deafening roar of laughter came from the crowd. It's hard to explain what it feels like when an entire stadium of people laughs at you at once.

"It really isn't the case," Buffett said. "It sounds like a very good method of operating, but it's much more disciplined than I actually am. If they stick fudge down in front of me"— he pointed to the box of See's—"I eat it!"

I felt my face turning red under the spotlight.

"Charlie and I live very simple lives," Buffett added. "But we know what we do enjoy and we now have the option of pretty much— Charlie likes to design buildings. He's no longer a frustrated architect. He's a full-fledged architect now. And, you know, we both like to read a lot. But I've never made a list. I can't recall making a list in my life.

"But, maybe I'll start!" Buffett said, triggering even more laughter. "You've given me an idea!"

In an instant, the spotlight shut off.

I staggered back to my seat, unable to make sense of what had happened. What I could make sense of were all the whispers and chuckles I heard as I passed through the aisles. I kept my head down, trying to avoid eye contact.

———

AFTER I SETTLED IN MY SEAT, Kevin leaned over and brought up a good point: our first two questions probably surprised Buffett, and if we wanted to get a good answer out of him, the next one needed to be simple and straightforward. I agreed, and we both pulled Brandon aside and told him his question needed to be completely clear so Buffett would have no choice but to answer it.

Kevin and I then stepped into the hallway with Brandon so he could practice projecting his voice and enunciating every word. We returned to our seats, and soon enough, Brandon was at the mic.

"Hi . . . I'm . . . Brandon . . . from . . . Los . . . Angeles."

It was the clearest sentence I could have asked for. The problem was Brandon was so clear, and enunciated so slowly, it sounded suspicious.

"If I'm in my twenties . . . ," Brandon continued, "and I'm starting a partnership . . . what advice do you have . . . about getting people . . . to put in money . . . *before* I have a track record . . . as a solo investor?"

There was a pause.

"Well," Buffett said, "you haven't sold me!"

Another wave of laughter shot from the crowd.

I wondered if Buffett had caught on to what was going on. Here was another twenty-something, also wearing jeans, also from Los Angeles, also at Station 8, and also asking another unusually specific question that had nothing to do with Berkshire's recent performance.

"I think people should be quite cautious about investing money with other people," Buffett said, "even when they have a track record, incidentally. There are a lot of track records that don't mean much. But overall, I would advise any young person who wants to manage money, and wants to attract money later on, to start developing an audited track record as early as they can. I mean, it was far from the sole reason that we hired Todd and Ted [who manage investments for Berkshire], but we certainly looked at their record. And we looked at a record that [Charlie and I] both believed and could understand, because we see a lot of records that we don't really think mean much.

"If you have a coin flipping contest," Buffett continued, "and you get 310 million orangutans out there and they all flip coins, and they flip them ten times, you'll have 300,000 roughly that flipped [heads] ten times in a row successfully. And those orangutans will probably go around trying to attract a lot of money to back them in future coin flipping contests.

"So it's our job," he went on, "when we hire somebody to manage money, to figure out whether they've been lucky coin flippers or whether they really know what they're—"

"Well . . ."

A voice cut Buffett off.

". . . when you had his problem, didn't you scrape together about a hundred thousand dollars from your loving family?"

It was Charlie Munger.

"Yeah," Buffett said. "Well, I hope they kept loving me after they gave me the money."

Buffett chuckled again.

"Well, I . . . it . . ." he continued, stammering, "it was very slow, and it should have been very slow. As Charlie has pointed out, some people thought I was running a Ponzi scheme, probably. And other people may not have thought it, but it was to their advantage to sort of scare people, because they were selling investments in Omaha.

"To attract money, you should deserve money. And you should develop a record over time that does it. You should explain to people why that record is a product of sound thinking rather than simply being in tune with a trend or simply just being lucky. Charlie?"

"You're starting in the game and you're twenty-five years old," Munger repeated, with a sense of thoughtfulness in his voice. "How do you attract money?"

I'll never know what Charlie Munger was thinking, but perhaps he too noticed Buffett wasn't giving us straight answers. I felt like Munger was saving me from another round of humiliation.

He said that the best way to raise money before you have a track record is to do it from people who already believe in you and trust you, because they've seen you do other things in the past. Those people can be family, friends, college professors, former bosses, or even the parents of your friends.

"It's hard to do when you're young," Munger added, "and that's why people start so small."

Munger and Buffett's conversation veered off to hedge funds, and then they moved on to the next question. Brandon returned to his seat. Although he had to endure some laughter, at least we had gotten a response.

We had one more shot. It was up to Corwin.

After Buffett fielded a question from Station 7, Corwin headed to the mic. The journalist asked a question, then the analyst.

The spotlight flashed on Station 8.

Corwin was leaning in, holding the sheet of interview questions with one hand, pulling up his sagging pants with the other.

He began asking the question, but I couldn't hear him.

His microphone was shut off.

Buffett's voice boomed. "We'll take a five-minute or so recess. I thank you for coming! And I hope you come next year!"

Just like that, Buffett ended the Q and A.

Corwin just stood there, under the spotlight, holding up his pants.

———

MY FRIENDS AND I MADE our way out of the arena, overwhelmed with confusion and defeat. As we moved through the crowded halls, people stared at me. One guy patted me on the back and said, "Nice question, pal. I needed a good laugh."

Out on the sidewalk, people were still snickering at me. Kevin put a hand on my shoulder. "Don't let them get to you," he said.

We walked on in silence.

A few minutes later, Kevin gently spoke again. "It doesn't make sense . . . how could you have been so off with your question?"

"I wasn't off," I shot back. "It was Buffett who was off."

I told Kevin about the Avoidance List and how I had met Dan; how he'd promised to get me to Buffett, about the stories he had shared about working for Buffett; and about Dan's ideas to make the website and send the shoe.

Kevin began to squint.

"How could Buffett say he doesn't know about the Avoidance List?" I said, holding myself back from screaming. "I can't believe Buffett would lie like that."

Kevin just looked at me and said, "What if it wasn't Buffett who lied?"

CHAPTER TWENTY-THREE

MR. KINGGG!

soon learned that Kevin was right. Shortly after the shareholders meeting, Dan's girlfriend called and told me she'd been getting suspicious about him too. She contacted Buffett's assistant, who revealed that Dan never worked directly for Buffett.

I couldn't believe it.

When I called Dan, he denied it—and then he suddenly asked if anyone else was on the call, listening to our conversation. I told him no, and when I asked him more about his background, the conversation filled with tension. He answered my questions, but the details didn't add up. Dan hung up, and it was the last time we ever spoke.

Never before had I felt so betrayed. This wasn't just a stranger with a lie. This was someone I'd trusted, someone I cared about. That's what made the pain sear so deep.

Perhaps this was something I needed to learn the hard way. Some people are not who they say they are. My problem was that

I'd been so desperate to get to Buffett that I ignored the red flags about Dan that had popped up all around me. The lesson was clear: desperation clogs intuition.

At the same time, I hadn't been transparent either. I had an agenda from the moment I'd met Dan. The only reason I befriended him was to get to Warren Buffett. When I was on Dan's boat in San Francisco, I put him on the spot in front of his girlfriend. Although he twisted the truth, he never would have kept pushing the lie if I didn't keep pulling on it. My strategizing and lack of transparency backed him into a corner. Dishonesty breeds dishonesty.

My gloom was unshakable after I returned to LA from Omaha. A short time later, Corwin was trying to lift my spirits as we sat on a curb one afternoon, eating sandwiches in front of a grocery store.

"Dude," Corwin said, his mouth full, "I know you're upset, and I don't blame you, but at some point you have to let it go and move on."

I sighed, then bit into my sandwich.

"You got to get back to your routine," he went on. "Don't you have any other interviews lined up?"

"I've got nothing," I said. "And even if I did, I'd probably screw it up. Look what happened at the shareholders meeting. When I sent Andre up with that persuasion question, I packed it with so many details it turned Buffett against us. Not only can I not get an interview, I don't even know how to interview."

"You've got to stop being so hard on yourself," Corwin said. "Interviewing isn't easy. It's more than just asking questions. It's an art."

As we continued talking, the most inexplicable coincidence of my journey occurred. A black Lincoln with tinted windows pulled up to the curb and parked in front of us. The door swung open—and out came Larry King.

One of the most iconic interviewers in the world was walking into the grocery store right in front of me, and he was all alone. Larry King's show on CNN had run for twenty-five years. He'd interviewed more than fifty thousand people over his lifetime. *Why hadn't I tried to track him down before?* I knew he lived nearby and it was practically public knowledge where he ate breakfast every day.

But I sat motionless, watching him walk away through the store's sliding doors.

"Dude," Corwin said, "go talk to him."

I felt like I had sandbags on my shoulders.

"Just go into the grocery store," Corwin pressed.

I wasn't sure if I was dealing with The Flinch or if I was just depleted from the six months of rejection and humiliation.

"Come on!" Corwin said, nudging my shoulder, pushing me to stand. "He's eighty years old. How far could he have gone?"

I lifted myself off the sidewalk and walked through the store's sliding doors. I glanced around the bakery. No Larry. I jogged to the produce section: towers of colorful fruits, walls of vegetables. No Larry.

That's when I remembered he'd parked in a loading zone. *He must be leaving any minute now.*

I ran to the back of the store and dashed across the aisles, turning my head down each one. No Larry, no Larry, no Larry. I cut a sharp left, dodged a tower of canned tuna, and sped down the frozen food section. I sprinted to the front of the store and looked at every register. Still, no Larry.

I stopped myself from kicking a stray shopping cart. Once again, I'd blown it. When Larry King had been right in front of me, I didn't do a thing.

As I moped through the parking lot, I lifted my gaze and right in front of me, thirty feet away, was Larry King, suspenders and all.

In that moment, all the pent-up anger and energy inside me began to combust, erupting from my mouth, causing me to yell at the top of my lungs—

"*MRRRRR. KINGGGGGGGGGGGG!!!!!!*"

Larry's shoulders shot straight up. His head slowly turned around; his eyebrows arched toward his hairline, his mouth gaped open, and every wrinkle on his face sprung back. I sprinted toward him and said, "Mr. King, my name is Alex, I'm twenty years old, I've always wanted to say hi—"

He lifted a hand. "OKAY . . . *HI*," then he speed-walked away.

I followed in silence until we were finally out on the sidewalk, in front of his car. He unlocked the trunk, stuffed in his groceries, opened the driver-side door, and was about to climb inside, so I yelled again—

"Wait! Mr. King!"

He looked at me.

"Can I . . . can I go to breakfast with you?"

He looked around. A dozen people were on the sidewalk, watching the scene unfold.

Larry took a heavy breath, and then said in his gravelly Brooklyn voice, "*Okay, okay, okay.*"

I said thank you as he clicked his seatbelt. Before he shut the door, I called out, "Wait, Mr. King. What time?"

He looked at me—then slammed the door.

"MR. KING!" I shouted through the glass. "WHAT TIME?"

He turned on the engine.

I was now standing in front of his car, flailing my arms in front of the windshield. "*MRRRRR. KINGGGGGGG! WHAT TIIIIIME?*"

He glared at me, then at the crowd, and then shook his head and said, "*Nine o'clock!*" and then drove off.

———

I ARRIVED AT THE RESTAURANT the next morning. Larry King was in the first booth, hunched over a bowl of cereal, sitting with a few other men. Above their table was a large silver picture frame with photos of Larry interviewing Barack Obama, Joe Biden, Jerry Seinfeld, Oprah Winfrey, and more. There was an open seat at the table, but because I was embarrassed about how I'd acted the prior day, I didn't want to boldly pull back the chair and plop down. So from a distance, I gently waved a hand and said, "Hi, Mr. King. How are you?"

He acknowledged me with a lift of his head, mumbled gruffly, and then turned back to his friends. I assumed he wanted me to come back in a few minutes, so I took a seat at the table next to him, waiting to be called over.

Ten minutes passed.

Thirty.

An hour.

Finally, Larry stood up and stepped toward me. I could feel my cheeks lifting. But then he walked right past me and headed for the exit.

I lifted my hand. "Mr. . . . Mr. King?"

"WHAT IS IT?" he said. "WHAT DO YOU WANT?"

A sharp, familiar pain shot through my chest.

"Honestly," I said in a depleted voice, "I just wanted some advice on how to interview people."

Then, a slow smile appeared on his face. It was as if his eyes were saying, "Why didn't you say so before?"

"All right," he said. "Sometimes when people are starting out and feel they don't know how to interview, they look to the people they admire—maybe it's Barbara Walters or Oprah or myself—and they see how we interview and they try to copy that. That's the *biggest* mistake you can make. You're focused on what we're doing, not why we're doing it."

He explained that Barbara Walters asks thoughtful questions that are strategically placed, Oprah uses loads of enthusiasm and emotion, and he asks the simple questions that everyone wants to ask.

"When young interviewers try to copy our styles, they're not thinking about *why* we have these styles. The reason why is because these are the styles that make us the most comfortable in our seats. And when *we* are the most comfortable in our seats, our *guests* are the most comfortable in their seats—and that's what makes for the best interviews.

"The secret is: there is no secret," Larry added. "There's no trick to being yourself."

He checked his watch.

"Listen kid, I really gotta go—" He looked me in the eye, then shook his head again as though debating something in his mind. He put a finger in my face and said, "All right. Monday! Nine o'clock! *See ya' here!*"

When I showed up on Monday, all the seats were taken at Larry's table, but he waved me over anyway and asked why I was so interested in interviewing. I told him about the mission, and as soon as I asked if I could interview him, he said, "All right, *I'll do it.*"

We talked a bit more about the mission, then he said he had someone he wanted me to meet.

"Hey, Cal," he said, turning to one of his friends at the table. "Can you give this kid a few minutes?"

Cal wore a sky-blue fedora with horn-rimmed glasses. He seemed to be in his fifties, decades younger than the rest of Larry's crew.

Larry told me that Cal Fussman was a writer at *Esquire*, where he'd interviewed Muhammad Ali, Mikhail Gorbachev, George Clooney, and dozens of other icons for the magazine's "What I've Learned" column. Larry asked Cal to share some more interview advice with me.

After Cal and I peeled off to a nearby table, I told him about my prior interviews.

"No matter how much I prepare," I said, "things don't go the way I plan. And I can't figure out why."

"How are you doing the interviews?" Cal asked.

He nodded along as I told him I spent weeks, sometimes months, researching my questions. Then his eyelids narrowed when I said I brought my notepad filled with questions into the sessions.

"Are you bringing your notepad because it relaxes you," he asked, "or because you're afraid that without it you won't know what to ask?"

"I'm not sure," I said. "I've never thought about that."

"Okay, let's try something," Cal said. "Come back to breakfast tomorrow. You'll have a seat at the table. Don't think of it as an interview. Just eat breakfast and relax."

I spent every day the next week doing exactly that. Each morning, I sat next to Cal and watched how Larry ate his Cheerios with blueberries, how he pushed his bowl away after he ate the final blueberry, no matter how much cereal was left; how Larry talked on his flip phone; how he interacted with strangers who came over to say hello and ask for a picture. Larry couldn't have been kinder to each of them, which made me wonder how crazy I must've looked when I chased him in front of the grocery store.

At the end of the week, Cal told me to bring my audio recorder to breakfast the next day. "But leave your notepad at home," he said. "You're comfortable now. Just sit at the table and let your curiosity ask the questions."

The following morning, everyone was in their usual positions. Larry was across from me, hunched over his Cheerios; to his right was Sid, one of Larry's best friends for more than seventy years; next was Brucey, who went to middle school with them; Barry, who also grew up with them in Brooklyn; and then there was Cal, with his sky-blue fedora. I was halfway through my omelet when I asked Larry how he got started in broadcasting.

"When we were kids," Sid said, jumping in. "Larry used to roll up sheets of paper, pretend it was a microphone, and announce Dodger games."

"When Larry used to describe movies," Barry added, "his description took longer than the actual movie."

Larry's dream was to be a radio broadcaster, he told me, but he didn't know how to get started. After graduating high school, he worked odd jobs—delivering packages, selling milk, working as a bill collector—until one afternoon when he was twenty-two years old. Larry and a friend were walking down the street in New York City when they bumped into a man who worked at CBS.

"He was the guy who hired radio announcers," Larry said. "He was also the guy who announced between shows: *This is CBS! The Columbia Broadcasting System!*"

Larry asked him for advice on how to break into the industry. The man advised him to go to Miami, where a lot of stations were nonunion and had open slots. Larry jumped on a train to Florida, slept on a relative's couch, and began searching for a job.

"I just knocked on doors," Larry said. "There was this small station where I took a voice test and they said, 'You sound pretty good. Next opening, you've got the job.' So I hung around the station—I watched people read the news, I learned, I swept the floors—then one day, a guy quit on a Friday and they told me, 'You start Monday morning!' I stayed up all weekend, nervous as hell."

"Wait, what did you mean by 'knocked on doors'?" I asked. "How did you do that?"

Larry looked at me like I was in preschool. "*Bang! Bang! Bang!*" he said, pounding his knuckles on the table.

"It isn't a figure of speech," Sid said. "Larry knocked on the doors of different radio stations. He introduced himself and asked for a job. That's what we did in those days."

"That's all I could do," Larry said. "I didn't have a résumé. I didn't go to college."

"Okay, I get that that's what you did back then," I said, "but if you were starting out today, what would you do?"

"Same thing," Larry said. "I'd knock on doors. I'd knock on whatever doors I'd have to. There'd be many more places to knock. And look—nothing is new. We have the Internet, but nothing is new except the transmission. Human nature hasn't changed."

Cal explained that it's still a human being making the hiring decision. Only after looking you in the eye can someone get a sense if you're genuine. You may be using the same words in an email, but it's a different experience in person.

"People like human beings," Cal said. "People don't like random names in their inbox."

It dawned on me that when Spielberg gave me that early encouragement, when Elliott took me to Europe, or when Larry finally invited me to breakfast—those moments happened only after I met them in person and looked them in the eye.

Wait a minute . . .

For the past year, I'd been a random name inside Bill Gates' Chief of Staff's inbox. He took that original phone call with me because Qi Lu had asked as a favor, not because he knew me. I had taken it personally when the Chief of Staff stopped replying to me, but it wasn't personal at all. I was just a random name to him.

And I knew exactly how to fix that.

CHAPTER TWENTY-FOUR

The Final Bullet

FOUR WEEKS LATER, LONG BEACH, CALIFORNIA

I pulled back a chair at the lobby espresso bar of the Westin hotel. I was at the main lodging for the TED conference, and over the course of my journey, I'd never been in such a perfect position.

As I looked around, a wave of déjà vu washed over me. In the dining area twenty feet away was the table where I'd had my first meal with Elliott. That meeting with Elliott had taken place one year earlier, almost to the day. The timing was so eerie it felt like fate was smiling upon me.

My mood was high to begin with, because minutes earlier I'd just finished having breakfast with Tony Hsieh. When he heard why I was at the Westin, he invited me to watch the TED live-stream in his RV parked in front of the hotel.

But all this hadn't come together easily. Four weeks earlier, I'd reached out to Stefan Weitz, my Inside Man at Microsoft. I knew Bill Gates' Chief of Staff attended TED every year, so I asked Stefan if I could meet with the Chief of Staff at the event for five minutes, in person. If this didn't work, I swore to Stefan I'd never ask again. This was my final bullet.

Stefan agreed and sent the Chief of Staff email after email for weeks. When he didn't get a reply, he even had one of his colleagues email the Chief of Staff. Stefan's generosity had always been astonishing, but this time it left me speechless.

The day before the conference, Stefan still hadn't received a response. Then at 7:27 p.m. the night before, a reply arrived. Yes, the Chief of Staff said, he'd be at TED; and yes, he'd like to see me. He said he'd meet me after the conference's first session, around a quarter past ten, at the lobby espresso bar.

Now here I was, looking up at the clock on the wall. It read 10:14 a.m.

"Sir," the barista said, "what can I get for you?"

"Just a minute, please," I said. "My guest should be here any moment."

A short while later, the barista was in front of me again, asking if I was ready to order.

I glanced up—10:21 a.m.

"Sorry," I said. "He must be running late. Just a few more minutes, please."

I looked across the lobby and scanned the faces emerging from the rotating glass door. The next time I looked at the clock, it read 10:31 a.m. My gut sensed something was wrong, but I brushed it off. The conference's first session was probably running behind.

Time began to slow. Then I heard again, "Sir, are you going to order?"

It was 10:45 a.m. The barstools next to me were still empty. After all I'd been through, after everything I did to get to this point, this was how it was going to end?

I pulled up an old email from the Chief of Staff's assistant and called her office line, forcing myself to take deep breaths.

"Hi, Wendy. It's Alex Banayan. I know we had this 10:15 appointment today, and I'm sure he's really busy—I'm grateful he even gave me an appointment—but I just wanted to make sure everything is okay. It's been thirty minutes now and he hasn't showed up."

"What are you talking about?" she said. "He called me and said *you* didn't show up."

"*What?*"

Apparently, there were two lobby espresso bars, one at the hotel and one at the convention center, and I was at the wrong one.

I clutched my phone and tried to hold myself together, but I couldn't. Tears formed in my eyes as I poured my heart out to Wendy, explaining everything I'd gone through the past two years to get this meeting.

"Okay," she said, "give me a little time. Let me see what I can do."

An hour later, I got an email from Wendy. She said the Chief of Staff was going to the airport that afternoon at 4:30 p.m. His town car would be in front of the Westin valet, and he'd agreed to have me ride with him to the airport and talk in the car.

I was too drained to throw a fist in the air, but I still felt a faint smile on my face. This time, I knew there was only one Westin valet.

———

I PASSED THE TIME INSIDE Tony Hsieh's RV, watching the TED live-stream on a flat-screen TV, and then going out for lunch with Tony's friends. On my way back, I traced the route from the Westin valet to the RV, timing it at just about a minute. I set my phone alarm for 4:10 p.m., guaranteeing I would get there early.

As I lounged on a soft brown couch in Tony's RV, a man stepped onto the bus. The sun shined through the window behind him, so all I saw was a silhouette. He slowly lowered himself onto the couch across from me. His face looked familiar. He was an older man with thin white hair, a white beard, and a round belly. I looked closer, and that's when I realized—this was Richard Saul Wurman, the founder of TED.

"You," he said, looking my way, "what do you think of this thing?" He was pointing to the TV displaying the live-stream. The founder of TED was literally asking me what I thought of his conference.

I shared with him what I thought, and before I knew it he was telling me the entire story of how he started TED. He enthralled me with story after story and I felt like I'd broken the wisdom piñata and was trying to stuff as many nuggets into my pocket as possible.

"You want to know the secret to changing the world? Stop trying to change it. Do great work and let your work change the world."

"You won't get anywhere significant in life until you come to the epiphany that you know nothing. You're still too cocky. You think you can learn anything. You think you can speed up the process."

"How does one become successful? You'll get the same answer if you ask that to any other older, wiser, and more successful person: you have to want to do it very, very badly."

"I don't understand why people give speeches with slides. When you speak with slides, you become a caption. Never be a caption."

"I live my life by two mantras. One: if you don't ask, you don't get. And two: most things don't work out."

ERRH-ERRH-ERRH-ERRH!
My phone was blaring. It was 4:10, but he was talking a hundred miles a minute and there was no way to excuse myself without

cutting him off. His insights were so good I didn't want to leave. Plus, I couldn't just walk out on the founder of TED. *Whatever,* I thought, *I'll just hit snooze this one time.*

He kept going and going and then—

ERRH-ERRH-ERRH-ERRH!

He kept talking over the alarm. It was like I was on an express train with no local stops. I felt I couldn't leave while he was mid-story. And the Westin valet was a minute away. *I'll just hit snooze one more time.*

I kept sitting there, waiting for him to take a damn breath. I couldn't decide if this was one of the greatest conversations of my life or a hostage situation. I kept checking the time, and then—

ERRH-ERRH-ERRH-ERRH!

"Genius," he said, "is the opposite of expectation."

"*Genius,*" he repeated, looking at me with deep, knowing eyes, "*is the opposite of expectation.*"

ERRH-ERRH-ERRH-ERRH!

I didn't know what else to do, so I just jumped up and said, "I might regret this one day, but I have to go," and before he could say another word, I sprinted off the bus.

I dashed down the sidewalk, cut a left up the hotel's driveway, and spotted the town car. A driver in a suit and tie stood out front. While catching my breath, I checked the time—I'd made it with a minute to spare.

The driver and I made small talk while I kept my back to the car, glancing at the Westin's rotating glass door, until finally, the Chief of Staff stepped out.

He was holding a leather bag in one hand and a phone in the other. His hair was dark and thick with subtle streaks of gray, which perfectly complemented his blazer and black Ray-Bans. He approached the car and lowered his sunglasses.

"So, you must be Alex."

I introduced myself and we shook hands. "Please," he said, motioning toward the car, "come on in."

We took our seats and the car pulled out of the driveway.

"Tell me," he said, "how is your project going?"

"Oh, it's going really well," I said, and I began to list one thing after another, saying whatever I could to show momentum.

"So," he said, "I take it you still want to interview Bill."

I said it was my biggest dream.

He nodded silently.

"Who else have you interviewed?"

I pulled out my wallet and took out the note card that had the names of the people I wanted to interview, with the ones I already had checked off in green. The Chief of Staff held the note card with two hands and slowly moved his eyes down the list, examining it like a report card.

"Ah, Dean Kamen," he said. "We know him well.

"Larry King," he went on. "That must have been an interesting one."

As he was about to say the next name, an unexpected sensation overtook me and I cut him off.

"*It's not about the names,*" I said, my voice louder than I'd anticipated.

He turned his head to me, bewildered.

"It's not about the names," I repeated. "It's not about the interviews. It's about, well, I just believe that if all these leaders come together for one purpose—not to promote anything, not for press, but really, just to come together to share their wisdom with the next generation, I believe young people could do so much more—"

"All right," he said, slicing his hand up. "I've heard enough . . ."

My whole body tensed.

He looked at me, swung his hand down, and said, ". . . We're in!"

STEP 5

TAKE THE THIRD DOOR

CHAPTER TWENTY-FIVE

The Holy Grail: Part I

B ill Gates.

Nearly everyone knows the name, but most don't know the whole story. Behind the nerdy glasses and magazine covers, there's the boy who read the entire *World Book Encyclopedia* at age nine. At thirteen, his hero wasn't a rock star or basketball player, but the French emperor Napoléon. One night at dinnertime he hadn't left his room, so his mom yelled, "Bill, what are you doing?"

"I'm thinking!" he shouted.

"You're thinking?"

"Yes, Mom, I'm thinking. Have you ever tried thinking?"

While that might sound obnoxious, for some reason, I found it a bit endearing. As I dug deeper into Gates' life, I started to see him as the most relatable unrelatable person in the world.

On one hand, in eighth grade he spent his free time in the computer room with his friend Paul Allen, teaching himself how to code on the ASR-33 Teletype. That's totally unrelatable. While most kids in high school were sneaking out of the house at night to go to parties, Gates was sneaking out to go code at the University of Washington computer lab. That's even more unrelatable. On the other hand, he used his computer skills to help his high school automate the class schedules—and rigged the system to put himself in the classes with the best-looking girls. Now, that's relatable.

After high school, he majored in applied math at Harvard. Why did he choose that major? Because he'd found a loophole. He figured out a way to get priority registration in whatever classes he wanted because he claimed he was "applying math" to economics or "applying math" to history. Bill liked to rebel just for the sake of it, so he ditched classes he *was* signed up for and went to ones he wasn't.

The man the media portrays as an awkward, uncool geek was famous in college for staying up hours past midnight playing high-stakes poker. In his twenties, he blew off steam by sneaking onto construction sites in the middle of the night and racing bulldozers across the dirt. While he was starting Microsoft, he would take breaks from coding by climbing into his Porsche, flooring the gas pedal, and racing on the highway.

And his love for speed wasn't limited to driving. As I read stories about him closing major software deals, I felt like I was watching a chess prodigy play ten opponents at once, jumping from board to board, making dozens of moves a minute without blinking, beating them all. At an age when his friends were just graduating college, he was battling in the conference rooms of some of the world's biggest companies—IBM, Apple, HP—and negotiating contracts with people twice his age. With the chess prodigy metaphor in my mind, I realized that Gates has played the coding game, the sales game, the negotiating game, the CEO game, the public figure game, the philanthropy game—all at the highest levels—and has won each one.

He grew Microsoft into the world's most valuable company

in 1998, making him the wealthiest person on the planet. To put that in perspective, Oprah Winfrey is incredibly rich; so are Mark Zuckerberg, Howard Schultz, Mark Cuban, Jack Dorsey, and Elon Musk. Well, at the time I was preparing for my interview, Bill Gates' assets were worth more than all of theirs *combined*.

After stepping down as CEO of Microsoft, Gates could have retired, lounged on a yacht, and enjoyed every material pleasure the world has to offer. Instead, he jumped over to new chessboards to take on even harder challenges—feeding the world's poor, revolutionizing clean energy, stopping the spread of infectious disease, and bringing quality education to students in need. I already knew that the Bill & Melinda Gates Foundation was the largest philanthropic foundation in the world, but I had no idea its efforts have helped save the lives of more than five million people. Because of how Bill Gates has chosen to spend his fortune, he's helped cut the rate of infant mortality in half. In the next five years, it's projected his programs will save the lives of another seven million children. If there was ever a real-life superhero, it was Bill Gates.

I used everything I learned about him to plan my interview. I wrote dozens of questions on my notepad and color-coded them by subject. From sales to negotiating, I felt like I was creating my own treasure map.

A week before my meeting with Gates, I went to breakfast with Larry King and Cal Fussman and asked for advice on handling the interview.

"Just remember what I told you before," Larry said, pointing a finger. "The secret is: there is no secret. Just be yourself."

"And be just as relaxed as when you were here interviewing Larry," Cal added.

When I left breakfast, I felt they didn't understand the kind of pressure I was under. I didn't have the luxury to relax. This wasn't just another interview. For the past three years, I'd gone out of my way to stake the entire mission on this moment. I'd sworn to my publisher, agent, and family, that when I finally got the chance to interview Gates, I would draw out a piece of advice from him that would change my generation. Something that would radically transform people's careers forever. The Holy Grail.

I needed help from someone who had done something similar. I'd heard that for his book *Outliers*, Malcolm Gladwell had interviewed Gates for the "10,000 Hour Rule" chapter. If anyone could relate to what I was up against, it had to be Gladwell. So I used the Tim Ferris cold-email template and Gladwell responded a day later.

> From: Malcolm Gladwell
> To: Alex Banayan
> Subject: RE: Mr. Gladwell—advice on Bill Gates interview?
>
> my advice? bill gates is the easiest person you will ever interview because he is exceedingly smart and direct and perceptive. make sure you have read widely and deeply about his life so you don't waste his time. and then let him talk. he will take you in surprising directions if you let him.
> good luck!

As much as I was grateful for Gladwell's encouragement, it didn't calm me down. The stakes in my head were too high and I was too intimidated by Gates to relax. I needed something to move him off the pedestal in my mind.

I tried visualizing what he looked like when he was my age. I imagined him in a worn-in T-shirt and jeans, lying on his dorm room bed. A story I'd read came to mind. It took place during his sophomore year at Harvard. Gates was nineteen years old when Paul Allen barged into his dorm room and threw a magazine on the desk.

"Bill, it's happening without us!" Paul yelled.

On the cover of the magazine was a smooth, pale-blue box with lights, switches, and ports. It was the Altair 8800, the world's first minicomputer kit. Bill tore through the article and realized that although MITS, the company that invented the Altair, had already created the hardware, it still needed software. Microsoft wasn't even an idea at the time, but Bill and Paul wrote a letter to Ed Roberts, the founder of MITS, and offered to sell software to run it. Bill and Paul wanted to seem more legitimate, so they wrote the note on letterhead stationery from a company they had started in high school called Traf-O-Data.

A few weeks passed with no response and Bill had to be wondering, *Did the founder of MITS throw the letter in the trash? Did he find out I'm a teenager?*

Years later, Bill learned that the founder of MITS not only read the letter, but also liked it so much he wanted to buy the software. He called the phone number on the letterhead and a random woman answered—Bill and Paul forgot their letterhead still had the phone number of their friend's house from high school.

They didn't know that though, so back in Bill's dorm room they debated how to follow up. Bill handed the phone to Paul.

"No, you do it!" Paul said. "You're better at this kind of thing."

"I'm not going to call," Bill shot back. "You call!"

I guess even the person destined to be the world's richest man suffered from The Flinch. Eventually, they came up with a compromise—Bill would call, but say he was Paul.

"Hello, this is Paul Allen from Boston," Bill said in his deepest voice. MITS was a small company, so he didn't have trouble getting through to the founder. *"We've got some software for the Altair that's just about finished, and we'd like to come out and show it to you."*

The founder was receptive and said they could come out to their office in Albuquerque, New Mexico, to demo the software. Bill was overjoyed. He had only one problem—he didn't actually have any software.

In the weeks that followed, Bill spent every minute he could coding. Some nights he didn't go to bed at all. One evening, Paul walked in and found Bill asleep on the floor by the computer terminals, curled up like a cat. Another night, Paul saw Bill passed out in his chair, using the keyboard as a pillow.

After eight long weeks, Bill and Paul finished the software for the Altair. When deciding who should fly out to Albuquerque to make the pitch, they used simple logic: Paul should go—he had a beard.

Paul boarded a plane with the software safely in his hands. As the plane took off, he mentally went over the demo and realized, *Oh, my God. I didn't write a loader for this thing.* A loader is the code that tells the computer, "This is software." Without it, the code would be useless.

Hunched over a foldout table, Paul scribbled all the code on a notepad from brute memory, finishing just before the plane's wheels hit the ground. He didn't even have a way to test it.

The following day, Paul arrived at MITS headquarters and the founder gave him a tour. They stopped at a desk with an Altair 8800 on top. It was the first time Paul had seen one in person.

"All right," the founder said. "Let's do it."

Paul took a breath, loaded the software, and . . . it worked. Paul and Bill closed the deal, signed the contract, and that's how they sold their first piece of software.

For me, a single lesson stood out among the rest. Although his talent for coding was remarkable, none of this would have happened if Gates hadn't pushed through his fears in his dorm room, picked up the phone, and called MITS. It was his ability to do the hard, uncomfortable thing that made this opportunity possible. The potential to unlock your future is in your hands—but first you have to pick up the damn phone.

Although that was a good lesson, I felt it was far from the Holy Grail. When I sat down with Gates, I would need to dig up an insight that was surprising, powerful, and life-changing—something no interviewer had gotten before.

To me, the Holy Grail was a living, breathing truth. It's what motivated me to trudge through the mud the past two years. And now that I was so close, I was even more adamant I was going to get it.

The morning before the interview, I packed my duffel bag, placed my notepad in my backpack, and headed to Seattle.

CHAPTER TWENTY-SIX

The Holy Grail: Part II

I stepped down a golden-lit hallway, a single door at the end.

An assistant asked me to stay put as she disappeared behind it, leaving me to stare at the towering, frosted glass door. I looked closer at the dark leather handle with silver trim, studying it as if it held a clue. Even the slightest detail could lead me to the Holy Grail, and because I didn't know where it was buried, no detail could be overlooked.

After all, I couldn't just walk in there and say, "Yo, Bill. What's the Holy Grail?" You can't do that. And you can't just hope Bill Gates will give you a clue. He's not going to point to a Buddha statue on his desk and say, "Ah . . . you see that Buddha? I keep it there to remind me of the secret to business . . ." I would have to find the clues myself and I wouldn't have much time. Because I would need to be fully present when our conversation began, my only chance to find visual clues would be right when I walked in.

And then, in what felt like slow motion, the frosted glass door cracked open. Directly in front of me was Bill Gates, sipping a Diet Coke. He smiled and lifted the can as if to say cheers.

"Hey, there," he said. "Come on in . . ."

The moment I stepped through the doorway I felt like I was on the '90s game show *Supermarket Sweep*—the one where the contestants have to sprint through a grocery store, find the most expensive items, throw them in their cart, and then race to the checkout before the buzzer goes off. Except I had to spot all the details I could, memorize them as fast as possible, figure out which ones were clues that would help me find the Holy Grail, and do it all before we began talking. As Gates walked over to the sitting area of his office, all I heard in my head was, "*ON YOUR MARK . . . GET SET . . . GO!*"

Gates' desk was made of wood; it was tidy; there were two monitors on top; behind his desk was a tall leather chair the color of malt whiskey; sunlight streamed through floor-to-ceiling windows, illuminating the glass of five picture frames on the wall. One was a photo of Gates laughing with Warren Buffett, another of Gates with Bono, and a third was a close-up of a mother cradling an infant in what appeared to be a third-world country. Below the picture frames was a polished oval coffee table with two books stacked on top. One of the books was by Steven Pinker and I made a mental note: "buy books by Steven Pinker." At either end of the sitting area were two ivory-gray armchairs, a brown couch in between. Gates sat in an armchair and I noticed his loafers were black and round-toed, with tassels on top. I made another mental note: "buy loafers with tassels." He had on dark slacks and his socks bunched low. He wore a golf polo: relaxed fit; dark gold, almost mustard-brown. His—

My mental buzzer went off.

"So, is this your first book?" Gates asked.

Gates' signature high-pitched voice was even higher pitched in person, making me feel like he was genuinely excited to meet me.

He congratulated me, saying he was impressed by the people I'd interviewed. Then he asked how I met Qi Lu.

Gates' Chief of Staff entered the room, greeted me, and took a seat beside me on the couch. "I figure with forty-five minutes," he said, "we should probably get right into it to maximize our time."

I placed my audio recorder on the table and glanced at my notepad. I thought I'd begin by taking Gates back to when he started his first business.

"I was reading about your Traf-O-Data days from high school," I said. "What did you learn from that experience that later helped you with Microsoft?"

"Well," Gates said, "Paul Allen and I worked together on that. It actually was good for us because that was a very limited microprocessor . . ."

Gates started slowly, and then, as if with a flick of a switch, he shifted in his chair, fixed his gaze at the wall, and turned into an audio version of the *World Book Encyclopedia* in double-time.

". . . The very first microprocessor comes out in '71. It's the 4004, which could hardly do anything. Paul saw that and showed it to me and he knew we couldn't do much. Then the 8008 comes out in '73 and he asked if I could write a BASIC for that and I said no—no, no, I had those dates wrong—'72 was 8008 and '74 is 8080 . . ."

I'd come searching for details and now I was buried under an avalanche of them.

". . . we decided we can only do special purpose stuff, so we got a third partner who knew how to wire wrap stuff up, and it all came out of the fact that we knew people had those tubes that measure traffic on the ground and punch these funny paper tapes. We'd always thought there must be a way to do that by computer. We'd actually been getting people to process them by hand; we'd look at them and write numbers down, then card punch them, put them in a batch computer and . . ."

The avalanche kept coming and I couldn't keep my head above the snow.

"...so I went off to college, Paul got a job back there, and we kept discussing whether we should do hardware or software, when we should start it, and then eventually we started as a pure software company in 1979. No, no—we started the software company in '75. Yeah, sorry, '75. We moved up to Seattle in '79 . . ."

Ten minutes sped by, but it felt like ten seconds. A pulsating fear spread through my body. *What if the entire interview flashes by in what feels like forty-five seconds?*

Right then, the office door opened.

"Sorry to interrupt," a woman said, poking her head in. "But I have Jenn on the line. She asked if I could get you."

"Okay," Gates said, pushing himself out of his armchair.

"I'll be back," he said to me. "One sec."

The Chief of Staff leaned over. "Family," he whispered.

It was like a rescue helicopter had arrived.

The door shut.

I slouched on the couch, letting out a breath.

———

I FRANTICALLY FLIPPED THROUGH my notepad, looking over my questions.

"Is this . . . is this helpful?" the Chief of Staff asked me. "This angle for the stories?"

I'd asked the Chief of Staff to sit in on the interview in case I needed help, and now he was offering it. My first question wasn't thoughtful at all. At this point, I should've said, "Yeah, I could use some help," but I was too afraid the truth would make me look like an amateur.

"Uh, yeah," I said, "I think this is good."

"Okay," the Chief of Staff said. "Great."

I turned back to my notepad. If anything could lead me to the Holy Grail, it had to be a tactical business question, and probably something about sales. Without a doubt the most important sale of Gates' life was the IBM deal he closed at its Boca Raton office in 1980. He was twenty-five and IBM was the biggest tech company in the world. Because Gates was able to close that deal, it put Microsoft in the position to dominate the software industry for decades. After IBM, he struck a deal with HP, and the dominoes kept falling. Gates would tell PC executives, "Are you going to bet on some operating system that second-raters use, or are you going to bet on the one endorsed by IBM?" It was the tipping point of Gates' success, yet no biography I'd read explained *how* he closed the deal.

"I told my friends about the IBM Boca story," I told the Chief of Staff. "One question they wanted me to ask was: If Bill were teaching a five-minute class on how to handle major sales meetings, what would he teach?"

"That's good," the Chief of Staff said. "I like that."

The office door opened.

Gates returned to his armchair and I asked my question.

"At the time," he said, "I was young, and I *looked younger.* IBM had people around the table who were initially quite skeptical of me." He explained that the first step in a sales meeting is having to blast through skepticism, and the best way to do that is by overwhelming people with your expertise. Gates would talk fast and dive immediately into the details—character sets, computer chips, programming languages, software platforms—to the point that it became undeniably clear he wasn't just some kid.

"Almost anytime they asked us how long it would take to do something," Gates said, moving on, "we'd kind of say, 'Well, we can do it quicker than we can *tell you* how long it takes to do it! So when do you want it? Like, hours from now?'"

His advice to overpromise isn't new, but Gates was selling IBM on his speed in a way that was obviously impossible. In reality, it took Microsoft months to deliver the software. But that didn't matter in the long run. What mattered is that Gates understood that one of the problems large companies have is they move slowly—so he was selling them on what they needed most.

Gates then told me something that completely flipped what I thought I knew about structuring a deal. He bet it would be *better* to take less money from IBM than to squeeze it for all it was worth. He believed that other companies would come into the PC market, and if he could close the IBM deal, other PC companies would make even more lucrative deals with Microsoft.

"So the deal would be monetized *somewhat* with IBM," Gates explained, "but *more* with the other companies coming in."

Gates wanted to be paid in something more valuable than cash: strategic positioning. It's better to make a fair deal today that sets you up for more deals down the road than a great deal that doesn't set you up for anything. The takeaway was clear: choose long-term positioning over short-term profits.

Reflecting back, I should have been grateful for the lessons Gates was sharing. But instead I just sat there thinking, "*Really . . . ? That's it? Where's the Holy Grail?*"

It's taken me a long time to understand why I was so blind. I was part of the BuzzFeed generation, and because Gates' insights weren't tweetable or packaged in a listicle like "10 Surprising Secrets from the World's Richest Man," I didn't recognize their value. I figured the Holy Grail had to be buried somewhere else, so I asked Gates about his negotiating secrets.

"What was it like negotiating with people who were so much older and more experienced than you?"

"Well, IBM had certain constraints," he replied. He then began telling me about source code and unlimited liability, which seemed to have nothing to do with negotiation. I couldn't understand why he wasn't answering my question.

Only with hindsight can I see he *was* answering it, just not how I wanted. It wasn't until I later listened to the recording that I understood what he was saying.

During the IBM negotiation, Gates knew he had to keep Microsoft's source code secret, yet he also knew he couldn't tell IBM not to take the source code because that was the very thing it was buying. Gates figured out what IBM was scared of—a major lawsuit—and used that to form a strategy. In the contract, he insisted on unlimited liability if IBM accidentally disclosed the source code. That meant if any employee even unknowingly leaked the code, Microsoft could sue IBM for perhaps billions. That scared IBM's attorneys so much that the company chose not to even *take* the source code, which is exactly what Gates wanted. The lesson: figure out your opponent's fears, then use them to your advantage.

"That was hugely strategic," Gates said, grinning. "Steve Ballmer and I thought that through."

All of that went over my head during the interview, though. So I took a breath and made the question more specific. "How did you negotiate with Ed Roberts?" Roberts was the founder of MITS, the company that bought Gates' first piece of software.

I was hoping to hear a secret checklist like, "One, sit up in the chair; two, shake their hand at an angle; three, when there's a minute left, stand up, look them in the eye, and say this . . ." But of course Gates didn't give me any of that. Instead he told me all about the life of Ed Roberts. Then he told me all about the business model of MITS.

Again, only looking back can I see his answer made sense. He was saying it's critical to become an expert on the background of the person you're dealing with. When it came to the founder of MITS, Gates learned everything he could about his personality, his quirks, his successes, and his dreams. On top of that, Gates learned about his business model, financial constraints, capital structure, and cash flow problems.

But again all that went over my head. I checked my watch. Time was running out. I panicked and asked a third time. "What are three negotiating mistakes people make?"

Gates let out a sigh. He looked at me as though he couldn't understand why I didn't get it. He began to answer, and it essentially sounded like: *Well . . . not doing what I just said . . .*

I sat there thinking, "What's wrong with this guy? Why won't he give me a real answer?" It never crossed my mind that it was me who wasn't getting it.

Gates told me to ask for their advice, spend as much informal time with them as possible, and get them to take me under their wing. I can see now that Gates was essentially telling me to stop worrying about the BuzzFeed tricks. The best negotiating tactic is to build a genuine, trusting relationship. If you're an unknown entrepreneur and the person you're dealing with isn't invested in you, why would he or she even do business with you? But on the other hand, if the person is your mentor or friend, you might not even need to negotiate.

It was the last thing I expected to hear from the business world's chess grandmaster. I thought he'd share battle-tested secrets, but instead he was telling me to befriend my opponent so I wouldn't have to battle.

The Chief of Staff cleared his throat.

"You have time for one more question."

——

I FLIPPED THROUGH THE PAGES of my notepad. There were still so many unasked questions.

Screw it, I thought. *If I have one final minute with Bill Gates, I might as well have some fun.*

I tossed my notepad to the side.

"What's your most memorable, crazy, funny hustle story from early on?"

Gates took a moment to think.

"Well," he said, uncrossing his arms, "there were lots of funny negotiations with Japanese companies." His gaze lifted as though he was watching a movie in his mind's eye. I could feel his excitement as he told me about a meeting with a group of Japanese executives. Gates was pitching them as hard as he could, explaining things over and over, until finally at the end he asked if they wanted to make a deal. The executives huddled together. They talked to each other in Japanese for a minute, then five minutes, then ten. Twenty minutes passed. Finally, they gave their verdict.

"Answer is . . ."—dramatic pause—*". . . maybe."*

"Which in Japanese pretty much means no," Gates said. "Then we told them, 'Oh, your lawyer speaks such good English!' And then they said, *'Oh, but he speaks terrible Japanese!'* "

The Chief of Staff and I broke into laughter. It's as if all my tension from the past forty-five minutes had shattered.

Gates shot straight into another story about a different Japanese executive. The man had flown out to Seattle, showed up at Gates' office, and began saying how great Microsoft was, piling on compliment after compliment. Gates got nervous. Microsoft was late delivering software to the executive's company, so it didn't make sense. The executive kept being extraordinarily kind, lavishing all this praise, and Gates wondered: What does he want? Did he want to buy more software? Finally, the executive got to the point.

"Mister Gates . . . what we want to buy . . . is . . ."—another dramatic pause—*". . . you."*

The three of us laughed again, and for the first time, it felt like this wasn't an interview anymore. We were just three guys having a good time.

"What did you say?" the Chief of Staff said, laughing. " *'Answer is maybe'*?"

We joked around a bit more, then the Chief of Staff bent down and zipped up his bag. Gates took the cue and pushed himself out of his armchair.

"How old were you during those Japanese negotiations?" I asked.

"The big years in Japan were when I was between nineteen and twenty-three. My friend and business partner Kay Nishi deserves a lot of credit for that. It was he and I going around. We'd stay in the same hotel room that had two single beds. People would be calling us in the middle of the night. I remember one night we got to sleep for like three hours straight and I woke Kay and said, '*Hey, what's wrong with business? Nobody's called for three hours!*'"

Gates continued for a bit more, and I noticed that a sense of warmth had spread throughout the room. It made me regret not starting the interview like this in the first place. But it was too late. Gates shook my hand and said goodbye. He walked toward his desk and I headed for the door. Before stepping out, I turned my head over my shoulder, grasping for one final glimpse. Just when things had started feeling right, it was over.

CHAPTER TWENTY-SEVEN

The Third Door

TWO MONTHS LATER, THE STORAGE CLOSET

I felt like I was trapped in an old nightmare. Once again I was hunched over my desk, my head in my hands.

You've got to be kidding . . .

When I had first met Gates' Chief of Staff at TED, not only had he said Gates would do an interview, but he'd also said he would help me secure an interview with Warren Buffett. Gates and Buffett were best friends, so if there was anything that would sway Buffett, this had to be it. The Chief of Staff eventually contacted Buffett's office, and while I'll never know what happened, the Chief of Staff then sent me the following email:

> Please no more calls to Warren's office. Thanks . . .

I couldn't believe it. Not only was the answer still no, but I'd been so persistent I got myself blacklisted.

No business book ever talked about this. No inspirational quote warned me about the dangers of *over*-persistence. Not once had I stopped to ask myself, "Am I being the kind of person people want to help?" Instead I just kept calling Buffett's assistant week after week. And after months of hearing no, I still flew to Omaha and sent her a freaking shoe. I was so obsessed with achieving my goal I was blind to how I came across. I'd dug myself into such a deep hole that even Bill Gates couldn't pull me out.

I should've learned about the dangers of over-persistence a long time ago, when I was harassing Tim Ferriss by sending him thirty-one emails. Ferriss wanted nothing to do with me. He agreed to the interview only because of my Inside Man at DonorsChoose. Though because Ferriss ultimately said yes, I took that as a win. It was only now, because Buffett ended in failure, that I was taking the time to reflect. Life will keep hitting you over the head with the same lesson until you listen.

And I must not have been listening to a lot of lessons, because Buffett wasn't the least of my problems. Ever since I left Bill Gates' office, I'd sent out more interview requests and received even more no's from Lady Gaga, Bill Clinton, Sonia Sotomayor, Michael Jordan, Arianna Huffington, Will Smith, Oprah Winfrey—and when I'd circled back to Steven Spielberg, even he'd said no.

I'd thought the rejection from Spielberg had to be a mistake. When we first met, he'd looked me in the eye and *told me* to come back to him. So a friend from Summit had introduced me to the co-president of Spielberg's TV production company so I could explain the situation in person. The copresident personally passed along my request, but Spielberg's response was still no. The copresident tried other angles, sending the request a second time and then a third. Still no.

What the hell was going on?

I slammed my laptop shut and paced across the storage closet, but the cramped space made me even more frustrated. I pulled out my phone and texted Elliott.

Could use some advice. U around?

My phone rang before I put it down.

"That was fast," I said.

"Of course it was fast," Elliott replied. "What's going on?"

"I'm going crazy. Bill Gates' Chief of Staff told me to build momentum, so I built momentum. Malcolm Gladwell wrote about the tipping point, and I hit my tipping point. I'd thought once I'd interviewed Bill Gates, everything would fall into place. But I'm still no better off."

"You *idiot*. You asked that stupid question when we first met and I told you *there is no tipping point*. It's all just little steps."

I fell silent. He *had* said that.

"A tipping point only appears in hindsight," Elliott added. "You don't feel it when you're in the trenches. Being an entrepreneur is about pushing, not tipping."

"Fine, I get that," I said. "But you know what pisses me off? All these no's I'm getting are of zero help. They tell me, *Oh, we love what you're doing! Unfortunately his schedule is just overwhelmed.* Of course he's busy. But so is Bill Gates. If he really wanted to do it, he'd make the time. What am I supposed to do when I'm not only getting rejected, but I'm not even being told the real reason they're saying no?"

"Dude, that's the story of my life. They're called *bullshit no's*. I get them a thousand times a week. You just have to build a pipeline so when you get a bullshit no from one person, there's still thirty others to work on.

"You want to know why a pipeline works?" Elliott went on. "A year and a half ago, when you first cold-emailed me asking for advice, you didn't know that a month earlier I'd made it my New Year's resolution to find someone to mentor."

I was stunned.

"Crazy, right? There's no way you could've known that. My

point is that I'm sure I wasn't the first person you emailed for advice. You asked dozens of people, and because of an external factor you couldn't have predicted, one of those things worked. You have no way of knowing what's going on in the lives of the people in your pipeline. You can't anticipate their mood or how generous they're feeling. All you can do is control your effort."

"But what if all thirty things in my pipeline are clogged?"

"Then you have to do two things: One, think bigger. And two, think differently."

"Come on, man. Give me something concrete."

"I can't give you all the answers, but I'll give you an example. For the Summit conference we organized in Washington, D.C., we couldn't get a single person to give the main keynote. People were busy. Blake Mycoskie from TOMS said he couldn't come. It was just a disaster. So we had to think bigger: Bill Clinton. And we had to think differently: we hosted a fundraiser for his foundation so he *had* to come. Once he was in, we called Russell Simmons—who had already said no—and we asked him if he could give the opening remarks for Bill Clinton, so now he said yes. Then we planned the event to coincide with Ted Turner's travel schedule in D.C. Doing that, plus having Clinton confirmed, led to Ted Turner saying yes. Blake Mycoskie still told us he had other commitments, so we changed the request and asked him to moderate a Q and A with his hero, who we knew was Ted Turner. Boom. Now Blake was in. You just have to give people an offer they can't refuse."

An idea was coming to me. "I wonder if—"

"Yes."

"I was going to say, I wonder if—"

"Yes. Yes, yes, yes. Whenever you wonder, the answer is yes. People don't want to do small shit. You need to think bigger and think differently. Don't 'I wonder' through life. Just make it happen."

ONE WEEK LATER, CENTRAL PARK, NEW YORK CITY

I zipped up my jacket and followed Elliott through the crowd. It was an hour past dusk. Directly in front of us was an outdoor stage lit up in lava-red concert lights. John Mayer was under the spotlight, slinging his guitar strap over his shoulder and triggering the roar of sixty thousand fans.

I'd come to New York to take meetings to reboot my interview requests and build my pipeline. Elliott invited me to this festival and we were now making our way to the stage. As we moved forward, Elliott spotted someone he knew, waved, and headed his way.

I stood back to let them catch up. A minute later, Elliott grabbed my shoulder and pulled me forward. "Matt," Elliott said, "have you met Alex?"

Elliott's friend shook his head, looking uninterested. He was about forty years old and had broad shoulders.

"You'll love him," Elliott said. "Alex is working on a project that's everything you stand for. He's interviewed Larry King, Bill Gates . . ."

Matt's eyelids slightly widened. Elliott told me to tell Matt my *Price Is Right* story, and when I did, Matt laughed the whole way through. Elliott jumped in again. "Alex, tell Matt that analogy you told me. You know, the three doors one."

Elliott and I had been on the phone a few days earlier when he'd asked if I noticed a commonality in the people I'd interviewed. I'd told him I'd been playing around with an analogy.

All the people I'd interviewed treated life, business, and success the same way. In my eyes, it was like getting into a nightclub. There are always three ways in.

"There's the First Door," I told Matt, "the main entrance, where the line curves around the block. That's where ninety-nine percent of people wait around, hoping to get in.

"Then there's the Second Door, the VIP entrance. That's where the billionaires, celebrities, and the people born into it slip through."

Matt nodded.

"School and society make you feel like those are the only two ways in. But over the past few years, I've realized there is always, always . . . the Third Door. It's the entrance where you have to jump out of line, run down the alley, bang on the door a hundred times, crack open the window, sneak through the kitchen—there's always a way. Whether it's how Bill Gates sold his first piece of software or how Steven Spielberg became the youngest studio director in Hollywood history, they all took—"

"—the Third Door," Matt said, a smile spreading across his face. "That's how I've lived my whole damn life."

I looked over at Elliott, who was grinning.

"Alex," Elliott said, "you know Matt created Lady Gaga's social network, right?" Before I could respond, Elliott added, "Didn't you tell me you want to interview her?"

Of course Elliott knew the answer to that. He was the one who'd introduced me to Lady Gaga's manager a year earlier. I'd tried building a relationship with the manager ever since; meeting with him at his office, emailing and calling him. But every time I'd asked for an interview, the answer was no. Just a few weeks earlier, he'd rejected my request again.

Yet still, of all the musicians in the world, I felt no one represented the spirit of the mission better than Lady Gaga.

"I would love to interview her," I said.

Matt looked at me and nodded.

"Well," Matt said, "Elliott is friends with her manager. Why doesn't Elliott call him and set it up?"

I didn't want to admit I'd been rejected, so I said it was a good idea.

As John Mayer began to sing "Waiting on the World to Change,"

Elliott spotted another friend and jumped over to say hello. Matt and I talked a bit more about the mission, and then he took out his iPhone and began swiping through photos. He tilted the screen in my direction. On it was a picture of him with Lady Gaga, her arms around him backstage at a concert. Matt swiped again and there was another photo of the two of them, this time in an office. Gaga was on top of a desk with her arms in the air.

Matt continued swiping—a photo of him at a golf tournament with Condoleezza Rice, skateboarding on a half-pipe with Tony Hawk, ringing the NASDAQ opening bell with Shaquille O'Neal, backstage at a show with Jay-Z, and then sitting on a couch with Nelson Mandela.

There was a gravitational force radiating from Matt and I could feel myself being sucked in. I asked him how he started his career and he told me one Third Door story after another. After training to be a U.S. Army Ranger and getting injured, Matt went off to start a hedge fund. From there, he created a tech platform for electronic trading, began investing in start-ups including Uber and Palantir, and then got a call from 50 Cent that eventually led him to Lady Gaga. We had been talking for nearly half an hour when I felt a hand slap on my back.

Elliott said we needed to head out, so Matt and I exchanged contact information.

"If you're ever in San Diego," Matt said, "let me know. You can come by my ranch."

I heard Elliott faintly whispering, *"When it's in front of you . . . make your move,"* but when I glanced at him, his mouth wasn't moving. The voice was in my head.

"You know what?" I said. "I'll actually be in San Diego next month. I could use a place to stay."

"Done," Matt said. "We have a two-bedroom guesthouse. It's all yours."

CHAPTER TWENTY-EIGHT

Redefining Success

T hat's *perfect*," Cal said.

I was back at Larry King's breakfast table, and I'd just told Larry and Cal that in a few days I would be interviewing Steve Wozniak, the cofounder of Apple, who built one of the first personal computers with his bare hands. Elliott's advice to create a pipeline had worked.

"The best part is that you won't have the same problem you had when you interviewed Bill Gates," Cal added. "This time, you can't be nervous. He's *the Woz*."

"Where are you doing the interview?" Larry asked.

"At a restaurant in Cupertino."

"When I was starting out," Larry said, "I did an interview show at Pumpernik's deli in Miami. Restaurants are great. Everyone just wants to have fun."

"Alex, do me a favor," Cal said. "Don't take your notepad. Try it as an experiment. If the interview fails, you can blame me."

I was hesitant, but I thought it was worth trying after what had happened with the Bill Gates interview. A few days later, I boarded a plane and within hours I was walking up to Mandarin Gourmet, a restaurant two blocks from Apple headquarters. I was standing in front of the entrance when my phone rang. It was my friend Ryan.

"The Woz?" he asked as I told him what I was up to. "Bro, I know you were having trouble getting interviews, but Woz peaked like twenty years ago. Look at the *Forbes* list. He's not even on it. I don't get why you're doing this. Actually, you know what? Maybe it's good you're interviewing him. Try to figure out why Woz never became as successful as Steve Jobs."

Before I could respond, out of the corner of my eye I saw Steve Wozniak striding toward me, wearing sneakers and sunglasses. A pen and green laser pointer were clipped to the chest pocket of his shirt. I hung up my phone and greeted him, and then stepped inside.

The restaurant was a sea of white tablecloths. As soon as we sat, I picked up a menu but Wozniak motioned for me to put it down. He called over the waiter and ordered for both of us with the enthusiasm of a kid who could get all the desserts he wanted. Our table was soon overflowing with fried rice, vegetable chow mein, Chinese chicken salad, sesame chicken, honey walnut prawns, Mongolian beef, and crispy egg rolls. Even before our first bite, Wozniak already seemed to be the happiest person I'd ever met. Whether he was telling me about his wife, his dogs, his favorite restaurants, or the road trip he was about to take to Lake Tahoe, Wozniak seemed to love everything about his life.

He told me that he met Steve Jobs in 1971, just a few miles from where we were sitting. Jobs was in high school and Wozniak was in college. A mutual friend of theirs named Bill Fernandez introduced them. The moment they met, Wozniak and Jobs hit it off and spent hours sitting on a sidewalk, laughing and sharing stories about pranks they'd pulled.

"One of my favorite pranks was during my first year of college," Wozniak told me. "I built a TV jammer, which you could hide in the palm of your hand. You could turn a knob and jam any TV set you wanted, making the show go fuzzy with static."

Wozniak said that one night he and a friend went over to the common room of another dorm to mess around. There were about twenty students sitting around watching a color TV. Wozniak sat in the back, concealed the jammer in his hand, and made the TV malfunction.

"For the first few tries, I had my friend get up and hit the TV— *bonk*—and the TV would go perfect! Then I jammed it again. After a while, my friend hit the TV harder and harder, but if he smacked that TV enough, it worked. By the end of half an hour, I had the whole group of college kids pounding the TV with their fists, and if it was a show they really wanted to see, they would hit the TV with chairs."

Wozniak kept visiting the dorm to see how far he could take this. One time, he noticed a few students were at the TV set trying to fix it, and one guy had his hand on the middle of the screen and his foot in the air. Wozniak quickly turned the jammer off. When the guy took his hand away from the screen or put his foot down, Wozniak turned the jammer on. The guy stood there, with his hand in the middle of the screen and his foot in the air, for half an hour as everyone else watched the TV show.

As Wozniak told me about another prank, a woman with short brown hair joined our table. "Woz," she said, "did you show him the laser pointer test?"

Wozniak introduced his wife, Janet. He unclipped the green laser pointer from his shirt and held it close to my face, telling me it could detect "how much brains" I had. When he shined it into my right ear, green light appeared on the opposite wall.

"Holy crap!" he said. "Your head is completely empty."

Glancing down, I spotted a second laser pointer he was holding under the table. Woz and I let out a laugh. He clipped his laser pointer back on his shirt and told his wife about my mission. He shared with her the names of the people I was interviewing.

"You know," he said, turning to me and lowering his voice, "I don't know why you're interviewing me. I'm not a successful mogul like Steve Jobs or anything like that . . ."

His words trailed as though he was baiting me for a response. It felt like he was testing me, but I didn't know what to say, so I did the only thing I could think of—I stuffed an egg roll in my mouth.

"When I was a kid," Wozniak said, "I had two goals for my life. The first was to create something with engineering that changes the world. The second was to live life on my own terms.

"Most people do things because that's what society tells them they should do. But if you stop and do the math—*if you actually think for yourself*—you'll realize there's a better way to do things."

"Is that why you're so happy?" I asked.

"Bingo," Wozniak said. "I'm happy because I do what I want every day."

"Oh," his wife said, laughing, "he does *exactly* what he wants."

I was curious about the difference between Wozniak and Steve Jobs, so I asked what it was like founding Apple when it was just the two of them. Wozniak shared a handful of stories, but what stood out most were the ones that made it clear how different their values were.

One story took place before Apple was formed. Jobs was working at Atari and was assigned to create a video game. He knew Wozniak was a better engineer, so he made a deal: if Wozniak would create the game, they would split the seven-hundred-dollar pay. Wozniak was grateful for the opportunity and built the game. As soon as Jobs got paid, he gave his friend the three hundred and fifty dollars he had promised. Ten years later, Wozniak learned that Jobs hadn't been paid seven hundred dollars for the game, but rather *thousands* of dollars. When the story broke in the news, Steve Jobs denied it, but even the CEO of Atari claimed it was true.

Another story took place early in Apple's growth. At the time, it seemed obvious Jobs would be the company's CEO, but it wasn't clear where Wozniak would fit in on the executive team. Jobs asked him what position he wanted. Wozniak knew that managing people and dealing with corporate politics were the last things he wanted to do. So he told Jobs he wanted his position capped at engineer.

"Society tells you that success is getting the most powerful position possible," Wozniak said. "But I asked myself: Is that what would make me happiest?"

The final story Wozniak shared took place around the time Apple filed for its initial public offering. Jobs and Wozniak were set to make more money than they ever imagined. Leading up to the public offering, Wozniak found out that Jobs had refused stock options to some of Apple's earliest employees. To Wozniak, these people were family. They helped build the company. But Jobs refused to budge. So Wozniak took it upon himself and gifted some of his own shares to the early employees, so they all could share in the financial rewards. On the day the company went public, those early employees became millionaires.

As I watched Wozniak lean back in his chair, cracking open a fortune cookie and laughing with his wife, I could hear the words Ryan had told me before the interview ringing in my ears.

But the only thing that came to mind was: Who's to say that Steve Jobs was more successful?

CHAPTER TWENTY-NINE

Staying an Intern

THREE WEEKS LATER, MIAMI, FLORIDA

I leaned against the balcony railing and looked at the city as the sun began to set, the palm trees silhouetted by hues of pink and orange. We were on the twentieth floor of a high-rise condo and Armando Pérez was showing me the beauty of his hometown. It felt like the scene from *The Lion King*, where Mufasa looks over the cliff and says, "*Simba, everything the light touches is our kingdom.*"

Armando's finger shot to the left. "Look, there's Marlins Park."

To the right. "That's my charter school, SLAM."

"That hotel is where I hang out.

"Down there is the boat I take out onto the ocean.

"See that white building right there, next to Grove Isle? That's Mercy Hospital. That's where I was born."

If anyone saw me standing beside Armando, they probably would have recognized him by another name—the Grammy Award–winning rapper and musician Pitbull.

Thinking differently and building a pipeline was continuing to pay off. First had come Wozniak, now Pitbull, and just this morning I'd received another confirmation from Jane Goodall. The mission was starting to bear fruit and I couldn't have been happier.

Pitbull led me inside where a few of his friends were lounging on a couch. He reached for a red Solo cup, filled it to the brim with vodka and soda, and then we headed back out to the patio. As we sat, I noticed how different Pitbull seemed from the fist-pumping persona I'd seen hours earlier at his concert. Now his energy was calming. His movements were slower. I decided not to start with a question and just ease into a conversation, seeing where it would go. He soon told me that ever since he was a kid, he loved looking for new challenges.

"A true hustler is always looking for the next one," he said. "It's like playing a video game—let's say Mario Bros. Okay, you beat the first level, now you got to beat the second level, now you got to beat the third level. Once you beat the game, you're like, 'Whoa, whoa. Where's the next game? Where it at?'"

I felt my thoughts being pulled in a new direction.

What's his key to constantly leveling up?

How do you keep your success growing, when you're already at the top of your game?

Once you've made it, how do you maintain it?

This must've been what Cal had meant when he said to let my curiosity ask the questions. I asked Pitbull to walk me through the video game levels of his life, hoping I'd spot his secret along the way.

"What was your level one?" I said.

He reached for his cup, took a swig, and then sat silently for a few moments. In the early eighties, he told me, he came out of his mother's womb with cocaine in his blood. When his father took off, Pitbull's mother raised him on her own, using drug money to make ends meet. They were constantly on the move. Pitbull had to

switch high schools eight times. Drug dealing was all he saw growing up, so it was only natural he got caught up in it too. I could see
the pain in his eyes as he reflected on it.

"I sold everything, dawg," he said. "I had my time, and I sold it
all."

He sold ecstasy, weed, cocaine, and heroin. In high school, Pitbull
never kept any drugs on him; instead he hid them in girls' lockers
around school. When he made a sale, he would tell the buyer which
locker to get the product from. One day, the principal grabbed Pitbull, threw him in his office and said, "I know you're selling drugs!
Let me check your pockets!" Pitbull emptied his pockets. "Damn it!
Let me see your shoes!" Pitbull took off his shoes. "Your hat!" The
principal was getting more and more frustrated, and then Pitbull
said, "You know what? *Why don't you check this?*" and pulled down
his pants.

Soon after that, the principal printed out a diploma, handed it to
Pitbull, and told him to leave campus and not come back.

"He just fucking gave it to me," Pitbull said. "I never actually
graduated high school. But I still went and got a photo studio to
take my own graduation pictures. I took one smiling and another
one with my middle finger up. Both photos are still hanging up at
my *abuela's* house."

Though in all that time, Pitbull stressed, he never did any cocaine himself. He saw how it affected his parents and didn't want
that for his own life. Now that he'd "graduated" and survived the
world of drug dealing, it was time for level two of his video game:
becoming the biggest rapper in Miami.

"I started to understand the opportunity I had if I really focused,"
Pitbull said. "That's number one in anything: understanding the
opportunity you have. I knew that if I wanted to make money rapping, I had to write to music. So I started writing rhymes. I didn't
know what a record was at the time. I just wrote rhymes, rhymes,
rhymes, rhymes."

Pitbull also knew that if he wanted to be the next king of Miami's rap scene, he had to learn from the king at the time: Luther Campbell, the leader of the hip-hop group 2 Live Crew.

"Not only was Luther Campbell the biggest guy down here," Pitbull said, "but he did it as an entrepreneur. For one, he was able to press his own records, promote them himself, and sell millions. He taught me that independent mindset. No one's going to envision your vision the way you envision your vision."

Pitbull signed his first deal with Campbell's record label and got an advance of fifteen hundred dollars. Pitbull couldn't have had a better mentor at the time, because in 1999, Napster upended the music industry by allowing people to download songs without paying. The artists who prospered, for the most part, were the ones with that entrepreneurial mindset.

"The best thing I learned from Luther Campbell," Pitbull said, "was that there's nothing better than to be an intern in life. The best CEOs in business started out as interns. Because when you go from intern to CEO, no one can bullshit you. But all you can do is help them. 'Look, I already did that job. I know exactly what it took to make that happen.'"

Pitbull's talent for rapping, plus the lessons he learned from Luther Campbell, finally paid off. Pitbull's debut album *M.I.A.M.I.* became certified gold.

"What was the next level of your video game?" I asked.

Pitbull said that although he became the biggest rapper in Miami, he had trouble breaking into the mainstream. His most successful single at the time peaked at thirty-two on the *Billboard* Hot 100. He wanted to hit number one. So he sought out new experts to collaborate with and learn from—music executives who worked with David Guetta, Flo Rida, and Chris Brown; songwriters who produced number one hits with Katy Perry, Lady Gaga, and Britney Spears.

"I'm constantly studying the game," Pitbull said.

After years of repositioning his sound and brand, he released the album *Planet Pit*, which not only earned him his first Grammy win, but also included a number one record.

His video game continued. The next level: turning himself into more than a musician. Pitbull wanted to stand for something. He wanted to use his influence for good, so he began working with a charter school in Little Havana called SLAM, where he's helping kids from the same neighborhood he grew up in. In a part of town where street corners are covered in chain-link fences and run-down liquor stores, SLAM's brand-new seven-story school is a beacon of hope. At the same time, Pitbull also became more intentional with his lyrics, using them to highlight the influence of Latinos in America.

> *Latin is the new majority, ya tú sabe [Latin is the new majority, yeah you know]*

> *Next step: la Casablanca [Next step: the White House]*

> *No hay carro, nos vamos en balsa [If there's no car, we'll get there in a raft]*

That song, "Rain Over Me" featuring Marc Anthony, went number one in six countries. Pitbull's political commentary didn't stop there, because in 2012 President Obama asked Pitbull to help campaign for his reelection. Two years after that, Pitbull performed at the Fourth of July celebration at the White House.

As Pitbull reached for the red Solo cup again, a moment of quiet crept up in our conversation. Something told me not to say anything and just let the moment sink in.

"Last month," Pitbull said, breaking the silence, "I was walking into a meeting with Carlos Slim Jr. in Mexico. I told him, 'I don't really know what you guys got going on in your world, but I want to learn. *Hey, I'll intern for you.*'"

"Seriously?"

"One hundred percent, *papo*. I told him, 'I just want to be around you to see what you're talking about, how you're doing things. I don't have a problem being down here for a month, getting dough-nuts, making coffee, I don't care.'"

The look in Pitbull's eyes made me feel like he wasn't kidding. A part of me couldn't believe it—here's one of the most famous musicians in the world, who can headline Madison Square Garden, yet he seems dead serious about fetching coffee for Carlos Slim Jr.

Our conversation continued and Pitbull kept tapping on the idea of being an intern in life. He said that while he can now walk around record labels like a king, the following day he'll be walking through the halls of Apple or Google taking notes. It's that duality that makes him, him. And that's when I realized Pitbull's key to continued success: it's about *always* staying an intern.

It's about humbling yourself enough to learn, even when you're at the top of your game. It's about knowing that the moment you get comfortable being an executive is the moment you begin to fail. It's about realizing that, if you want to continue being Mufasa, at the same time you have to keep being Simba.

CHAPTER THIRTY

The Collision

T his is Mr. H. He goes everywhere with me."
I'd just stepped into Jane Goodall's hotel room, and she
was introducing me to her stuffed animal monkey.

Goodall motioned for me to follow her to the couch, and then asked me to hold her stuffed animal as she reached for a cup of tea. As I sat beside her, the seventy-nine-year-old anthropologist couldn't have made me feel more at ease. Nothing about this initial greeting foreshadowed how I would walk out of this interview—anxious, disoriented, and completely conflicted. Goodall made me see myself in a new way, and frankly, I didn't like what I saw.

Our conversation began simply, with Goodall telling me about a toy chimpanzee her dad gave her when she was two. The gift was significant, because while bombs dropped on London during the Second World War, there were times Goodall's family didn't even have enough money to afford an ice cream cone. Goodall carried that toy chimpanzee wherever she went and her obsession with animals grew. Her best friend was her dog, Rusty; her favorite books were *Tarzan of the Apes* and *The Story of Doctor Dolittle*; she daydreamed about living among primates and being able to talk to them. As she grew older, she became determined to pursue her biggest dream: studying chimpanzees in the jungles of Africa.

Goodall couldn't afford college, but that didn't deter her. She continued reading books on chimps while working as a secretary and a waitress, which were among the few jobs women in England could get in the 1950s. At twenty-three, she finally saved enough money for a ticket on a ship to Africa. After hitting shore in Kenya, Goodall ended up at a dinner party where she described her obsession with animals to another guest, who recommended she contact Louis Leakey.

Leakey was one of the most prominent paleoanthropologists in the world. He was born in Kenya but of British descent, held a doctorate from Cambridge, and his research focused on understanding how humans and apes evolved. There couldn't have been a better mentor for Goodall, except for one thing.

While his wife was pregnant, Leakey had an affair with a twenty-one-year-old woman who worked as an illustrator on his book. He took the woman on trips across Africa and Europe and they eventually began living together. Leakey's wife filed for divorce and Leakey married his illustrator, moving with her back to Kenya. Then Leakey began *another* affair—this time with his assistant. Leakey's second wife found out and he ended the affair, and his assistant moved to Uganda. Now Leakey's office had an opening, and it was right around then when he got a call from Jane Goodall.

Here were two people: a twenty-three-year-old woman with a dream and a fifty-four-year-old man with the key to that dream. And now they were destined to collide.

Goodall arrived at Leakey's office, which was housed in a museum in Nairobi. They roamed the exhibits and talked about

African wildlife. Leakey was impressed and, naturally, gave her a job as his assistant. Goodall grew close to Leakey. He mentored her. She traveled with him on fossil-hunting expeditions. Then, just as Goodall felt her dream of studying the chimps was within her grasp, Leakey made sexual advances.

For some reason I stopped thinking about Goodall and started imagining my sisters in this situation. Talia was eighteen. Briana was twenty-four. The thought of either of them working for years toward their biggest goal, traveling to another continent to achieve it, and then right before they make it a reality, the mentor who holds the key implies, *If you have sex with me, I'll give it to you*, made me disgusted in a way I'd never felt before.

Although Goodall was terrified of the idea of losing her dream, she told me she still rejected his advances.

"I have two sisters," I said to Goodall, shifting on the couch. "When Leakey came on to you—how did you deal with that?"

I braced myself for an explosion of emotion. But Goodall replied softly, "I just expected that he would honor what I said. And he did." Then she sat back, as if to say "end of story."

I'd expected dynamite, but there wasn't even a spark.

"How did that *feel*," I asked, "right in that moment?"

"Well, I was very concerned," Goodall said, "because I thought if I just reject his advances, maybe I'll lose my chance at the chimps. He never explicitly proposed anything; it was just the way he was, you know? But of course, I rejected it anyway. And he respected it because he was a decent person. He wasn't a predator.

"He just fell for my charms," she added. "He wasn't the only one either. So I'm kind of used to it."

A part of me felt like Goodall was defending Leakey. In my view, he was her mentor and should have been looking out for her. What he did felt like an injustice. But Goodall's response seemed as if she was shrugging it off and saying, "Hey, that's how the world works."

Goodall explained that Leakey not only respected her decision not to have an affair, but also granted her funds to study the chimps. She then spent three months living in the jungle with the wild chimpanzees, crouching behind bushes and observing that they use tools just like humans. Before Goodall's research, the very definition of human beings was that we were the only species who used tools, so Goodall's findings rocked the scientific community and forever redefined the human-ape relationship. Since then, Goodall has continued her research, publishing thirty-three books, receiving more than fifty honorary degrees, and becoming a Dame of the British Empire and a Messenger of Peace of the United Nations.

Goodall and I moved on to other topics. Though, as much as I tried to stay present, I couldn't stop thinking about the Louis Leakey story. I became frustrated with myself. Goodall had said it wasn't a big deal. If it didn't bother her, why did it bother me?

Goodall and I wrapped up the interview and said goodbye. I climbed into a cab and headed for the airport. As I pressed my head against the window, I couldn't stop wondering how my sisters would have felt in the position Leakey had put Goodall in.

And then an unexpected thought entered my head . . . *This is the first time I've ever left an interview and wanted to share what just happened with my sisters.* I usually called my best friends or mentors, who I suddenly realized were all . . . male.

My mind began flashing over all the interviews I'd done so far— Tim Ferriss, Qi Lu, Sugar Ray Leonard, Dean Kamen, Larry King, Bill Gates, Steve Wozniak, Pitbull—and, as if I was looking at my reflection for the first time, it was shockingly, and embarrassingly, clear: male, male, male, male, male, male, male, male.

How could I have never noticed this before?

When I'd come up with my list, it was me with my *male* friends dreaming up whom we wanted to learn from. When I brainstormed questions before an interview, it was me and my *male* friends thinking about what we wanted to learn. Not once had it crossed my mind to wonder whom my *sisters* or *female* friends wanted to learn from. I was so stuck inside my own bubble that I was blind to anything outside of my one-sided version of reality. And just because I didn't know I had a bias didn't mean I was free of guilt. I was the perfect example of a guy claiming to care about equal treatment, but not once had I ever looked within myself and asked if I was walking the walk.

It made me wonder how many men like me were out there. Just as I'd been sitting with my male friends thinking about whom to put on my list, there must be male executives in boardrooms with their male friends thinking about whom to hire and whom to promote. Just like my friends and me, those executives probably don't know their instincts are to give preference to people who look like them. It's the biases we don't know we hold that are the most dangerous.

My cab pulled up to the airport curb and I slung my duffel bag over my shoulder, but it felt heavier than before. I dragged my feet through the terminal. The view out the windows darkened as the San Francisco fog rolled in. I made my way to my gate and couldn't stop wondering: *How could I have been so blind to something so obvious? How did I not even know I was part of the problem?*

I didn't know the answers, but I knew what I had to do first.

I·headed straight to see my sisters.

CHAPTER THIRTY-ONE

Turning Darkness into Light

rushed home full of questions. But when I sat with my sisters in our living room, I found out I didn't even understand what I didn't understand.

"You just left an interview with one of the most accomplished women in the world, and all you can talk about is that she got hit on by her mentor?"

That was Briana. She's three years older than me, was in her third year of law school, and for as long as I've known her, she's been fighting for what she believes.

"Even during the interview," Briana continued, "when you asked Goodall about it *again*, she told you it wasn't a big deal. Her response to Leakey's advances was everything I hope I would do if that happened to me."

She stood up from the couch. "I think I know why you were so upset. It's because you see a sexual advance as an act of disrespect.

Sometimes it is, but it isn't always. For my whole life, you and Dad were always like this. Dad made it clear that if a guy even showed interest in me or Talia, it was an act of aggression—which is why you got so triggered.

"And I'm surprised it took you this long to realize that women deal with these kinds of things all the time. You've been living with women your entire life. You grew up with two sisters, a mom, and nine girl cousins who were your best friends. I can even remember you reading *I Know Why the Caged Bird Sings* in high school. If anybody should have realized this stuff earlier, it should have been you."

My gaze lowered and I stared at my feet. When I looked over to my younger sister, Talia, she was sitting there quietly, taking it all in. I knew I'd be hearing from her soon.

"I'm not trying to make you feel bad," Briana added. "I'm just trying to make a point. If even *you* didn't understand the issues women face, and you grew up *surrounded* by women, imagine what it's like for guys who didn't."

A silence settled over the living room, and then Talia took out her phone. She pulled up a meme on Facebook and put the screen in front of my face.

"What's the matter?
It's the same distance!"

As I stared at the image, Talia said, "I bet you're focusing on the wrong part. It's not only all the extra obstacles women face that bothers me—it's that sentence on the bottom. It's the fact that most men won't even acknowledge our reality. There are problems women face that most men will never understand . . . because they never try to understand."

———

IT'S HARD TO KNOW FOR SURE why I hadn't experienced Maya Angelou's memoir the way Briana assumed I had. When I'd read *I Know Why the Caged Bird Sings* as a teenager, I was so overwhelmed by the African American experience that it was all I'd focused on. Maya Angelou was born in an era when you could see a black man dangling from a tree, or look out a window and see hooded Klansmen setting fire to a cross. When Maya Angelou was three years old, she and her five-year-old brother were placed on a train car all alone headed to the South, with nothing more than a nametag tied to their feet. Angelou and her brother were received by their grandmother and taken to her home in Stamps, Arkansas, a town clearly divided between blacks and whites.

Only now, as I picked up Maya Angelou's memoir again, did I try to see it through the lens of her gender. One afternoon, when she was eight years old, Angelou was headed to the library when a man grabbed her arm, yanked her toward him, pulled down her bloomers, and forced himself on her. He then threatened to kill her if she told anyone what had happened. When Angelou finally reported who raped her, the man was arrested. The night after his trial, he was found dead, kicked to death behind a slaughterhouse. Shaken and traumatized, Angelou internalized it as if her words caused that man to die. For the next five years, Angelou didn't speak.

As time wore on, she faced even more obstacles. She got pregnant at sixteen, worked as a prostitute and madam, and was a victim of domestic violence. At one point, a boyfriend drove her to a romantic spot by the bay, beat her with his fists, knocked her unconscious, and kept her captive for three days. These events, though, are not what define her. What defines Maya Angelou is how she turned darkness into light.

She channeled her experiences into works of art that made waves in American culture. She became a singer, dancer, writer, poet, professor, film director, and civil rights activist, working alongside Martin Luther King Jr. and Malcolm X. She wrote more than twenty books, and I Know Why the Caged Bird Sings spoke so directly to the soul of readers that Oprah Winfrey has said: "Meeting Maya on those pages was like meeting myself in full. For the first time, as a young black girl, my experience was validated." Angelou won two Grammy Awards and was the second poet in American history, preceded only by Robert Frost, to recite a poem at a presidential inauguration.

And now I was about to pick up the phone and give her a call. A friend of mine had helped arrange the interview. Angelou was eighty-five years old and had recently been discharged from the hospital, so the interview was just fifteen minutes long. My goal was simple: not only to ask the questions my sisters had come up with, but to listen and, hopefully, understand.

———

MY SISTERS BOILED DOWN THEIR QUESTIONS into four obstacles. The first was how to deal with darkness. There's an expression Maya Angelou coined called "rainbow in the clouds." The idea is that when everything in your life is dark and cloudy, and there's no hope in sight, the greatest feeling is when you find a rainbow in your cloud. So I asked Angelou, "When someone is young and just starting out on their journey, and she or he needs help finding that rainbow, in mustering the courage to keep going, what advice do you have?"

"I look back," Angelou said, her voice soothing and wise. "I like to look back at people in my family, or people I've known, or people I've simply read about. I might look back at a fictional character, someone in A *Tale of Two Cities*. I might look at a poet long dead. There may be a politician, could have been an athlete. I look around and realize that those were human beings—maybe they were African, maybe they were French, maybe they were Chinese, maybe they were Jewish or Muslim—I look at them and think, 'I'm a human being. She was a human being. She overcame all of these things. And she's still working at it. *Amazing*.'

"Take as much as you can from those who went before you," she added. "*Those* are the rainbows in your clouds. Whether they knew your name, or would never see your face, whatever they've done, it's been for you."

I asked what someone should do when they're searching for rainbows, but all they see are clouds.

"What I know," she said, "is that: it's going to be better. If it's bad, it might get worse, but I know that it's going to be better. And you *have* to know that. There's a country song out now, which I wish I'd written, that says, 'Every storm runs out of rain.' I'd make a sign of that if I were you. Put that on your writing pad. No matter how dull and seemingly unpromising life is right now, it's going to change. It's going to be better. But you have to keep working."

Angelou once wrote, "*Nothing so frightens me as writing, but nothing so satisfies me.*" When I had shared that quote with my sisters, they'd said it resonated with them. In many ways, that applies to any kind of work you love. Briana's passion for special education law had turned into her dream, but now that dream was turning into a cold reality of applying to firms and wondering if she was good enough. I brought up that quote to Angelou and asked how she dealt with that fear.

"With a lot of prayer and much trembling," she said, laughing. "I have to remind myself that what I do is not an easy thing. And I think that's true when any person begins doing what he or she wants to do, and feels called to do—not just as a career, but really as a calling.

"A chef, when she or he prepares to go into the kitchen, has to remind herself that everyone in the world, who can, eats. And so preparing food is not a matter of some exoticism; everybody eats. However, to prepare it really well—when everybody eats some salt, some sugar, some meat if they can, or want to, some vegetables— the chef has to do it in a way that nobody has done it before. And so this is true when you are writing.

"You realize everyone in the world who speaks, uses words. And so you have to take a few verbs, and some adverbs, some ad- jectives, nouns, and pronouns, and put them all together and make them bounce. It's not a small matter. So you commend yourself for having the courage to *try* it. You see?"

The third obstacle was dealing with criticism. In Angelou's autobiography, she wrote about joining a writer's guild. She read aloud a piece she'd written and the group ripped it apart.

"You wrote that it pushed you to acknowledge that if you wanted to write," I said, "you had to develop a level of concentration found mostly in people awaiting execution."

"In the next five minutes!" Angelou said, laughing again. "It's true."

"What advice do you have for a young person who's dealing with criticism and looking to develop that same level of concentration?"

"Remember this," she said. "I'd like you to write this down, please. Nathaniel Hawthorne said: *Easy reading is damn hard writing.* And that's probably just as true the other way around; that is, easy writing is damn hard reading. Approach writing, approach what- ever your job is, with admiration for yourself, and for those who did it before you. Become as familiar with your craft as it is possible to become.

"Now, what I do, and what I encourage young writers to do, is to go into a room alone, close the door, and read something you've written already. Read it aloud, so you can hear the melody of the language. Listen to the rhythm of the language. Listen to it. Before you know it, you'll think, '*Mmmh*, it's not too bad! That's pretty good.' Do it so you can admire yourself for *trying*. Compliment yourself for taking on such a difficult, but delicious, chore."

Obstacle four was an issue Briana was confronting. As she looked for a job, every job description she found said, "Prior experience required." But how could she get prior experience if all the jobs *require prior experience*? In Angelou's autobiography, she faced a similar problem.

"I read when you were hired as the associate editor of the *Arab Observer*," I said, "you bluffed your way into the job by inflating your skills and prior experience and, when you were hired, you had to really learn how to swim. What was that like?"

"It was hard," Angelou said, "but I knew I could do it. That's what you have to do. You have to know that you have certain natural skills, and that you can learn others, so you can try some things. You can try for better jobs. You can try for a higher position. And if you seem assured, somehow your assurance makes those around you feel assured. 'Oh, here she comes, she knows what she's doing!' Well, the thing is that you're going to the library late at night and cramming and planning while everybody does their thing.

"I don't think we are born with the art," she added. "You know, if you have a certain eye you can see depth and precision and color and all of that; if you have a certain ear, you can hear certain notes and harmonies; but almost everything is *learned*. So if you have a normal brain, and maybe a little abnormal, you can learn things. *Trust* yourself."

I had one minute left. I asked if she had just a single piece of advice for young people as they launch their careers.

"Try to get out of the box," she said. "Try to see that Taoism, the

Chinese religion, works very well for the Chinese, so it may also work for you. Find all the wisdom that you can find. Find Confucius; find Aristotle; look at Martin Luther King; read Cesar Chávez; *read*. Read and say, 'Oh, these are human beings just like me. Okay, this may not work for me, but I think I can use one portion of this.' You see?

"Don't narrow your life down. I'm eighty-five and I'm just getting started! Life is going to be short, no matter how long it is. You don't have much time. Go to work."

As time passed, I became even more grateful for this conversation, because if I'd waited much longer it wouldn't have happened. Almost exactly a year after this phone call, Maya Angelou passed away.

CHAPTER THIRTY-TWO

Sitting Down with Death

Months had passed since my conversation with Maya Angelou, and the solace she'd given me had washed away. I was experiencing a level of sadness I didn't know I could feel. My dad had just been diagnosed with pancreatic cancer.

He was only fifty-nine. And I was watching him wither away. Seeing my dad's full head of hair fall from his scalp, eighty pounds waste away from his body, and hearing him cry in the middle of the night filled me with a pain I'll never be able to fully put into words. There was such a deep sense of despair, of helplessness, as if I was on a raft, looking out at my dad as he drowned in the ocean, spitting up water, and no matter how far I stretched my hand, I couldn't reach him.

But as overwhelming as those thoughts were, this wasn't the place to linger in sadness. I was now sitting in the lobby of The Honest Company's headquarters, minutes away from interviewing

Jessica Alba, which meant that for the next hour, I needed to com-
pose myself, focus on the mission, and stop thinking about death.

I was escorted down a hallway. Bright sunlight filled the open
workspace. On one wall were a hundred bronze butterflies. On
another were dozens of shining white ceramic mugs spelling the
word "HONESTY." Everything about the company seemed positive and upbeat, and I wanted the interview to be that way too.

As I turned a corner and approached Jessica Alba's office, I reflected on the magnitude of what she's accomplished. She's the
only person in Hollywood history to simultaneously be both a
leading actress *and* the founder of a billion-dollar start-up. The
Honest Company has grossed $300 million since its inception and
her movies have grossed an estimated $1.9 billion worldwide. She's
also the only person in the world to have been on the cover of both
Forbes and *Shape* magazine in the same month. She didn't climb one
mountain and then climb another. She climbed two mountains at
the same time. And I was here to find out how she did it.

I greeted her and sat on an L-shaped couch in her office. During
my research, I'd noticed that whenever Alba spoke about her mom,
she always had the most uplifting things to say. And a few weeks
earlier, while at Larry King's breakfast table, Cal had told me one
of his favorite questions is "What's the best lesson your dad ever
taught you?" I thought if I combined these two elements, we'd immediately go to a positive and profound place.

I asked Alba what the best lesson was that she learned from her
mom. She took a moment to think, running her fingers over the
fringes of her ripped jeans. I sat back, feeling I'd hit the bull's-eye.

"I learned," Alba said, "to try to make the most of moments. You
know, my mom's mother passed away when my mom was in her
early twenties . . ."

Don't think about it. Don't think about it.

"When I was a mean teenager," Alba continued, "my mom

would say, 'You need to be nicer to me, because I am not going to be around forever.'"

She paused, almost as though she was looking inside herself. "You just never think life's going to stop," she said, "until it stops."

I couldn't take it anymore. I had to redirect the conversation.

I'd seen YouTube clips where Alba glowed as she told the story of how she started her company. It went like this: she was twenty-six, pregnant with her first child, and after the baby shower she was washing a onesie in the laundry and was shocked by the allergens in the "child safe" detergent. That inspired her to create a company committed to safe and toxin-free products. In every video clip, Alba's eyes lit up as she talked about helping create happier, healthier lives, which made this the perfect topic.

"How did you start The Honest Company?" I asked.

"I was thinking about mortality," she said, "my own mortality."

"At twenty-six?"

"When you bring life into the world," she said, leaning forward, "it forces you to see how life and death are so close to each other. You realize: *this person wasn't here, and now they are. And now they can just as easily die.* And it's not just a baby that should have access to healthy products; it needs to be everybody. It needs to be me. I don't want to die early. I don't want to get Alzheimer's. I'm terrified of that. My mom's father had it. And then my mom had cancer. My aunt had cancer. My grandmother had cancer. My great-aunt had cancer. My cousin's son had cancer. So . . . I just don't want to die."

I couldn't speak. But that didn't matter, because Alba just kept talking about death and cancer, death and cancer, death and cancer—until I became physically nauseous.

"My dad just got diagnosed with pancreatic cancer," I blurted.

The first time I had ever said those words, I couldn't get them out without tearing. As weeks passed, I could say the words, but I didn't believe it. Now I just felt numb. Through all my stages, the reactions I got were the same. Most people put their arms around me, saying everything was going to be okay; others gave me that kind, soft-spoken "I'm so sorry"—which left me totally unprepared for Alba's response. She slapped her hand down on the couch and said, "Oh, shit. *Fuck*."

Her words felt like a bucket of ice water being splashed in my face. And the strangest thing about it was that it lifted a weight off my shoulders I didn't even know was there.

From this point on, this no longer felt like an interview.

We spent the next thirty minutes talking about cancer in our families. She told me about dealing with her mom rushing to the emergency room, throwing up for three days, and then doctors cutting out pieces of her intestines. Alba put her parents on special diets, got them off harmful medications, set them up with a nutritionist, and they both lost fifty pounds. I told her I had set my dad up with a nutritionist who specialized in helping cancer patients, but my dad wouldn't follow her advice or even see her a second time.

"It's the craziest thing," I said.

"For my parents," Alba replied, "I just had to say, 'Look. If you guys want to be around to see your grandchildren graduate high school or get married, you need to figure it out. It's not okay anymore. You have to do whatever it takes.' So, they did."

Somehow her words made me feel less alone.

"It's just horrible to be sick," she added, letting out a breath. "And then, as I hear about more women having endometriosis and hysterectomies and hormonal cancers, breast cancer, cervical cancer, and all this—I'm in this rut, you know? I'm just like: *What the hell is happening?* Obviously the culprit is a combination of things, but I finally asked myself, 'What's within my control?' And what's within my control is what's in and around my home."

"The first time I bought something from your website," I said, "was after my dad's diagnosis. I know this sounds weird, but the cancer makes his bowel movements smell really bad, and I didn't want to get him a regular air freshener, because I don't know what chemicals are in it. And you guys are one of the only companies with a nontoxic air freshener, the essential oil one. And I told my dad, 'This is your best friend. Use this every day.' And it helped."

Alba's eyes gleamed as if I'd just handed her a gift.

"You and I know that what we put in our bodies, what we're inhaling, what's in our environment—it affects our health," she said. "Our parents' generation is like: 'If I can get it at a store, it's fine. If they're selling it to me, it's okay.' And we're like: 'No, that shit ain't right.' It's so hard because our parents are so afraid to try something new."

"That's the story of my life," I said.

"My grandmother recently found out she has diabetes," Alba went on. "I'm sure she's had it for a while, but she would never go to the doctor. She's had strokes and all that, and they could have been diabetes-related strokes, but she won't acknowledge it. So last night we were at dinner and my grandpa was giving her all this cake and ice cream. I was like, 'She could literally have a seizure right now and go into a coma! What are you guys doing?' They just don't want to accept reality."

"It scares the shit out of me," I said. "I have no idea how you dealt with it with so many family members. I'm drowning with just one."

"I think it's different when it's your dad," she replied.

"I feel like as technology gets better and we can save more lives," I said, "the things that are killing us are getting more extreme; the toxins, the pollution."

"I think that's why we struck a chord," Alba replied, "because people are seeing it."

"The crazy part is—I know you talk a lot about your company helping babies—but you're also doing this for my dad. You're doing it for literally the thing that's hurting me the most."

Her eyes widened, and then an epiphany hit me. "This is crazy!"

I said, lifting off the couch. "All of *this*"—I pointed to the view out of her glass door where some of her five hundred employees worked—"all of *this* is because *you* grabbed death by the collar, sat it down at the table, and asked yourself, 'What am I going to do with my life?'"

Now *she* looked like she'd gotten splashed with ice water.

"It's true!" she said.

"You could have just continued a very successful acting career and been content with that, but instead you—"

"Exactly!" she said.

"It's mind-blowing— Wow— If—" My energy was so high I could barely get a sentence out. "If we had this conversation two months ago, we wouldn't have been talking about any of this. I'd never had to think about death before. But now I see your company in an entirely new way."

Many celebrities create businesses that are a reflection of their lives on the mountaintop. They create fragrances or clothing lines, but Alba created a business that's a reflection of her lowest point. She tapped into her humanity. She created something that resonates with all people. *That* was her key to ascending her second mountaintop: to first go back down to her deepest valley.

"Facing death," Alba said, "makes you sensitive to how delicate life is. Everything is so"—she snapped her fingers —"in a *moment*. It forces you to think about all of your decisions in a different way. What really matters? What are you spending your life doing? What are you going to do when you stare your biggest fear in the eyes?"

———

I BARELY NOTICED OUR HOUR was up, but it didn't matter, because we just kept talking. I took out my phone and pulled up the meme Talia had shown me, of the man racing the woman with all the extra obstacles in front of her.

"I want to see what you think of this," I said.

Alba held my phone in her hand and stared at the image. Then, she laughed. I'd shown the image to a dozen people by now and no one had responded like this. It may have just been in my head, but Alba's laugh seemed to have a hint of sadness.

"It's funny . . . because it's so true," she said. "If everyone could choose to be a white dude in America, born into a family that cares about his education, everyone would probably choose that, because it's really much easier."

Alba continued staring at the meme. "I think you can remove some of those hurdles in the road, if you surround yourself with the right people," she said. "If you try to go it as a lone wolf, if you're just angry and fighting the system the whole time, no one is going to want to be around you because you're always going to be mad, fighting the good fight. But if you can run the race with grace, dignity, and integrity, it makes it a lot easier to get to the finish line.

"Nobody is in control of who they are when they're born," she continued. "You're born into the family you're born into and you're born into the circumstances you're born into. So you just have to take what you can from where you're at and not compare yourself to other people. You have to look at your path and know that whatever got you there, and where you're going, is unique to you. You weren't supposed to be any other way.

"And it's so easy to get distracted," she added. "The man in the left lane is still going to get to his finish line. He doesn't care. He may look over at you in the beginning, but then he's off. If you're constantly looking over your shoulder at him, you'll never finish your race. And you know what? The obstacles women face just make for better businesses. Because in the end, we know how to deal with some shit. This man in the cartoon won't be equipped, because you really only learn if you've gone through it."

Alba looked at the meme again, and then handed my phone back.

"What got you interested in working on this project in the first place?" she asked.

I told her how I had started out staring at the ceiling and how the journey unfolded. Then she asked if I'd found a pattern from my interviews.

"I'd love your take on it," I said. "My theory is that every single one of these people treats life and business . . . like a nightclub."

She let out a small laugh. As I told her the rest of the Third Door analogy, she kept nodding her head.

"I like that," she said. "It's so true. My cofounders and I always say here that it's tough to find job candidates who are intelligent and focused, but who are also dreamers. The dreamer part is that entrepreneurial spirit—where if this door is closed and that door is closed and that door is closed—*how the hell are you going to get in?* You just need to figure it out. You need to use common sense, build relationships; I don't care how you get in, but you've got to get in somehow."

"So you literally hire based on the Third Door?" I asked, laughing.

"Yes! I don't care where you got your degree. I don't care about your past work experience. I care about how you solve problems. I care about how you take on challenges. How do you create new ways of doing things? It's about having that hustle, that drive. That's *everything* when it comes to the best people here. It's all about the Third Door."

CHAPTER THIRTY-THREE

The Impostor

The founder of TED had told me, "I live my life by two mantras. One: if you don't ask, you don't get. And two: most things don't work out."

And now I had just made my most far-fetched ask yet, and it was working out better than I could've imagined. I had asked Qi Lu if he would introduce me to Mark Zuckerberg over email and Qi immediately responded saying he'd be happy to. I looked around the storage closet, shaking my head in disbelief. Just three years earlier I had to crouch in a bathroom to talk to Tim Ferriss. Now a single email connected me to Mark Zuckerberg.

Following Qi's advice, I drafted a paragraph telling Zuckerberg about the mission and that I was attending Startup School, a conference he was scheduled to speak at the following week. I asked if we could meet there. Qi then Facebook-messaged my note to Zuckerberg, and sixteen hours later, I got this:

To: Alex Banayan (cc: Stefan Weitz)
From: Qi Lu
Subject: (no subject)

Here is what I got back from Mark:

Sure, please pass along my email address to him and I'll
try to find a few minutes to speak to him before I have
to leave. I can't promise I'll have time but if I have a few
minutes then I will meet him.

His email address is **********

                              Best,
                              Qi

I knew exactly who I wanted to call first.

"Holy . . . shit," Elliott said.

Elliott talked with a level of excitement that sounded like trumpets blasting the most triumphant song I'd ever heard. He advised me to write an email that wouldn't require much on Zuckerberg's part, so he could easily reply with "Sounds good." Elliott helped draft the email and I sent it off.

To: Mark Zuckerberg (cc: Qi Lu)
From: Alex Banayan
Subject: See you Saturday

Hi Mark,

Qi Lu told me about your reply and passed along your
email address. Qi's been like a guardian angel the past
few years and I'm so grateful for him—and he's said incredible things about you.

> I can pop by backstage after your speech at Startup School for a couple of minutes. If you end up not having time to talk, totally understand. Does that sound good?
> Either way, I really appreciate you and thanks for being such a big inspiration.

I paced across the storage closet and refreshed my email every hour. But there was no reply. Two days before the event, I emailed Qi again, asking if it was okay to send a follow-up message. Qi replied asking what I was talking about. "Mark replied back to you almost immediately."

That's impossible. Wait . . . What if . . .

I checked my spam folder:

> Viagra
> Viagra
> Viagra
> Mark Zuckerberg
> Viagra
> Viagra
> Viagra

Even Gmail couldn't believe Mark Zuckerberg would email me.

> To: Alex Banayan (cc: Qi Lu)
> From: Mark Zuckerberg
> Subject: RE: See you Saturday
>
> Good to meet you. Qi is a great person and I'm glad you got connected with him.
> I'll try to make a few minutes for us to catch up after my Startup School talk on Saturday. I don't have much time, but I'm looking forward to meeting you briefly.

I forwarded Zuckerberg's and Qi's emails to the Startup School event organizer, gave her the context, and asked how I should get backstage. Then I called Elliott and told him the good news.

"Don't send Zuckerberg another email," Elliott said.

"But shouldn't I confirm?" I asked.

"No. Never oversell. He already said yes. At this point, all you have to do is show up."

Although that didn't feel right in my gut, I had ignored Elliott's advice too many times in the past only to find out he had been right. I wasn't going to make that mistake again.

"Well, Mr. Big Shot, congratulations," Elliott said. "You have a meeting with The Zuck. Welcome to the big leagues."

ONE DAY LATER, PALO ALTO, CALIFORNIA

The restaurant was packed and our table was crowded with pita, hummus, and chicken kebabs. It was the night before the Startup School event and I was having dinner with Brandon and Corwin, who would be coming with me the following day. As the waiter placed our bill on the table, I checked my email and saw the event organizer's reply:

Hi Alex,

I'm unable to grant your request for tomorrow. I will need any requests to come from Mark's team.

I replied explaining I didn't know anyone on his team and that I'd been introduced through Qi Lu. The event organizer didn't respond. Each passing hour made me more nervous. I emailed again, but heard nothing back.

Late that night, I emailed a friend from Summit who knew the team organizing the event. I told him the situation and asked what to do. The following morning, he messaged me back.

> Is your email from zuck legit? The head of the event just emailed me saying you tried to get backstage by sending a fabricated email from zuckerberg . . .

———

CORWIN AND BRANDON huddled around my laptop in the kitchen of Corwin's parents' house.

"Just email Zuck and explain what's going on," Brandon said.

"I don't think it's a good idea," I replied. "Elliott told me to play it cool."

"Dude, it's just an email," Corwin said.

My lips pressed.

"Fine, if you're not going to email Zuck," Corwin went on, "then at least email Qi Lu."

I shook my head. "I know if I just see the event organizer face-to-face today and let her go through the emails on my phone, it will clear this all up. We don't have to bother Qi Lu about this."

I shut my laptop and we headed for the car. Half an hour later, Corwin turned a corner and pulled into the outdoor parking lot of De Anza College. The three of us climbed out and looked around at the campus' beige buildings. Hundreds of attendees sprawled the grounds, most carrying laptops and iPads. The line for the main entrance curved around the building. I spotted another entrance in the back of the building, where I assumed VIPs entered to go backstage.

I sped over to the main registration table and asked to speak to the event organizer. After a few minutes of waiting, I was told she wouldn't see me. There was no chance I was going to miss my meeting with Zuckerberg. I frantically tracked down the event organizer's phone number and she answered.

"Hi, this is Alex Banayan, the person who emailed you last night about my meeting with Mark Zuckerberg. I just wanted to—"

"Let's cut to the point," she said. "We know you forged that email. We contacted Mark's PR team and they said they don't have you on their list of approved meetings. We contacted Facebook's security team and they said they have no record of you. And on top of all of that, we know that's not even Mark's real email address. If I were you, I would drop the act before you get yourself in serious trouble. Goodbye."

I didn't know what to do. I was afraid of being overly persistent and bothering Qi Lu on a Saturday afternoon, but I needed help. I figured I could call Stefan Weitz, who worked with Qi at Microsoft. Stefan answered immediately and said he would handle it. A minute later, I was cc'ed on an email to the event organizer. Stefan assured her the email was 100 percent real, and if she still had any concerns, she could call him on his cell.

Two hours passed. The event organizer still hadn't replied to Stefan's email. I texted him the event organizer's phone number. Stefan called, but she didn't answer. I was running out of options. There was an hour to go until Zuckerberg's speech and I didn't have a backup plan. I sent another email.

> To: Mark Zuckerberg (cc: Qi Lu)
> From: Alex Banayan
> Subject: RE: See you Saturday
>
> Just got to Startup School and the staff is being tricky about being backstage. Should I still try to come back there for a few minutes or is there a simpler place for us to catch up?

I checked my watch a bit later—thirty minutes left. There was no response from Zuckerberg, so I decided to take matters into my own hands.

It made sense that Zuckerberg would arrive through the VIP entrance on the other side of the building. When he was getting out of his car, maybe I could tell him I was the person Qi Lu introduced him to, and then Zuckerberg could tell the event organizer who I was. It was the only plan I could think of, so Brandon, Corwin, and I walked over to the driveway leading up to the speakers' entrance. We found a large, shady tree and sat down. A bit later, as we were talking and fidgeting with twigs on the ground, I noticed a man's head emerge from around the corner, then disappear. A minute later, the same man popped out again, whispered into a radio, and then disappeared once more.

Before I knew it, the silhouettes of a woman and a much larger man were moving toward me. They stopped a couple yards away, as if they didn't want to get too close. The walkie-talkie in the man's hand made it clear he was security. He took a step forward and glared down at me.

"Do you mind if I ask what you're doing here?" the woman said. I recognized her voice.

"Hi, I'm Alex," I said lifting my hand, giving a gentle wave. "I'm the person who—"

"I know who you are," the event organizer said. "Why are you sitting under this tree?"

"Oh . . . we're sitting here because . . . our car is parked right there and we just wanted some fresh air."

My car *was* parked right there, but she and I both knew the real reason I was under this tree. I wish I had the courage to say, "Look, I know you think I'm an impostor, and I know you're just doing your job, but I have to do my job too. A president of Microsoft introduced me to the founder of Facebook, and the last thing I'm going to do is not show up. If you don't believe my email is real, that's on you. By all means, ask Mark when his car pulls up." But I couldn't say any of that. I just stared at her.

Her eyes hardened. "I know what you're trying to do," she said. "You need to leave the premises immediately."

The security guard took an ominous step forward.

"If you don't leave now," he said, "we'll call the police."

I imagined Zuckerberg's car pulling up and him stepping out, seeing me with my arms handcuffed behind my back, blue and red lights flashing, and as I'm hauled away I'm screaming, "Mark! *Please!* Tell them we have a meeting!"

I lowered my head, told the security guard we didn't want any trouble, and walked away.

———

I COULDN'T FORGIVE MYSELF. This was the *one time* I hadn't needed to jump over a Dumpster or bang on a door a hundred times to use the Third Door. I sent one email to Qi, and Mark Zuckerberg said, "Come on in!" But of course, the nightclub bouncer saw me, grabbed my arm, and said, "Not so fast, punk."

What made me feel even worse was the thought that I'd let Qi Lu down. I sent an email explaining what happened. Qi replied within minutes.

> Stefan told me about this, and I am sorry things didn't work out. I sent a Facebook message to Mark right after Stefan contacted me, but Mark didn't respond. In retrospect, if you had called me at the time, I could have called the head of the event to let you in.
>
> If you can wait, one suggestion is to try this again next year at the next Startup School. Because Mark already agreed, it's kind of a rain check, and I can contact the

head of the event beforehand so that he can ask his staff to let you in. If you cannot wait that long, I can try to message Mark again, but I'm not sure whether he will respond, as he didn't for the previous message I sent.

I thanked Qi and asked if he could try one more time now. My thinking was that this was never going to be fresher in Zuckerberg's mind. If it would ever happen, it would be now. Qi sent Zuckerberg a second message. Three days later, Qi emailed me back.

I sent the message to Mark via Facebook message on Thursday, and so far Mark has not responded.

Following past patterns, this unfortunately means that Mark is not open to that possibility, as otherwise he would have responded. I am sorry Alex that I wasn't able to be of more help on this. Hope there could be other ways that you get to meet with him.

Over the next few weeks, I desperately tried to salvage the situation. An early Facebook employee I'd met at Summit contacted Zuckerberg's security team; Bill Gates' office contacted Zuckerberg's assistant; Matt Michelsen, the founder of Lady Gaga's social network whom I met through Elliott, introduced me to one of Zuckerberg's attorneys. Matt then took me to Facebook headquarters to meet with the company's chief marketing officer. Still, there was no word from Zuckerberg.

As months passed, what killed me most about this failure was the lack of closure. There was no postmortem. A part of me felt that I never had a good strategy in the first place. This hadn't even been a real meeting with Zuckerberg. His email basically implied he would shake my hand and talk for a minute. That was great, but

I should've asked Qi to introduce me to Zuckerberg's chief of staff, someone whom I could sit down with, explain what I was doing, and who could then set up a full interview.

But another part of me knew that it didn't matter. Even if it was just a minute-long meeting, Qi Lu had thrown me a perfect Hail Mary. I'd caught it at the one-yard line with no defenders around. All I had to do was take two steps forward to the end zone, but I *still* fumbled.

CHAPTER THIRTY-FOUR

The Greatest Gift

I beat myself up for weeks, thinking about sitting under that tree, failing to meet Zuckerberg; then I thought about how I sent that shoe, failing to back off from Buffett; and even when I'd managed to get to Bill Gates, I failed to ask the right questions. There were moments when I felt like my journey was one long, pathetic string of mistakes. But I stopped thinking about my pain as soon as I was in the presence of Quincy Jones.

"Where you from, my man?"

His deep eighty-one-year-old voice landed on my ears like the notes of a baritone sax. Quincy wore a royal-blue robe that swept down to his ankles. I sat beside him on a sofa in the circular living room of his Bel-Air home.

"Born and raised in LA," I replied.

"No"—he shook his head—"I said where you *from*."

"Oh. My parents are from Iran."

"That's what I thought."

"How'd you know?"

Instead of answering directly, he launched into a wild story about his travels in Iran when he was eighteen; attending parties thrown by the Shah and sneaking out at night, meeting up with young revolutionaries trying to break the Ayatollah out of jail. Then he told me the story of when he dated a Persian princess.

"*Khailee mamnoon*," Quincy said, laughing as he tossed out phrases in Persian. "I was in Tehran, Damascus, Beirut, Iraq, Karachi, everywhere. I've been traveling for sixty-five years, all over the planet."

I'd researched his background before this interview, but now I was realizing how little I truly knew about the man. I already knew he'd been nominated for more Grammy Awards than any other music producer in history. I knew he'd produced Michael Jackson's *Thriller*, the highest-grossing album of all time, as well as "We Are the World," the highest-grossing single of all time. He'd worked with some of the greatest performers of the twentieth century, from Frank Sinatra to Paul McCartney to Ray Charles. In the world of film, he produced *The Color Purple* with Steven Spielberg, which was nominated for ten Oscars. In television, he created *The Fresh Prince of Bel-Air*, which was nominated for an Emmy. As a mentor, he helped launch the careers of Will Smith and Oprah Winfrey. Quincy Jones is undeniably one of the most important figures in the history of entertainment, and now he was asking me, "You got a pen?"

I pulled one out of my pocket. He grabbed a sheet of paper from under the coffee table. He began drawing curvy letters, teaching me how to write in Arabic. Then he taught me how to write in Mandarin. Then Japanese. I had hated learning languages in school, yet Quincy made them seem as if they were the keys to the universe.

"Look here," he said, pointing up to the living room's arched ceiling. Twelve large wooden beams radiated from the center like rays from the sun. "That's *feng shui*," he said. "They symbolize the twelve notes of the musical scale, the twelve apostles, the twelve signs of the zodiac . . ."

He pointed around the room. Surrounding us were dozens of ancient-looking artifacts—a Chinese sculpture of a boy on a horse, a bust of an Egyptian queen—and each of them seemed to have its own vortex of energy.

"I've got Nefertiti over there," Quincy said. "I've got Buddha there. The Tang dynasty there. Japan there. That's Picasso there. Over there, that's a model of the original SpaceX rocket. Elon gave me that. He's my neighbor."

My head spun and Quincy smiled, as though he knew something about me that I didn't.

"It's a hell of a world out there," he said. "You've got to go to know."

Our conversation moved faster and faster. One second he was talking about meditation, the next about nanotechnology; one minute he was talking about architecture (*"Frank Gehry always says to me—he's a Pisces too—he says, 'If architecture is frozen music, then music must be liquid architecture.' All great art is emotional architecture."*) and the next he was talking about directing (*"When Spielberg came to my studio, he said he directs the same way I conduct. He creates a strong structure, and on top of that, he improvises. You have to give people room to put their personalities on it."*). Gems of wisdom kept dropping and I sat back on the couch, absorbing each one.

> *"I teach the musicians I mentor to become themselves. To know themselves and to love themselves. That's all I care about . . . Know yourself and love yourself."*

> *"Young people are always chasing. It's because they think they're in control of everything. They have to learn to be connected to the universe. Just let it happen to you."*

"There's a statute of limitations that's expired on
all childhood traumas. Fix your shit and get on with
your life."

Quincy reached under the coffee table for a book. He flipped through pages of black-and-white pictures. "Chicago in the thirties," he said, pointing to the photos. "This is where I spent my childhood. My daddy was a carpenter for the most notorious black gangsters on the planet. They didn't fuck around, man. I wanted to be a gangster when I was young. I saw guns and dead bodies every day."

He pulled up his sleeve and pointed to a scar on the back of his hand. "You see that? Seven years old. I went to the wrong block. Some guys took a knife, used it to nail my hand to a fence, and then stuck an ice pick in the back of my head. I thought I was going to die."

Some summers his dad took him to Louisville to visit his grandmother, a former slave. She would tell Quincy to go to the river and grab rats that still had their tails moving. She fried the rats with onions on her coal stove for dinner.

When Quincy was ten, his family moved to Seattle. One night, when he and his friends were breaking into a recreation center to steal food, he stumbled into a room with a piano. It was the first time he'd seen one. When Quincy's fingers touched the keys, he remembers it feeling like a moment of the divine. "Everything changed for me," he said. "I loved music so much I wrote songs until my eyes would bleed."

Quincy learned to play any instrument he could get his hands on—violin, clarinet, trumpet, sousaphone, B flat baritone horn, E flat alto peck horn, French horn, and trombone. He began sneaking into nightclubs to meet jazz musicians who passed through town. When he was fourteen, Quincy slipped into a club and met a blind teenager who was two years older. They hit it off and the older teen began to mentor Quincy. They became close friends. That blind teenager was Ray Charles.

"I met McCartney when he was twenty-two; Elton John, seventeen; Mick Jagger; all those guys. I found Lesley Gore when she was sixteen."

Lesley Gore's "It's My Party," which Quincy produced, was one of the biggest songs of 1963.

"How did you find her?" I asked.

"Through her uncle, who was Mafia. He went to Joe Glaser, who worked with Al Capone. Back when I came up, *everything* in music was Mafia. The booking agencies with Duke Ellington, Louis Armstrong, Lionel Hampton—*all* Mafia. It was fucked up, man. There were exploitations of blacks like you cannot believe. Back then is when I learned that if you don't have a master, a negative, or a copyright, you're not in the music business. I learned the hard way."

Quincy had composed ten original songs for the iconic bandleader Count Basie. A music executive named Morris Levy called Quincy into his office to sign a publishing contract. The contract was on the table—and all of Levy's cronies were behind him. "You can ask for anything you want," he told Quincy, "but you're only getting one percent."

"I signed the contract," Quincy told me, "and before I walked out of his office, he owned all my shit."

Quincy laughed gently as if recounting a fond memory, but for some reason I felt my whole body stiffen.

"I was young and I learned my lesson," Quincy said. "The second time I did Basie's album he asked me, 'What are we going to do about the publishing?' I told him, 'Nothing. I'll publish it myself.' He said, 'Now you're getting smart, kid! Why didn't you think of that the first time?'"

Quincy laughed some more.

"The Mafia took all my shit," he added. "I'm still getting it back."

"That's *fucked up*," I said, my anger surprising us both. With hindsight, I can see where it came from. I was still so upset over what happened with Zuckerberg that even the smallest reminder of being screwed by someone in a position of power set me off.

"It's all good, man," Quincy said, putting his hand on my shoulder. "That's how you learn."

As Quincy and I locked eyes, something within me clicked. I felt as if my body had been an overinflated tire and Quincy had just hit a valve, all the excess pressure rushing out.

"You have to cherish your mistakes," he said. "You have to get back up no matter how many times you get knocked down. There are some people who face defeat and retreat; who become cautious and afraid, who deal with fear instead of passion, and that's not right. I know it seems complex, but it's relatively simple. It's: *let go and let God.*

"You can't get an A if you're afraid of getting an F," Quincy added. "It's amazing, the psychology of growing in your field, no matter what you do. Growth *comes* from mistakes. You have to *cherish* them, so you can *learn* from them. Your mistakes are your greatest gift."

———

WE SPENT THE REST of the evening talking for hours about everything from the pyramids in Egypt to the samba dancers at Rio's Carnival. Quincy was making me realize that I'd spent the past five years constantly looking up—*up* at the richest man in the world, *up* at the most successful investor, *up* at the most famous director. And now it was hitting me how badly I wanted to go *wide*—to travel and explore and absorb the magic of the far corners of the world. Quincy was instilling a new hunger in me. It felt like as one stage of my life was closing, a new one was beginning.

"I feel like a different person," I said as our conversation wound down. "You know, you taught me something tonight I wasn't expecting to learn."

"What's that?" he said.

"You taught me to be a full person, a person of the world."

"That's amazing, man. It's true. Nat King Cole used to always tell me: 'Quincy, your music can be no more or no less than you are as a human being.'"

"That's what the world gives you," I said.

"No," Quincy said, correcting me. "That's what *mistakes* give you."

It was as if he was going to keep repeating that lesson until it sank in. And now it had. In a moment of clarity, it dawned on me that advice from Bill Gates was never my Holy Grail. My mistakes on my way to get to him were what changed me most.

I'd always seen success and failure as opposites, but now I could see they were just different results of the same thing—trying. I swore to myself that from now on I would be unattached to succeeding, and unattached to failing. Instead, I would be attached to trying, to growing.

It's almost as though Quincy could see the gears turning in my head, because he slowly put his hand on my shoulder and said, "You got it, man. You got it."

Before I could think of a response, he just looked at me and said, "You're a beautiful, beautiful human being. Don't ever change, motherfucker."

CHAPTER THIRTY-FIVE

Getting in the Game

THREE MONTHS LATER, AUSTIN, TEXAS

W e stepped toward the nightclub and approached a line so chaotic it looked like a mob. Matt Michelsen, the founder of Lady Gaga's social network, pulled me close and led me through the crowd. Broken beer bottles littered the ground, the moonlight glinting off the shards. A pack of bouncers guarded the entrance.

"The party is at capacity," one said, stepping forward.

"We're with Gaga," Matt replied.

"She's already inside. No one else is getting in."

There was a brief silence, then Matt stepped forward too. He said something into the guard's ear. The guard hesitated—then stepped aside.

As soon as the door opened, the thump of techno music made my whole body vibrate. Matt and I pressed through the crowd on the dance floor. Hundreds of people were gawking in one direction, holding their phones in the air, taking pictures. Standing on an elevated VIP platform, under a glowing white light, was one of the most famous pop stars in the world. Lady Gaga's platinum-blond hair dangled past her waist. She balanced on shoes at least ten inches high.

The VIP platform was packed and a bouncer guarding the stairs said there was no way in. This time, Matt didn't bother talking to the guard. We moved to the front of the platform, directly below where Lady Gaga was standing.

"Hey, L.G.!" Matt yelled.

She looked down and her face lit up. "Get up here!"

"It's too packed," Matt replied. "They won't—"

"Get the fuck up here!"

Seconds later, two bodyguards grabbed us by the arms and led us up the platform. Matt headed straight to Gaga. I stayed back, giving them space.

Minutes later, Matt pointed in my direction. A bodyguard gripped my shoulder, pulled me through the crowd, and planted me next to Matt and Lady Gaga. Matt put his arms around us both, pulling us in.

"Hey, L.G.," he shouted over the music. "Remember that thing I told you about called the Third Door?"

She smiled and nodded.

"And remember that story I told you about that kid who hacked *The Price Is Right*? The same kid who went with his friends to Warren Buffett's shareholders meeting?"

Her smile grew bigger and she nodded even more.

"Well," Matt said, pointing at me, "he's standing right here."

Gaga's eyes widened—she turned to me, flung her arms up, and gave me a giant hug.

———

EVER SINCE ELLIOTT INTRODUCED ME to Matt at the concert in New York City, Matt had become a mentor. I'd stayed at his guesthouse for weeks at a time, traveled with him to New York and San Francisco, and when I'd found myself in trouble with Zuckerberg, he immediately tried to help. Even when it came to setting up an interview with Lady Gaga, I didn't have to ask. Matt brought it up himself and offered to make it happen. He's that kind of guy.

The afternoon after I met Gaga in the nightclub, I was on a couch in Matt's hotel suite when he walked in, his phone to his ear. Matt paced across the room. When he hung up, I asked who he was talking to. He said it was Gaga—and she was in tears.

Matt sat down and explained the situation. Gaga's first two albums had been blockbusters and catapulted her to the top of the music industry, but then, just in the past year, she had broken her hip, underwent emergency surgery, been confined to a wheelchair, and had to cancel twenty-five dates of her tour. She then fought with her longtime manager over the direction of her career, and when Gaga fired him, it made headlines. Her manager, the one who had rejected my interview requests in the past, told his side of the story to the press, but Gaga remained quiet, which only raised more questions. And then just weeks later, Gaga released her third album, *ARTPOP*, which critics ripped to shreds. *Rolling Stone* called it "bizarre." *Variety* labeled some of the songs "snoozeworthy." Gaga's previous album sold over a million copies in its first week. *ARTPOP* didn't sell a quarter of that.

That was four months ago, and now Gaga was about to step back into the spotlight. In two days she would film a segment on *Jimmy Kimmel Live* in the afternoon, perform a concert at night, and give the South by Southwest Music keynote the following morning.

The keynote worried her most. It wouldn't be a short speech in front of her fans. This would be an hour-long interview in a ballroom full of music executives and journalists, many of whom were friends with her former manager. Gaga feared some would be hoping to see her fall flat on her face. It wasn't hard to imagine the kinds of questions she might be asked: *Do you see* ARTPOP *as a failure? Was firing your manager a mistake? Will your crazy outfits work against you now that your album sales have dropped?*

That's why Gaga had called Matt in tears, asking for help. She felt misunderstood. She knew she had been true to herself when she'd made *ARTPOP*, but she couldn't find the words to explain what the album meant. The next few days were Gaga's chance to start a new chapter in her career and she didn't want the baggage of the past year weighing her down.

After Matt finished explaining this to me, he called one of his employees and within an hour they were sitting beside me in the hotel suite, brainstorming a narrative Gaga could use throughout the week. Matt's employee was in his late twenties. I knew he had studied business in college, and all I heard coming out of his mouth were buzzwords: "*ARTPOP* is about *collaboration!*" "*Synergy!*" "*Connection!*"

I wanted to scream, "*That's not how you describe an artist's soul.*" But I felt it wasn't my place to say anything, especially after how generously Matt had treated me. He was arranging for me to interview Gaga later this week, and on top of that, he was letting me stay in the extra room in his hotel suite. So I remained quiet.

But ideas rumbled within me. I had already read Gaga's biography, buried myself in articles about her, and studied *ARTPOP*'s lyrics endlessly. As I listened to Matt and his employee, I felt like a basketball player sitting on the bench, legs twitching, dying to get in the game.

An hour into their brainstorm, Matt looked at me, frustrated. "Don't you have anything to contribute?"

"Well . . ." I said, trying to hold myself back; but instead, almost uncontrollably, lessons I'd learned from my journey combusted with everything I'd read about Gaga and it all erupted from my mouth. "Art is emotional architecture, and if we view Gaga through that lens—her foundation, her wooden beams—it all traces back to her childhood. When she was a kid, she went to Catholic school and felt stifled. The nuns measured her skirt. They made her follow their rules. Now when Gaga wears dresses made out of meat, she's still rebelling against those nuns!"

"Everything Gaga stands for is creative rebellion!" Matt said.

"Exactly! The founder of TED once told me, 'Genius is the opposite of expectation,' and now that makes perfect sense! Whether it's her music or outfits, Gaga has always gone against expectations." I jumped off the couch, feeling alive in a way I'd never felt before.

"Gaga's hero is Andy Warhol," I went on, "and using a Campbell's Soup can as a subject is also the opposite of expectation! Critics slammed *ARTPOP* for being too fringe and not resonating with the masses like her last album, but what if that was the point? Gaga's album *had to* come out the way it did! All of her art is the opposite of expectation. It only makes sense that if she was at the peak of Top 40, she had to do the opposite. *ARTPOP* wasn't Gaga losing her touch. *ARTPOP* was Gaga being completely herself!"

I kept going and going until I fell back on the couch to catch my breath. I looked up at Matt.

"Congratulations," he said. "You have twenty-four hours to write that up."

———

IT WAS PAST MIDNIGHT. Matt was out at an event and I was alone in the hotel suite, my eyes glued to my laptop. The river of words that had flowed earlier had dried up. By morning I had to give Matt a one-page document of the talking points, plus a PowerPoint that he would present to Gaga.

When I'd been on the couch earlier watching Matt and his employee, I had visualized everything I would do if I got in the game. But now that I was in, it felt like no matter how hard I tried to jump, my feet were glued to the court.

Minutes stretched into hours. I went to bed, hoping I'd find inspiration in the morning. Though as I lay under the covers, I couldn't sleep. My mind kept churning, and I don't know why, but I began thinking about a video of Steve Jobs I'd watched on YouTube years earlier. He was introducing the "Think Different" marketing campaign and talking about the importance of defining your values. It was one of the most brilliant speeches I'd seen. I pulled the covers off and reached for my laptop. I rewatched the speech and again it blew me away. All I could think was: *I need to show Gaga this video. This has the magic I'm missing.*

But I wouldn't be in the room with her the next day. And even if I would be, I couldn't force Lady Gaga to watch a YouTube video. So I emailed Matt:

> This is it . . . trust me on this and watch all seven minutes: https://www.youtube.com/watch?v=keCwRdbwNQY

A short time later, Matt walked into the hotel suite.

"Did you watch the video?" I asked.

"Not yet. I'll watch it now."

Finally, it felt like things were back on track. Matt disappeared into his bedroom and I could hear him watching the video through the open door. Then Matt emerged with a toothbrush in his mouth and his phone in his hand, barely watching as the video played. When the speech ended, Matt didn't notice. He returned to his room without a word.

I yanked the covers over me. Not only had my plan not worked, but it was the fourth quarter, and I was all out of ideas.

I WOKE UP BEFORE DAWN and headed to the lobby to continue writing. As much as I tried, the words just didn't have the impact I knew they could. Then Matt called.

"Come to the room," he said. "My meeting with Gaga moved up. We only have two hours now."

I hurried to the suite, opened the door, and that's when I saw Matt standing at the kitchenette counter, his laptop in front of him and headphones in—watching the Steve Jobs video in full screen. His eyes were fixed. When the video finished, Matt slowly turned his head.

"I have an idea," he said.

I stayed silent.

"I'm going to sit Gaga down . . . and show her this video."

"YESSSSS!" I shouted.

The exhilaration of the moment overtook me and I whipped out my laptop and rewrote the entire page of talking points within a minute, perfectly channeling everything I'd said the day earlier. Matt knew Gaga in a way I never could, so his edits lifted the words to new heights. Now all we needed was the PowerPoint.

Matt had to be at Gaga's house within the hour, so I stayed behind to finish. There was something thrilling about being under this kind of stress, as if the game clock was counting down 10 . . . 9 . . . 8 . . . As Matt called to say he was walking in—the buzzer sounded—and I hit send.

An hour later, my phone vibrated. It was a text from Matt.

Home run. Everyone crying over here.

————

THE NEXT TWO DAYS WERE a whirl. Late that night, I went to a Snoop Dogg concert to join Matt and Lady Gaga. After grabbing a Red Bull from the bar, I spotted them on a sofa in the VIP section. Matt motioned for me to sit beside Gaga. I plopped down and she put her arm around me. With her other arm she reached for my Red Bull, took a gulp, and handed it back.

"Alex," she said, "sometimes . . . sometimes something is so deep inside you, you can't express it yourself. For the first time, you expressed it for me in words.

"And that Andy Warhol line," she added, smiling and swirling her hand in the air. "Incredible."

After Gaga and I finished talking, Kendrick Lamar came over and sat beside me on the couch. Snoop Dogg continued performing on stage, rapping my favorite songs. I got up and danced, feeling freer than ever.

The next evening, as Matt and I headed to Gaga's concert, I checked Twitter and saw she'd changed her profile name to "CREATIVE REBELLION." She tweeted:

> ARTPOP is creative rebellion. I don't play by the nuns' rules. I make my own. #MonsterStyle #ARTPOP

In what felt like a second later, I heard the thunderous cheers of thousands of fans as Gaga danced on stage. While she sang, a woman beside her chugged bottles of a green liquid. Gaga stood still under a spotlight and the woman gagged herself, throwing up on the pop star. Gaga called it "vomit art."

As I watched green liquid hurtling out of the woman's mouth and splashing onto Gaga's body, I cringed. Matt laughed. "Talk about the opposite of expectation, huh?"

Later that night, Gaga's interview on *Jimmy Kimmel Live* aired. Kimmel opened with a jab at Gaga's outfits, then he took another shot at *ARTPOP*. But Gaga didn't miss a beat. She hit back with the "opposite of expectation" line and the audience roared with applause.

In another blink, I was sitting in the front row of the keynote speech the next morning, right between Matt and Gaga's father. The houselights dimmed. Gaga stepped on stage in an enormous dress made out of plastic tarps. One of the first questions was about the "vomit art."

She explained how the idea originated and then said: "You know, Andy Warhol thought he could make a soup can into art. Sometimes things that are really strange, and feel really wrong, can really change the world . . . It's about freeing yourself from the expectations of the music industry and the expectations of the status quo. I never liked having my skirt measured for me in school or being told how to do things or the rules to live by."

Before I knew it, applause enveloped the room. The keynote was over and the audience was on its feet. Gaga received a standing ovation.

Matt headed straight to the airport and I went back to the hotel to pack. As I gathered my things, Matt sent me a screenshot of a text he had just received from Gaga:

> I don't even know what to say. I'm so grateful for everything u guys have done. U really supported me and I had wings today because of u. Hope I made u and Alex proud.

As I finished reading Gaga's text, another popped up on my phone. A friend from USC invited me to a party on campus. The friends I'd started college with were in the final semester of their senior year, celebrating graduation. I felt like, in my own way, I was too.

———

As I stared out of the airplane's window, watching clouds floating below, I couldn't stop thinking about how this Gaga experience came to be. In a way, it just seemed like a series of little decisions. Years ago, I chose to cold-email Elliott Bisnow. Then I chose to go to Europe with him. I chose to go to that concert in New York City where Elliott introduced me to Matt. Then I chose to spend time visiting Matt's home and building a relationship with him.

As my thoughts continued to unfold, a quote came to mind, from a seemingly unexpected source. It was from one of the Harry Potter books. At a critical moment in the story, Dumbledore says, "It is our choices that show what we truly are, far more than our abilities."

It's our choices . . . far more than our abilities . . .

I thought back to my conversations with Qi Lu and Sugar Ray Leonard. The message of that quote was the underlying lesson I learned during those interviews. While Qi Lu and Sugar Ray were both born with remarkable abilities, what made them stand out in my eyes were their choices. Qi Time was a *choice*. Chasing the school bus was a *choice*.

Different images began coming to mind, rolling in front of my eyes like a slide show. When Bill Gates sat in his dorm room, pushing through his fear and picking up that phone to make his first sale, that was a choice. When Steven Spielberg jumped off the Universal Studios tour bus, that was a choice. When Jane Goodall worked multiple jobs to save money to travel to Africa, that was a choice.

Everyone has the power to make little choices that can alter their lives forever. You can either choose to give in to inertia and continue waiting in line for the First Door, or you can choose to jump out of line, run down the alley, and take the Third Door. We all have that choice.

If there was one lesson I learned from my journey, it's that making these choices was possible. It's that mindset of possibility that transformed my life. Because when you change what you believe is possible, you change what becomes possible.

The plane's wheels hit the ground in Los Angeles. I carried my duffel bag and made my way through the terminal, feeling a gentle calm I'd never known before.

I stepped outside of baggage claim. When my dad pulled his car to the curb, he got out and I gave him a long hug. I tossed my duffel bag in the trunk and climbed into the passenger seat.

"So, how did the interview go?" he asked.

"It never happened," I said.

As I told him the story, my dad let out a big smile, and we headed home.

In loving memory of
David Banayan
1957–2017

ACKNOWLEDGMENTS

Four days before my dad passed away, he taught me one of the most important lessons of my life. I was at Elliott's Santa Monica apartment when I got the call from my dad's doctor. She'd just visited him at my parents' home and his condition had taken a sharp turn.

"From what I saw," she said, "he probably has a few days to live."

Nothing could've prepared me for what it was like to hear those words. Everything around me seemed to blur. I couldn't think. All I could do was feel. I felt an overwhelming isolation, gripped by fear and sadness, as if I was a small child who found himself suddenly separated from his parents amid a crowded train terminal, lost and alone, not knowing what to do.

In that moment, I did the only thing I felt I could. I called my older sister, Briana. After telling her the doctor's prognosis, I climbed into my car, picked her up, and headed to our parents' house. When we arrived, my mom and my dad's caregiver were sitting silently on the couch. My dad was in his favorite armchair, but he didn't look the same. Just two days earlier, I was with him for breakfast where he ate a full meal and moved around easily. Now he sat motionless with his eyes shut, but I could tell he wasn't sleeping. His skin had yellowed. His breathing was labored. My dad had opted for a natural death at home, so I fought my urge to call an ambulance.

"Dad?" I said.

When he didn't respond, I moved closer and put my hand on his, shaking it softly.

"Dad?"

I turned to my mom. She looked at me and subtly shook her head, as if no words could be said. I took a seat beside my sister on the couch. We sat in silence as the reality set in. We were watching our dad, the man who gave us life, slip into a coma.

A few minutes later, my dad's caregiver said it was time for him to take his pain medication. The caregiver stood above him, trying to feed him the pill, but my dad wouldn't open his mouth.

"David," the caregiver pleaded, "please open your mouth."

But there was no response.

I started to panic, not for us, but for my dad. I knew that if he didn't take his pain medication, his final days would be excruciatingly painful.

"David, please," the caregiver repeated.

She asked again and again, but my dad remained unresponsive.

Then my mom slowly stood up. She took the pill in her hand and then kicked off her shoes. She knelt down beside my dad, gently placing her hand on his.

The moment my mom spoke—the moment her voice landed on my dad's ears asking him to open his mouth—his mouth opened seamlessly. My dad not only took the pill, but he swallowed it easily.

I began to sob, my chest plunging toward my knees. But I wasn't crying out of sadness. Rather, I was crying about the beauty of it. As I watched my mom kneeling beside my dad, it was as if my dad wanted to teach me that, at the end of life—when you don't have access to money or possessions, when you can't even open your eyes—all you'll have left is your heartbeat, your breath, and your soul's connection to those you love.

So, Dad, my first thank-you goes to you. I could use a hundred pages to write everything I want to say to you, but that still wouldn't feel like enough. So for now, I'll just say: I love you, and I miss you . . .

The next thank-you goes to my mom, who I had always known was a superhero, but during the final year of my dad's life showed me that I hadn't seen the half of it. Somehow the excruciating pain she went through transformed her into an even more phenomenal woman. Instead of becoming consumed by fear, she became more fearless. Instead of hardening her heart, she opened her heart more. Mom, I am so proud to be your son. I am who I am because of who you are.

I want to thank my sisters, Talia and Briana, who are not only my most cherished friends, but also my greatest teachers. At the time of our dad's death, as I felt like emotional bombs were dropping on us every day, the fact that the three of us were in the trenches together, and that I could look over my shoulder and see you two beside me, made me feel that, in the end, everything would be all right. I am so grateful we get to do life together.

Thank you to my grandparents, great-grandparents, aunts, uncles, and cousins, because before I was on my dorm room bed and staring at the ceiling, I was sitting on your couches and around your dinner tables, feeling completely loved. And thank you to Mike Eshaghian and AJ Silva, who have joined us for this ride with steady minds and open hearts.

A particular thank-you is in order for my grandma, who we affectionately call Momina, and who's best known in this story for her phrase *jooneh man*. At the end of my journey, when I became more certain about my decision not to return to college,

Cal Fussman sat me down and reminded me that I still hadn't apologized to my grandma for breaking my promise.

I pushed back. I told Cal that my grandma knew I wasn't planning on returning to college and my relationship with her was great. It didn't need to be explicitly said.

"You swore on her life and broke the promise," Cal said. "It needs to be said."

I was reluctant, but I still went to my grandma's house one night to have the talk. We were halfway through dinner when I finally mustered the courage.

"I don't know if you remember," I told her, "but years ago I swore to you I would finish college and get my master's. I said *jooneh man*."

My grandma put down her fork.

She looked at me silently, as if she'd been waiting years for me to say these words.

"I broke the promise, and"—tears welled in my eyes—"I'm sorry."

The silence that followed made me feel even worse.

Then my grandma said, "It's . . . okay." She took a heavy breath. "I hope . . . I hope . . . I hope . . . that I was the one who was wrong to have asked you to make that promise in the first place."

———

THE FINAL MONTHS OF MY DAD'S LIFE were filled with more pain than I'd ever experienced. But it was also filled with a kind of love I didn't know existed.

Elliott would call multiple times a day to check on my dad's progress and how my family was holding up. As my dad's condition worsened, Elliott flew to LA more often, visiting my dad and sitting with him under his orange tree in our backyard. Elliott and my dad bonded over that tree. Elliott made a website for the tree. His brother, Austin, wrote a song about the tree. His best friend, IN-Q, created a poem about the tree. Elliott made two-dozen baseball caps with a logo of MR. BANAYAN'S ORANGE TREE on the front. No matter how much pain my dad was in, each time he was under the orange tree with Elliott, he'd light up.

When I had first cold-emailed Elliott, I dreamed of having a mentor. Not only was I lucky enough to get that, but I also got a best friend. But never in my wildest dreams could I have imagined he would become my brother.

Eventually, the time came for me to call Elliott and tell him my dad was slipping into a coma. Elliott was traveling for work and said he'd get to LA as soon as he could.

The next few days passed slowly. On the fourth afternoon, I was sitting under the orange tree with my sisters, searching for a pocket of calm amid the chaos of emotions. As the sun began to set, my aunt came out and asked us to come to my dad's bedside. At the exact moment I stepped inside, Elliott walked through the front door. He saw the look in my eyes and followed silently to my dad's bedside. We all stood in a circle around my dad—me, my sisters, mom, aunt, uncle, and Elliott—and held hands. A minute later, my dad took his final breath.

Many emotions flood me as I remember what it felt like to watch my dad die before my eyes. Many thoughts and theories swirl around my head too, and I'll always wonder whether my dad had waited until Elliott was in our house, holding my hand, before he passed away.

MY DAD TAUGHT ME ONE final lesson before he was laid to rest in the earth, and it happened to take place on the day of his funeral.

After the service in the chapel, six pallbearers carried my dad's casket out to the hearse. My mom, sisters, and I filed into another car and followed the hearse up to the gravesite. When we got out of the car, for some reason, the six pallbearers who carried my dad out of the chapel weren't by the hearse to carry the casket to the grave.

I began to worry, but I didn't have much time to think because a rabbi came over to talk to my family. I couldn't see what happened next, but I did hear the trunk of the hearse open and my dad's casket being taken out.

When I finally stepped onto the grass and looked out toward the processional, I saw my dad's casket being carried by my best friends.

My tears turned to wails as I lifted my head and looked up to the heavens. Again, I wasn't crying out of sadness, but at the beauty of it. It was as if my dad wanted to tell me, just a minute before he was set into the ground, that in life, there are friends, there are best friends—and then there are the best friends who carry your dad's casket.

Thank you to Kevin Hekmat, Andre Herd, Jojo Hakim, Ryan Nehoray, Brandon Hakim, and Corwin Garber, who've redefined the meaning of friendship, and who've proved that it truly is the most powerful force in the world.

I love you guys like family. Because you are family.

And I'm grateful my chosen family doesn't end there.

More than anyone else I've met, Cal Fussman is proof to me that God exists. The way Cal and I met feels like a miracle, and what Cal gave me was a miracle. On top of teaching me how to interview, Cal also taught me how to write, spending two hours a night with me, two or three times a week, for the past four years. He reviewed sentence after sentence and never lost patience. We edited some chapters together up to 134 times. And Cal's generosity didn't stop there. He adopted me into his family—*obrigado*, Gloria, Dylan, Keilah, and Bridgette—and his youngest daughter, Bridgette, is now my goddaughter, which is one of the greatest honors of my life. Cal, to say I'm incredibly grateful would be an understatement.

Thank you to the entire Bisnow family: Austin, IN-Q, Nicole, Deena, Mark, and Margot. Every time I'm with you all, no matter where in the world we are, I feel at home.

I'm grateful for my closest friends, from childhood to college to present day, who've brought more meaning, love, and fun into every part of life. Your collective energies are seeped into the lines of this book: Andrew Horn, Arturo Nuñez, Ben Nemtin, Brad Delson, Cody Rapp, Danny Lall, Jake Strom, Jason Bellet, Jesse Stollak, Jon Rosenblum, Kyla Siedband, Max Stossel, Maya Watson, Mike Posner, Miki Agrawal, Nia Batts, Noa Tishby, Olivia Diamond, Penni Thow, Radha Agrawal, Ramy Youssef, Ross Bernstein, Ross Hinkle, Sean Khalifian, Sophia Zukoski, and Tamara Skootsky.

And to my beloved friend Mallory Smith, who was a light in our lives and inspired my passion for reading since we were kids: you are missed and forever in our hearts.

———

THERE'S A QUOTE by Rabbi Abraham Joshua Heschel that particularly speaks to me.

"When I was young, I admired clever people. Now that I am old, I admire kind people."

When I first met Stefan Weitz, I was drawn to his intellect and ability to find ten solutions to every problem. Now as I reflect back, what blows me away most is his generosity and selflessness. Stefan, you put the full force of your reputation behind the mission when it was nothing more than an eighteen-year-old's pipe dream. People like you are who truly change the world. I'll be grateful to you for the rest of my life.

Thank you to Matt Michelsen, who not only put me in the game, but also brought me into his world and took care of me when I needed him most. Matt, you live the Third Door. I'm tremendously grateful for you, Jenny, and the three G's for the unwavering support and for always welcoming me into your home with open arms.

A special thanks to my earliest mentors, from high school to the initial days of the mission, who believed in me before I fully believed in myself. You all stoked the flame within me and I couldn't be more grateful: Calvin Berman, César Bocanegra, Dan Lack, Indra Mukhopadhyay, John Ullmen, Keith Ferrazzi, Kristin Borella, Michelle Halimi, and Richard Waters.

I want to give a special thank-you to Stewart Alsop, Gilman Louie, Ernestine Fu, and the whole team at Alsop Louie Partners. Not only did you bring me into the world of venture investing, but you also encouraged the writing of this book the whole way through.

I'm eternally grateful to my literary agent, Bonnie Solow, who thankfully didn't think I was crazy when I sent that "my 3 a.m. stream of consciousness" email. Bonnie, you have understood the heart of the mission since our first phone call. You masterfully guided this dream from idea to publishing deal to the book that's in our hands today.

Thank you to my editor, Roger Scholl, and my publisher, Tina Constable, for reasons that make me emotional just thinking about. Roger and Tina, as my dad was dying, you two treated me with a level of compassion and kindness that was almost unfathomable. Thank you for giving me time to feel my feelings, get some rest, and be there for my mom and sisters. It's well known that you both are masters at book publishing, but I want the world to know that it's your hearts that make you so remarkable.

Thank you both, and to the whole team at the Crown Publishing Group—Campbell Wharton, Megan Perritt, Ayelet Gruenspecht, Nicole McArdle, Owen Haney, Erin Little, Nicole Ramirez, Mary Reynics, Norman Watkins, Andrea Lau, and many more—for all you've done to make this book shine. A special thanks to Rick Horgan, who brought me into the Crown family and helped shape the vision of this book from the beginning. I'm grateful to Adam Penenberg for his meticulous edits, which kept the manuscript tight and clean. And I want to thank Kevin McDonnell for his masterful fact-checking and Ben Hannani for helping sift through early interview transcripts.

As I neared the end of the writing process, some of my dearest friends provided remarkable feedback and edits: Breegan Harper, Casey Rotter, Chaplain Kevin, Claire Schmidt, Dani Van De Sande, Julie Pilat, Michelle Zauzig, and Sam Hannani. Not only did you guys help refine the book, but you also reminded me why I wrote it in the first place.

I want to say—no, I want to shout—a giant, hallelujah-level thank-you to David Creech for working his magic on the book cover. And major thanks to my brother, Arturo Nuñez, for making it possible.

Thank you to the following authors, some of whom I know well and some of whom I've only exchanged emails with, who so generously guided me through the publishing process. You all are proof of the saying that there truly are good people in the world: Adam Braun, Adam Penenberg, Baratunde Thurston, Ben Casnocha, Ben Nemtin, Brendon Burchard, Cal Fussman, Craig Mullaney, Dan Pink, Dave Lingwood, Dave Logan, David Eagleman, Diane Shader Smith, Emerson Spartz, Esther Perel, Gary Vaynerchuk, Gina Rudan, Guy Kawasaki, Jake Strom, James Marshall Reilly, Janet Switzer, John Ullmen, Josh Linkner, Julien Smith, Keith Ferrazzi, Kent Healy, Lewis Howes, Malcolm Gladwell, Mastin Kipp, Neil Strauss, Rich Roll, Ruma Bose, Sam Horn, Seth Godin, Simon Sinek, Stanley Tang, Tim Ferriss, Tim Sanders, Tony Hsieh, and Wes Moore.

———

FOR YEARS, I'VE IMAGINED WHAT it would feel like to write the following words.

Below is a list of everyone who was interviewed for the mission, coordinated an interview, or tried to secure an interview. The massive size of this list is beautiful to me. It is the ultimate testament to what it took to make this book possible.

From the bottom of my heart, I thank each and every one of you:

Adrianna Allen

Ali Dalloul

Allie Dominguez

Allison Wu

Aman Bhandari

Amelia Billinger

Amy Hogg

Andrea Lake

Arturo Nuñez

Asher Jay

Barry Johnson

Ben Maddahi

Ben Schwerin

Bettie Clay

Bill Gates

Blake Mycoskie

Bobby Campbell

Brenna Israel Mast

Bruce Rosenblum

Cal Fussman

César Bocanegra

Cesar Francia

Charles Best

Charles Chavez

Chelsea Hettrick

Cheri Tschannel

Corey McGuire

Courtney Merfeld

Dan Lack

Daphne Wayans

Darnell Strom

Dean Kamen

Debbie Bosanek

Debborah Foreman

Drew Houston

Dylan Conroy

Elise Wagner

Elizabeth Gregersen

Elliott Bisnow

Franck Nouyrigat

Fred Mossler

Gerry Erasme

Gilman Louie

Hannah Richert

Howard Buffett

Jacob Petersen

James Andrews

James Ellis

Jane Goodall

Jason Von Sick

Jason Zone Fisher

Jennifer Rosenberg

Jesse Berger

Jesse Stollak

Jessi Hempel

Jessica Alba

Joe Huff

Joey Levine

Johnny Steindorff

Jon Rosenblum

Jonathan Hawley

Jordan Brown

Juan Espinoza

Julia Lam

Julie Hovsepian

Justin Falvey

Karla Ballard

Katie Curtis

Keith Ferrazzi

Kelly Fogel

Kevin Watson

Kristin Borella

Lady Gaga

Larry Cohen

Larry King

Lee Fisher

Lisa Hurt-Clark

Marie Dolittle

Mastin Kipp

Matt Michelsen

Max Stossel

Maya Angelou

Maya Watson

Michael Kives

Michelle Rhee

Miki Agrawal

Penni Thow

Peter Guber

Phillip Leeds

Pippa Biddle

Pitbull

QD3

Qi Lu

Quddus Philippe

Quincy Jones

Radha Ramachandran

Rebecca Kantar	Shira Lazar	Tom Muzquiz
Rick Armbrust	Simmi Singh	Tony DeNiro
Robert Farfan	Soledad O'Brien	Tony Hsieh
Romi Kadri	Sonja Durham	Tracy Britt
Ruma Bose	Stefan Weitz	Tracy Hall
Ryan Bethea	Steve Case	Van Scott
Ryan Junee	Steve Wozniak	Vivian Graubard
Samantha Couch	Stewart Alsop	Warren Bennis
Scott Cendrowski	Sugar Ray Leonard	Wendy Woska
Scott McGuire	Suzi LeVine	Will McDonough
Seth London	Tim Ferriss	Zak Miller

PERHAPS THE FINAL QUESTION THAT needs to be answered is: *Where do we go from here?*

After my dad's death, I became even more drawn to Quincy Jones' advice to travel to the far corners of the world, soaking up the wisdom and beauty of different cultures. Over the past year, my best friends and I traveled to Argentina, Brazil, Kenya, India, Japan, South Africa, and now I'm writing this from Australia, where Kevin and I are scuba diving in the Great Barrier Reef. The interview with Quincy Jones changed my life because it changed what I wanted out of life. And I couldn't be more grateful.

Traveling has given me space to look back at the past few years with fresh eyes. The more I reflect on my journey, the more I can see what the soul of the mission is truly about.

When I started, my focus was on gathering the wisdom of the greats so their hindsight could be my generation's foresight. And while that aspect remains, I've realized that the mission goes deeper. This book, and the mindset of the Third Door, is really about possibility.

I've learned that while you can give someone all the best

knowledge and tools in the world, sometimes their life can still feel stuck. But if you can change what someone believes is possible, their life will never be the same.

I dream of a future where more and more people are given that gift of possibility, no matter who they are or where they were born. I'm committed to doing whatever I can, and playing whatever role I can, to make this dream a reality. If you find yourself just as passionate about this idea as I am, if you want to help bring the Third Door mindset to the world, I want to hear from you. Call me, email me. Together, we can make a difference.

So, here's to the future.

Although my days of chasing interviews may be coming to an end, I feel like the larger mission is just getting started.

The day before his freshman-year final exams, **ALEX BANAYAN** hacked *The Price Is Right*, won a sailboat, sold it, and used the prize money to fund his quest to learn from the world's most successful people. Since then, Banayan has been named to *Forbes'* 30 Under 30 list and *Business Insider*'s Most Powerful People Under 30. He has contributed to *Fast Company*, the *Washington Post, Entrepreneur*, and TechCrunch and has been featured in major media, including *Fortune, Forbes, Businessweek*, Bloomberg TV, Fox News, and CBS News. An acclaimed keynote speaker, Banayan has presented the Third Door framework to business conferences and corporate leadership teams around the world, including Apple, Nike, IBM, Dell, MTV, Harvard, and countless others.